Free in Christ

Free in Christ

The Message of Galatians for Today

Edgar Andrews

Original Copyright © 1996, Edgar H. Andrews

All rights reserved. No part of this book may be reproduced, scanned, or distributed in any printed or electronic form without permission.

Unless otherwise indicated, Scripture quotations in this publication are from the Holy Bible, New King James Version. Copyright © 1988 by Thomas Nelson Inc. Used by permission. All rights reserved.

This Edition: 2017

ISBN: 978-0-9988812-2-5

Design and Typesetting by Great Writing Publications
Cover Concept and Design by Great Writing Publications
www.greatwriting.org
Taylors, SC, USA

Contents

Other Books by Edgar Andrews 9

Preface 11

Part 1: The Gospel of Grace 13
1. The Gospel of Christ (1:1–5) 14
2. The Gospel Perverted (1:6–9) 25
3. The Gospel Received (1:10–12) 30
4. The Gospel Preached (1:13–24) 36
5. The Gospel Shared (2:1–2) 42
6. The Gospel Threatened (2:3–5) 50
7. The Gospel to the Gentiles (2:6–10) 58
8. The Gospel Defended (2:11–14) 67

Part II: The Nature and Necessity of Faith 75
9. The Works of the Law (2:15–16) 77
10. Justified by Faith (2:16 89
11. The Law Dismantled (2:17–18) 101
12. United with Christ (2:19–21) 109
13. The Hearing of Faith (3:1–5) 121
14. The Faith of Abraham (3:6–9) 133
15. The Curse of the Law (3:10–12) 141
16. The Promise of the Spirit (3:13–14) 149
17. God's Covenant in Christ (3:15–18) 161
18. The Purpose of the Law (3:19–25) 168
19. All One in Christ (3:26–29) 180

Part III: The Spirit and The Believer 189
20. Heirs of God through Christ (4:1–7) 190
21. The Apostle's Concern (4:8–11) 203
22. The Apostle's Plea (4:12–20) 211

23. The Two Covenants (4:21–24) 222
24. The Two Jerusalems (4:25–31) 236
25. Freedom in Christ (5:1–6) 244
26. False Teachers (5:7–12) 256
27. The Law Fulfilled by Love (5:13–15) 265
28. Led by the Spirit (5:16–21) 273
29. Walking in the Spirit (5:22–26) 283
30. The Spirit of Meekness (6:1–5) 292
31. Sowing to the Spirit (6:6–10) 298
32. Glorying in the Cross (6:11–18) 306

Bibliography 317

Other Books by Edgar Andrews

God, Science and Evolution
From Nothing to Nature: A Basic Guide to Evolution and Creation
Christ and the Cosmos
The Spirit has come
A Glorious High Throne: Hebrews Simply Explained
Who made God? Searching for a Theory of Everything (see www.whomadegod.org for more information)
Preaching Christ

Preface

The epistle to the Galatians is an important book. As one commentator, Richard Longenecker, has written, "Historically, Galatians has been foundational for many forms of Christian doctrine, proclamation and practice. And it remains true today to say that how one understands the issues and teaching of Galatians determines in large measure what kind of theology is espoused, what kind of message is proclaimed, and what kind of lifestyle is practised."[1]

It is, perhaps, by the same token that Galatians is a controversial portion of Scripture. It raises issues over which believers still argue today, such as the role of "the law" and the work of the Holy Spirit in the believer. In this modest commentary, I have tried to deal openly and honestly with such controversies, so that even those who disagree with my interpretations may derive some benefit from reading these pages. Above all, I have sought to interpret Paul in a straightforward manner, taking his statements at their "face value" and seeking confirmation from other Pauline epistles wherever possible.

The central theme of the epistle is freedom in Christ, which is the birthright of every believer. Through faith in Christ, he has been delivered from the bondage and condemnation of the law and from the power of sin. He is free also to enjoy all that Christ has purchased, now and eternally, for his people by his death and resurrection. This freedom is mediated by the Holy Spirit through regeneration, union with Christ, and adoption as a child of God.

These are glorious doctrines, but Paul will not allow us to think of them *merely* as doctrines! In Galatians he explores in depth the practical and experimental dimensions of the work of the Spirit. Except, perhaps, for Romans chapter 8, no other epistle deals in such a soul-satisfying way with the Spirit and the believer as does Galatians. I have placed special emphasis on this subject because it tends to be neglected in many expositions of the epistle.

Preface

The chapters of this book have been kept short, to allow the reader time to reflect on one passage before moving on to the next. They are therefore suitable for use as daily readings. Equally, however, I have striven for readability, so that the commentary can also be read straight through, like an ordinary book.

Notes, many of which contain relevant quotations from other writers, will be found at the end of each chapter. In these the author and short-title system has been used, and the reader should turn to the bibliography to find full details of the source.

I would like to thank those who have read the manuscript prior to publication, both for their time and patience and for the many helpful suggestions they have offered. The end result, however, must remain my own responsibility!

Edgar Andrews
Welwyn, England
July 2017

[1] Longenecker, *Galatians*, p. xliii

Part I

The Gospel of Grace

1
The Gospel of Christ

Please Read Galatians 1:1–5

The epistle to the Galatians can be summarized by one simple question: what is the gospel? What is the real gospel, as opposed to false gospels or (to use Paul's own terminology) perverted gospels? Here, in his opening salutation, the apostle takes an early opportunity to summarize the content of the gospel (1:3–5).

Because it was Paul's custom to begin his letters with a greeting, it is easy to dismiss these "salutations" as mere formalities, having little bearing on the main theme of each epistle. This is a serious mistake, for the greeting often contains, in seed form, the apostle's mental preoccupations as he sets out to write to a particular church with its particular needs. This is especially true of Galatians 1:3–5, as we shall see.

Before we come to Paul's summary of the gospel, however, there are some important things for us to notice in the opening two verses of this chapter. These verses identify both the writer and the recipients of the letter.

Who was Paul? (1:1)

It would appear from this epistle that the greatest need of Paul's readers was to understand the true nature of the gospel. And since this gospel had been declared to them by the apostle himself, it was also necessary for them to understand who he was, and by what authority he spoke. Both of these needs can be discerned in these opening verses. Who is Paul? What is the gospel? The salutation anticipates both questions.

These questions are as important today as they were in the first century. We too need to know by what authority Paul and the other New Testament authors wrote what they did. We need to know the status of New Testament Scripture—whether it is merely man's attempt to explain the phenomenon of Jesus of Nazareth, or if it is indeed the timeless Word of God, mediated through human minds but not thereby adulterated or obscured, God's message to every age concerning his revelation of himself in Christ.

Paul is in no doubt about the answer. He was an **"apostle,"** one who was sent, a special messenger with a special message.[1] By whom was he sent? **"Not from men, nor through man, but through Jesus Christ and God the Father who raised Him from the dead"** (1:1). Paul's gospel did not originate with man, neither was he commissioned by men such as the other apostles. Gospel and commission alike derived from the risen Christ who had met him, so fatefully, on the Damascus road. If this is so, then we must heed what the apostle has to say, for what he writes is God's Word, not man's, and we neglect it at our peril.

To whom was the letter written? (1:2)

The recipients were **"the churches of Galatia"** (1:2), which had been founded during Paul's first and/or second missionary journeys in what we now call Asia Minor. There is an unresolved debate as to whether "Galatia" here refers to the ancient northerly kingdom of that name, inhabited largely by Gauls (or Galatæ), or to the larger Roman province which included the more southerly regions of Pontus, Phrygia, Lycaonia and Pisidia (Acts 13:14–14:26; 16:6).

Those who subscribe to the "North Galatian theory" argue that only the ethnic Gauls could truly be called "Galatians," and that certain details of Paul's ministry among them (such as Gal. 4:13) do not tally with the account in Acts of his work in the south of Asia Minor. If they are correct, this letter was addressed to churches founded during the apostle's second missionary journey, when Paul "had gone through Phrygia and the region of Galatia" (Acts 16:6), but not explicitly mentioned in Acts.

If, on the other hand, "Galatia" here refers to the larger Roman province of that name, the churches addressed would be those established during the first missionary journey, including Pisidian Antioch, Iconium, Lystra and Derbe. The advocates of this "South Galatian theory" point out that Paul often grouped churches according to the Roman provinces in which they were situated (for example, in 1 Cor. 16:1, 15, 19, Galatia, Achaia and Asia were all Roman provinces). The churches of South Galatia were also closer to the source of the false teaching he has to deal with in the epistle. This teaching, as we know from Acts and Galatians, had spread from Jerusalem to Syrian Antioch, and is highly likely to have reached the South Galatian churches also (Acts 15:1, 5; Gal. 2:11–13).

The South Galatian alternative is probably the more plausible. It would mean that the epistle was addressed to a group of recognizable churches whose origin is described in Acts, rather than to unknown churches situated to the north.[2]

What is the gospel? (1:3–5)

In verses 3–5 Paul greets his readers. But in doing so he also summarizes the essentials of the gospel. The word "gospel" simply means "good news." But what exactly is this good news? Normally, the word "gospel" in the New Testament has a very broad scope. When Paul preached the gospel, he preached "the unsearchable riches of Christ" (Eph. 3:8). Thus the gospel embraces everything that God has revealed concerning his Son. As we read in Romans 1:1–3, the apostle was "separated to the gospel of God ... *concerning His Son*, Jesus Christ." In Galatians, Paul almost always uses the word "gospel" in this comprehensive sense.

The distinctive nature of the gospel of Christ is also presented in another way in this epistle, namely by reference to the two "covenants" of which Paul speaks in Galatians 4. The old covenant is the law of Moses, given on Mount Sinai, and "gives birth to bondage" (4:24). In total contrast, the gospel is the new covenant, under which "Christ has made us free" (Gal. 4:26–5:1).

This is important to grasp if we are to understand the epistle to the Galatians. The question, "What is the gospel?" can be rephrased: "Under which covenant do believers in Christ find themselves?" We shall see, as we proceed through the epistle, that Paul equates the gospel of Christ with the new covenant of promise. The old covenant of works and the new covenant are as night and day.[3] They are totally at variance (see 4:29). They cannot be merged or blended into a twilight gospel. Yet this is exactly what was being attempted by those who troubled the Galatian churches. How, then, does Paul summarize this new covenant, the all-embracing gospel? We are told in verses 3–5.

Grace (1:3)

First of all, the gospel message tells of **"grace ... from God the Father and our Lord Jesus Christ"** (1:3). In Paul's day, "Grace!" was a common form of greeting. However, by adding the words "from God the Father and our Lord Jesus Christ," Paul transforms a mere greeting into a statement of enormous importance.[4] "Grace" means God's giving. It refers not so much to a specific gift, since there is a different (though related) Greek word for "gift," but rather to the whole context of God's dealings with his people (hence the idea of a "covenant"). "By grace you have been saved through faith, and that not of yourselves, it is the gift of God" (Eph. 2:8). Salvation and, thus, the faith by which it is appropriated are alike the gifts of God, "not of works, lest anyone should boast. For we are His workmanship ..." (Eph. 2:9–10).

This is something the Galatians had been slow to grasp, and many are like them today. Salvation is by grace, not works—not even by religious works; not even by a so-called "faith" that resides, like a sleeping giant, in human nature and can be roused by an effort of human will. Such "faith" is just as much a human work as are deeds of kindness and ethical behavior. No, salvation is entirely the work of God's grace, God's giving. Man contributes nothing, for even the faith that he must exercise in Christ is given him by God. Repentance? That also is a gift of God. "God has exalted [Christ] to His right hand to be Prince and Savior, to give repentance to Israel and forgiveness of sins" (Acts 5:31).

Peace (1:3)
As grace is the cause of salvation, so **"peace from God"** (1:3) is its consequence. "Peace!" was the conventional Hebrew greeting, but once again a common greeting is transmuted by the addition of the words, "from God."

Christ has "made peace through the blood of His cross" (Col. 1:20), so that, "Having been justified by faith, we have peace with God through our Lord Jesus Christ" (Rom. 5:1). This peace is not merely a "cessation of hostilities," but rather an ongoing experience for the believer (Phil. 4:6–7). By contrast, those who seek to be justified by the efforts of human nature, whatever form those efforts take, can never know peace. Why? Because they do not know how to rest in Christ. They must be ever striving for "assurance," ever revalidating their religious experience, ever refining their obedience. But he who rests in Christ has "entered His [God's] rest," and has "ceased from his works as God did from His" (Heb. 4:10).

There is a place for assurance, of course, for direct experience of God, for obedience to his Word, but our salvation is not based upon such things. It rests wholly and exclusively upon the perfect work of Christ on our behalf. It rests upon the sufficiency of God's grace in him, and there is no alternative foundation for our peace.

Jesus Christ (1:3)
The third thing Paul tells us about the gospel is that it concerns **"Jesus Christ, who gave Himself for our sins"** (1:3–4). It concerns Christ, for it is "the gospel of Christ" (1:7). It seems strange that Paul should have to emphasize what is, surely, obvious. Would anyone imagine that the Christian gospel could have any other centerpiece than Christ himself? Well, not in theory; but in practice many of us overlook the obvious. We shall see later in chapter 1 that Paul was called to preach *Christ*! Yet today, as then, men preach many things in the name of the gospel which are not centered upon Christ. They preach Christian ethics, church history, systems of doctrine, ecclesiology, religious experience,

eschatology—yes, even the Bible, without preaching Christ. Paul's gospel was a Christ-centered gospel, for he knew no other. The very purpose of the gospel is to provide a bride for Christ (Eph. 5:26–27; Rev. 21:2). The church is "His body, the fullness of Him who fills all in all" (Eph. 1:23). How can the gospel be anything but "the gospel of God ... concerning His Son Jesus Christ our Lord"? (Rom. 1:1–3).

Christ gave himself for our sins (1:4)
The Christ Paul preached was also a crucified Christ. To the Corinthians he wrote, "I determined not to know anything among you except Jesus Christ and Him crucified" (1 Cor. 2:2). Here in Galatians, he refers to "the offense of the cross" (5:11) and to his "glory ... in the cross" (6:14). Why does Paul insist on such an emphasis?

His insistence is not sentimental. It is the very essence of the true gospel that **"Christ ... gave Himself for our sins"** (1:4). For if Christ has died for our sins, then those sins need no additional, or alternative, or repeated, expiation. "By one offering He has perfected forever those who are being sanctified" (Heb. 10:14).

This emphasis upon the perfect, finished and unrepeatable work of Christ in purging the sins of his people sets the true gospel apart from all imitations. "With His own blood He entered the Most Holy Place once for all, having obtained eternal redemption ... He is the Mediator of the new covenant, by means of death ... that those who are called may receive the promise of the eternal inheritance" (Heb. 9:12–15). Christ did not die merely to make salvation possible. He died to *obtain* eternal redemption for those whom he would, in course of time, call to himself through the gospel preached to every creature.

Of course, this offends human pride. It destroys the idea that man can, or must, contribute something, however small, to his own salvation. In the marketing profession, the story is told of an unsuccessful product-launch. The product in question was a cake mixture which, in spite of good quality and competitive price, failed to sell. Then one of the marketing team had an idea. The manufacturer was persuaded to print in large letters on the package the legend, "Add an egg!" Sales immediately soared. The secret? Put the housewife in control! Give her something to do; allow her to make some contribution to the finished product, because it is human nature to want to do so.

This trivial example illustrates a profound reality. Human nature is proud of its achievements, its contributions. But what is acceptable, and even commendable, in everyday life, is not acceptable in the matter of salvation. Nothing is left for man to do, so "that no flesh should glory in His presence" (1 Cor. 1:29). Salvation is by grace, "not of works, lest anyone should boast" (Eph. 2:9).

Deliverance (1:4)

The fifth element of the true gospel identified here is that of deliverance.[5] Christ **"gave Himself for our sins that He might deliver us from this present evil age"** (1:4). A similar idea is expressed in Colossians 1:13: "He has delivered us from the power of darkness and translated us into the kingdom of the Son of His love."

Christ's death and resurrection do more than atone for our sins. They redeem (buy back) his elect people from their lost estate and transform their status. In Paul's day, a slave, having no rights and in total bondage to his master, could be redeemed by the payment of a suitable price, and set at liberty. His status was transformed. He had been a slave; he became a freeman. So Christ has paid the price of our redemption: "You were not redeemed with corruptible things like silver or gold ... but with the precious blood of Christ" (1 Peter 1:18). Since the ransom has been paid, those for whom it was paid are necessarily made free—free from "this present evil age," from the "power [authority] of darkness," and are put under a new authority, the kingship of Christ.

In part III of this book we shall see very clearly what it means to live as those who have been delivered from the authority of darkness. Paul writes of "the liberty by which Christ has made us free" (5:1), and expands upon the liberating work of the Holy Spirit in the believer, setting us free to serve righteousness instead of sin. "As He who called you is holy, you also be holy in all your conduct," exhorts Peter (1 Peter 1:14–19).

The will of God (1:4)
The sixth aspect of Paul's gospel is that our deliverance is **"according to the will of our God and Father"** (1:4). We often express this truth by saying that God is sovereign in the salvation of sinners. The idea is expanded in Ephesians 1:11: "In [Christ] we have obtained an inheritance, being predestined according to the purpose of Him who works all things according to the counsel of His will."

In his eternal counsels, God determined in advance to redeem a people for himself. He "predestined" them; that is, he predetermined their destination. If I board a train in London and travel to Edinburgh, my destination is determined long before I arrive, because Edinburgh always was the intended point of termination. So, Paul explains to the Ephesians, God "chose us in [Christ] before the foundation of the world ... having predestined us to adoption as sons by Jesus Christ to Himself, according to the good pleasure of His will" (Eph. 1:4–5). What is our destination? Romans 8:29 provides the answer: "Whom He foreknew, He also predestined to be conformed to the image of His Son, that He might be the firstborn among many brethren." Our destination, very simply, is to be like Christ.

All this is according to God's eternal purpose. He does not offer salvation to mankind on a take-it-or-leave-it basis. The fulfillment of his purpose cannot be left to the whim of man to accept or reject salvation. The conversion of a sinner to Christ is a sovereign work of God (though willingly received by the enlightened sinner). Only thus could he ensure the accomplishment of his purpose.

For God's glory (1:5)
The seventh and final element in the gospel preached by Paul is the glory of God: **"to whom be glory forever and ever, amen"**

(1:5). The whole redemptive process has only one object, namely that God might be glorified. "We have obtained an inheritance ... that we who first trusted in Christ should be to the praise of His glory" (Eph. 1:11–12). Have we been predestined and adopted according to the good pleasure of his will? Then it is "to the praise of the glory of His grace, by which He has made us accepted in the Beloved [Christ]" (Eph. 1:5–6).

Here, then, is another distinguishing mark of the true gospel. It brings all glory to God, and none to man. Nowhere here do we see the man-centered "gospel" so commonly promoted today. There is no hint here of promises of health and wealth, ease and comfort, as inducements to follow Christ. No, the authentic gospel exalts Christ, not ourselves. We are seen for what we are, miserable undeserving sinners, under God's righteous anger, helpless and hopeless. God is magnified as a gracious, merciful and sovereign Lord, working out his eternal purposes despite the rebellion of man and the opposition of Satan. "I will have mercy on whomever I will have mercy, and I will have compassion on whomever I will have compassion," said God to Moses (cited in Rom. 9:15). No wonder the inhabitants of heaven "fall down before Him who sits on the throne and worship Him ... and cast their crowns before the throne, saying, 'You are worthy, O Lord, to receive glory and honor and power; for You created all things, and by Your will they exist and were created' " (Rev. 4:10–11).

Summary

We have considered Paul's salutation at some length because it helps us to understand the content of the true gospel.[6] The great importance of this will emerge shortly. We have identified seven elements which distinguish the real gospel, the new covenant, from imitations. The genuine gospel features:

- the free grace of God as the *cause* of salvation;
- peace with God as the *result* of salvation;

- Christ as the *heart* of salvation;
- Christ's death and resurrection as the *means* of salvation;
- deliverance as the *hallmark* of salvation;
- the will of God as the *source* of salvation;
- the glory of God as the *purpose* of salvation.

Notes

[1] "The term apostle, in its native signification, signifieth no more than one sent; in its ecclesiastical use, it signifies one extraordinarily sent to preach the gospel" (Poole, *Commentary*, p. 640).

[2] Hendriksen, *Galatians and Ephesians*, pp. 4–14.

[3] Distinguishing the two covenants. Brown explains: "The one covenant or constitution is that from Mount Sinai; it is the order of things under which the Jews were placed at Mount Sinai to keep them a separate people, commonly called "the law." That constitution ... bringeth forth children who are slaves. The children of a constitution or covenant are the persons who are under it, and whose characters are formed by that constitution. The children of "the law" were the Israelites generally, and the Gentiles who submitted to it. It was formed on a servile principle, "do and live"; and as far as men were influenced by it only, they must have had a servile and not a filial character" (Brown, *Exposition of Galatians*, p. 100).

[4] "Paul *an apostle* (not an imposter) ... *grace to you*. These two terms, "apostle" and "grace" were loaded words in that situation, and if we understand their meaning, we have grasped the two main subjects of the Galatian Epistle."

"Although "grace" and "peace" are common monosyllables, they are pregnant with theological substance. In fact, they summarize Paul's gospel of salvation" (Stott, *Message of Galatians*, pp. 12, 16).

[5] The verb "deliver ... strikes the keynote of the epistle ... the Gospel is a rescue ... an emancipation from a state of bondage" (Lightfoot, *Galatians*, p. 73).

[6] "What the apostle has in fact done in these introductory verses of the Epistle is to trace three stages of divine action for man's salvation. Stage 1 is the death of Christ for our sins to rescue us out of this present evil age. Stage 2 is the appointment of Paul as an apostle to bear witness to the Christ who thus died and rose again. Stage 3 is the gift to us who believe of the grace and peace which Christ won and Paul witnessed to" (Stott, *Message of Galatians*, p. 19).

2
The Gospel Perverted

Please Read Galatians 1:6–9

There follows one of the most vehement passages in the whole of the New Testament. The apostle's pen is dipped in fire as he denounces perversions of the gospel and those who peddle them. In the strongest language he can command, Paul warns the Galatians that they court disaster if they turn from the gospel he had preached to **"a different gospel"** (1:6).

His words fall strangely on our modern ears, accustomed as we are to compromise and synthesis in the area of religious beliefs. All religions lead to God, we are told. We all worship the same God, though in different ways. Each denomination and creed contributes its own genius to our rich religious heritage, and our task is to weave these separate strands into one grand tapestry of faith. Creedal confrontation is "out." Mutual respect is "in." There are no absolutes, no certainties, in matters of faith, but only a hopeful seeking after truth.

Well, of course, we may take our choice. But choice there certainly must be! We cannot embrace both the uncompromising stand of Scripture and the bland platitudes of modern synthetical religion. If we follow Paul and Scripture, we shall no doubt be branded zealots, narrow-minded fundamentalists, and worse. But what does that matter, as long as we are true to the gospel as it really is?

Called in the grace of Christ (1:6)

The churches of Galatia had heard the gospel from Paul's own lips. He it was who had, at the human level, **"called [them] in the grace of Christ"** (1:6). There is some question in this passage as to the subject of the verb "call." Was it Paul who called them through his preaching, or was it God who called them through the work of his Spirit in their hearts? (compare with 3:2). Either could be intended, although the New King James Version prefers the latter rendering. Clearly, both are true and apposite to Paul's words of censure.

The gospel is to be preached "to every creature" (Mark 16:15). In this general sense, every person who hears the gospel is "called" with what we may term an "external call." All who hear, of course, will not believe. "He who believes and is baptized will be saved; but he who does not believe will be condemned" (Mark 16:16). However, the Bible speaks of another call which is both inward and effectual: "Whom He predestined, these He also called; whom He called, these He also justified" (Rom. 8:30). In Galatians 1 Paul refers to his own calling in the following terms: "It pleased God, who … called me through His grace …" (1:15; see also 1 Corinthians 1:26–31). It is quite clear that in these references the call is a gracious work of God, by which God's eternal purpose in election is actualized, both in time and in the experience of those called. This call is never rejected.

Such as are called are called **"in the grace of Christ"** (1:6); that is, the call is one element of God's gracious dealings with sinful people in Christ. God's grace is based upon the work of Christ, extended to us in the person of Christ and made effective in us by the Spirit of Christ (see 4:6). It is clear, therefore, that Paul regards the Galatians as real Christians, in spite of the strictures which follow in verses 6–9. He writes to those who are genuine believers, not apostates.[1] This is an important distinction. An apostate is someone who has once made a fair profession of faith in Christ, but who has subsequently denied that faith and turned his back upon Christ. Such people are described in Hebrews 6:4–8 and 10:26–31.

A different gospel (1:6–9)
The Galatians, though they were **"turning away"** from the true gospel to a **"different gospel"** (1:6), are not viewed by the apostle

as apostates. They are falling into error, however, and Paul is deeply concerned, even angry. His condemnation is reserved, not so much for the Galatians themselves, as for those who were leading them astray, **"who ... want to pervert the gospel of Christ"** (1:7). He writes with untypical ferocity. There is no other gospel, he declares, but that which he had preached to them. If he himself, or an angel from heaven, should return proclaiming an alternative gospel, such a preacher would be a bearer of falsehood and should be **"accursed,"** that is, vehemently rejected, by man and God alike. Any variant of the legitimate gospel was **"not another"** (1:7; i.e., not a gospel at all), but rather a perversion of the gospel.[2]

If Paul was sure that the Galatians were true believers, why was he so worried? If their spiritual state was not at risk, why did he not tolerate their deviations? Is there not room for differences of interpretation of the gospel? Perhaps Paul was making a lot of fuss about some rather minor issues. The answer to such questions lies in the very epistle itself. If we believe that "All Scripture is given by inspiration of God ..." (2 Tim. 3:16), then we must believe that what Paul wrote to the Galatians he wrote under the guidance of the Spirit of God. It is not merely Paul who was concerned, but God himself!

The reason for this concern is, surely, twofold. First of all, the gospel is the "glorious gospel of the blessed God" (1 Tim. 1:11). This could be rendered, "the gospel of the glory of the blessed God." We saw earlier that the very purpose of the gospel is to bring glory to God. What, then, is the effect of any deviation from that gospel, of any perversion? It is surely to detract from the glory of God; to diminish the **"grace of Christ"**; to belittle the sovereign mercy of the Almighty.[3] It is no small thing, therefore, to tamper with God's perfect provision for the salvation of his people. It is a grave offense against the majesty of God to embellish, or modify, the gospel to suit our own prejudices or convenience.

Would we dare to add brush-strokes of our own to "improve" a masterpiece by Rembrandt or Turner? Would we presume to rewrite the phrases of a Beethoven symphony, to attune them better to our ears? Of course we would not. Why then should we seek to improve upon the gospel, God's eternal masterpiece of saving grace? Some complain that the doctrine of election is too harsh, that the sovereignty of God is too fearsome, that the gospel needs to be softened to increase its appeal to men. This epistle was written to demolish such reasonings.

The second reason for Paul's concern is the danger of apostasy (falling away). The Bible makes it plain that the elect are eternally secure and cannot fall away (e.g., John 6:37–40; 10:26–30). However, it is possible for some who seem, for a while, to be real believers to turn their backs on all they once professed (see the parable of the sower, Matt. 13:1–23, and Heb. 6:4–12; 10:26–31). It is clear that Paul had this concern for the Galatians, for in Galatians 5:4 he thunders, "You have become estranged from Christ, you who attempt to be justified by the law; you have fallen from grace."

Whenever professing believers deviate from the truth of the gospel, or become involved with error, or dally with novel ideas that have no ground in Scripture, there is cause to fear for them, that they may become apostates. It is clear from Scripture, and particularly the passages cited from Hebrews, that we have a responsibility to warn such people of the danger facing them and, by presentation of the truth, to strive to restore them to sound faith. This is the major purpose of the Galatian epistle.

Summary

There is only one gospel, the gospel of "the grace of Christ." It is therefore impossible to modify or amend the gospel without destroying it. Through the preaching of this gospel of grace, the elect are effectually called out of spiritual darkness into fellowship with God.

Although Paul addresses them as true believers, the Galatians were in danger of embracing a perverted gospel, to the detriment of God's glory and with the attendant danger of apostasy. The purpose of the epistle is to restore the Galatian churches to sound, God-glorifying faith.

Notes

[1] "The experience of the Spirit in their lives, both at conversion and thereafter, is the reality on which he [Paul] builds" (Longenecker, *Galatians*, p. 107).

[2] "The false teachers ... [taught] that you must let Moses finish what Christ has begun. Or rather, you yourself must finish, by your obedience to the law, what Christ has begun. You must finish Christ's unfinished work" (Stott, *Message of Galatians*, p. 22).

[3] "If we cared more for the glory of Christ ... we too would not be able to bear the corruption of the gospel of grace" (Stott, *Message of Galatians*, p. 26)

3
The Gospel Received

Please Read Galatians 1:10–12

Paul now begins to elaborate the point he made in verse 1, namely, that his gospel is not "from men" but from God. It is not designed to please men, as if God had to cajole and entice them to believe. It is "the gospel of God" (Rom. 1:1), designed to promote the glory of God and of his Christ.

Pleasing God, or pleasing man (1:10)
"Do I now persuade men, or God? Or do I seek to please men?" asks the apostle (1:10). The Greek verb rendered "persuade" can also mean "appease," and that is its sense here.[1] We may therefore read this question along the following lines. "Is it my purpose to win the favor of men, or the favor of God?"

There was a time, he implies, when he did seek the praise of men. Like most of us, he enjoyed the plaudits of his fellows, who admired his advancement in the Jewish faith, and honored him for his outstanding zeal (see 1:14). Now, however, things are different. Since he became a **"servant of Christ"** (1:10) he can no longer aim to please men and indulge his religious pride.

In speaking thus, of course, Paul contrasts his own motives with those of the false teachers who pervert the gospel (1:7). Their object is to superimpose upon the gospel of God's free grace just this element of human achievement and pride which Paul now rejects. Their observation of the Mosaic law might please men, since it panders to man's natural pride. But it cannot please God, whose glory is diminished if grace is diluted (no matter how slightly) by human works.

The intrusion of human pride into the gospel is as great a problem today as it was for Paul. We see it in the personality cults which build up around well-known evangelists. We see it in the "good works" syndrome that emphasizes Christian charity to the neglect of gospel preaching. Of course, Christians should be "zealous for good works" (Titus 2:14), but these must follow gospel preaching, not replace it.

To please God, says Paul, is to serve Christ. To serve Christ is to preach Christ. To preach Christ is to proclaim "the grace of Christ" (1:6). We cannot minister effectively to men and women if we set out to please men. Too often a minister or church asks, "How can we attract people to our services? What can we offer that will please them? How can we be more popular with the world?" The result is a watered-down message, or "worship" aimed more at the gratification of emotions than the glorification of God. The fear of what people will think too often affects what ministers will preach. What is Paul's antidote to this? Please God, not man. Preach the grace of God in Christ—not what men want to hear, but what they need to hear!

A gospel revealed (1:11–12)

False gospels are designed to please men. They have their origin in human reasoning, driven by human desires. By contrast, the true gospel is revealed from heaven. Where can we look for truth and authority in matters pertaining to God? Whom are we to believe? Paul's answer is that we dare not trust man, who, as likely as not, perverts the gospel. We can trust only God, who declares the truth **"through the revelation of Jesus Christ"** (1:12). This revelation of Christ is preserved for us in the Bible, both Old and New Testaments. For, said Christ, "The Scriptures … are they which testify of Me" (John 5:39). So it is important for Paul to emphasize **"that the gospel which was preached by me is not according to man, for I neither received it from man, nor was I taught it"** (1:11–12). Paul's gospel was not even learned from the other apostles; it came to him by direct revelation.[2] The implications of this are weighty.

Firstly, it places Paul's preaching and writing in the same category of revelation as the Old Testament Scriptures which, Christ said, testify of him. The process of revelation was the same for both Testaments, and both together constitute the Word of God. The authority of the Old Testament, confirmed by Christ himself, thus extends to the New.

Secondly, the gospel is *unique*. There is only one authentic gospel. This is why, when Paul speaks of "a different gospel," he hastens to add that this is "not another" (1:6–7), but rather a perversion of the gospel. If we listen to men we hear a thousand different versions of the "gospel." Men promote the gospel of works, the gospel of decision, the social gospel, the gospel of liberation theology, the gospel of healing, the charismatic gospel, the sacramental gospel, and many more. Against all the inventions of man stands the one revealed gospel, the gospel of the grace of God in Christ.

Thirdly, the gospel was made known to Paul **"through the revelation of Jesus Christ"** (1:12), not just through some general revelation.[3] Hebrews tells us that "God ... has in these last days spoken to us by His Son, whom He has appointed heir of all things, through whom also He made the worlds; who being the brightness of His glory and the express image of His person, and upholding all things by the word of His power, when He had by Himself purged our sins, sat down at the right hand of the Majesty on high" (Heb. 1:1–3).

It would lead us too far from Galatians to explore these verses in detail, but they demonstrate the centrality of Christ to all of God's works, whether of self-revelation, creation, providence, redemption or sovereign rule. The gospel involves not simply the Christ of Calvary, but Christ in all his glorious attributes. Too often we forget that to preach the gospel fully we must preach "the unsearchable riches of Christ" (Eph. 3:8).

Fourthly, a revealed gospel must be a *perfect* gospel. If it is God's work, devoid of human input, it must be flawless and complete. It cannot be improved by additions or deletions, but only destroyed. This is why "Christ plus ... anything" is no gospel at all.

We have to be careful at this point. Some have suggested that "Christ plus the lordship of Christ" is a corruption of the gospel; others that "Christ plus creationism" is similarly flawed, and so on. This is not the case. The lordship of Christ, the creatorship of Christ, and many other aspects of Christ's person and work, are integral parts of the gospel, not additions. Indeed, the opposite is true, that if we preach a lesser Christ than the glorious person revealed in Scripture, we falsify the gospel by subtraction.

Let us be clear. The additions that adulterate the gospel are those that imply that Christ is insufficient, whether in his person or his work, to provide all the sinner's need. Any such suggestion must be rejected out of hand, for "Christ Jesus ... is made unto us wisdom, and righteousness, and sanctification, and redemption: That according as it is written, He that glorieth, let him glory in the Lord" (1 Cor. 1:30–31, KJV).

Fifthly and finally, a revealed gospel is an *unchangeable* gospel. It is "the everlasting gospel" that is to be preached "to every nation, tribe, tongue and people" (Rev. 14:6). Because it was conceived and executed by God himself, it is a changeless gospel. "God ... has saved us and called us with a holy calling, not according to our works, but according to His own purpose and grace which was given to us in Christ Jesus before time began" (2 Tim. 1:8–9).

There is, in every generation, a desire for something new. There are allegations that the gospel is somehow out of date, in need of modernization. We must adapt the gospel to our time, people say, so that men will understand. We have to adopt a modern idiom, a new approach, address the contemporary scene, lay aside time-worn concepts, and speak to today's people in today's language, using today's techniques. Thus preaching is "out," but dialogue is "in." Doctrine is divisive, but experience unites. Separation is old-fashioned, but "unity" is all. Evangelization is a business enterprise.

The Scriptures teach us otherwise. The content of the gospel cannot change, for it is eternally true. The method of its presentation is still "the foolishness of preaching," as it was in Paul's day (1 Cor. 1:21, KJV). The subject of the gospel is still "Jesus Christ and Him crucified" (1 Cor. 2:2).

Summary

The gospel is of divine origin, made known to Paul "through the revelation of Jesus Christ." It is revealed, unique, Christ-centered, perfect, complete and eternal in its conception, validity and effects. This revealed gospel differs from all "gospels" of human origin in that its purpose is to glorify God, rather than to please man.

Notes

[1] "Though 'persuade' is by far the most ordinary meaning of the word which occurs here, it is by no means its only meaning. It means also to 'conciliate,' to 'court favour.' In this sense it occurs in Matt 28:14; Ac. 12:20" (Brown, *Exposition of Galatians*, p. 17).

[2] "Paul's gospel given him by revelation was not a message that differed in kerygmatic content from that of the early church. Rather, it was a message that included a new understanding of what might be called the 'redemptive logistics' for these final days—e.g., (1) a direct outreach to the Gentiles apart from Judaism's rituals, (2) authentic christian living for Gentiles apart from a Jewish lifestyle, and (3) the equality of Jewish and Gentile believers in the Church" (Longenecker, *Galatians*, p. 24).

[3] "Revelation signifies an immediate conveying of the knowledge of Divine things to a person, without human means; and in that Paul ascribes the revelation of the gospel to Jesus Christ, be plainly asserts the Divine nature of the Lord Jesus Christ" (Poole, *Commentary*, p. 642).

4
The Gospel Preached

Please Read Galatians 1:13–24

Paul's epistles do not generally contain much biographical material, but Galatians is an exception. Nearly a quarter of the letter is taken up with accounts of the apostle's past. Why should this be?

It is certainly not that Paul had some specially close relationship with the Galatians, such as he obviously enjoyed with the Philippians, whom he called "my beloved and longed-for brethren, my joy and crown" (Phil. 4:1). The reason for the biographical detail in Galatians is, rather, that the Galatians needed to know certain important facts about Paul and his message. Without this background they would be unable to assess the true nature of the threat to their faith. Let us consider, therefore, what lessons Paul had for them out of his own experience.

Paul's knowledge of Judaism (1:13–14)

The apostle begins by reminding them of his **"former conduct in Judaism"** (1:13). He had been an outstanding servant of his former religion. He had **"advanced in Judaism beyond many of [his] contemporaries ... being more exceedingly zealous for the traditions of [his] fathers"** (1:14). He had demonstrated this zeal, in particular, by persecuting the church of God, that is, believers in Christ (1:13).

Unlike the Galatians, with their Gentile background, Paul understood the true nature of Judaism. To them, circumcision and the law of Moses were novelties, and novelty in religion can be enticing. We see this today, when people crave excitement and novelty in worship. This is simply a manifestation of human nature. It is likely, therefore, that the Galatians failed to see the implications of what they were being taught by their false instructors.

The teaching in question was of the kind recorded in Acts 15:5, where we read, "Some of the sect of the Pharisees who believed rose up, saying, 'It is necessary to circumcise them [Gentile believers], and to command them to keep the law of Moses.' " Because of his own impeccable upbringing in Judaism, Paul was eminently qualified to nail this lie. Indeed, it fell to him (with support from Peter and James) to oppose this teaching at the "Council of Jerusalem," that is, the gathering of apostles and elders called to consider the matter (Acts 15:2–21).

These false teachers (or "Judaizers") no doubt presented their teaching as both a requirement for salvation (see Acts 15:1) and a means of progress in Christian discipleship. The Gentiles (they argued) were not "proper" Christians until they had submitted to circumcision and embraced the law of Moses. This kind of teaching is common in our own times. I do not, of course, refer to Judaizers as such, but to those who, like the Judaizers, teach the need both to trust in Christ *and* fulfill some added experience or obligation. The Bible's message is uncompromising: "In [Christ] dwells all the fullness of the Godhead bodily; and you are complete in Him" (Col. 2:9–10).

Paul's separation (1:15–16)

The next element of his experience that Paul brings to their attention is his "separation" or "setting apart." The apostle was selected by God **"from [his] mother's womb,"** that is, before he was born (1:15). The purpose of this selection was that Paul should preach the gospel, particularly (though not solely) to the Gentiles. As Ananias was told, "He is a chosen vessel of Mine to bear My name before Gentiles, kings and the children of Israel" (Acts 9:15).

The implication is clear. If Paul was specifically chosen of God to proclaim the truth concerning Christ, then to refuse his gospel was to reject God's own messenger. The apostles, and Paul among them, were invested with particular authority. They alone were commissioned to define the content of the gospel revealed to them by the Lord. That is why it is dangerous to suppose, as some do, that apostles are with us today. Whether this teaching comes in the form of "apostolic succession," or of "restoration theology," it is wrong, for it implies that the gospel revealed in Scripture is incomplete.

Even when talking of the high privilege and responsibility to which God had called him, Paul is careful to acknowledge that he deserved no praise. He had been called only **"through ... grace"** (1:15). Unlike many religious leaders today, the apostles never sought glory or status for themselves. Paul refers to the gospel revelation he had received as "the dispensation of the grace of God which was given to me for you" (Eph. 3:2–3). He "became a minister according to the gift of the grace of God" (Eph. 3:7). In his own eyes he was "less than the least of all the saints," to whom "grace was given, that [he] should preach among the Gentiles the unsearchable riches of Christ" (Eph. 3:8).

This repeated emphasis upon God's grace, as the source of all he was, and all he accomplished in his ministry, is typical of Paul and of all true servants of Christ.[1] Like John the Baptist, they declare, "He must increase but I must decrease" (John 3:30). In service, as in salvation, the praise must go to God and not to man.

Called through grace (1:15)
Paul speaks here, not only of his separation, but of his calling: **"When it pleased God, who ... called me through His grace"** (1:15). This may refer to his apostolic calling, but it would be more consistent with Paul's normal usage to understand this as his call to faith in Christ. To the Romans he writes, "Whom He predestined, these He also called; whom He called, these He also justified; and whom He justified, these He also glorified" (Rom. 8:30). Paul particularly states that he was called "when it pleased God" (1:15). It is God who, in his own good time, reaches out in grace to revive those who are "dead in trespasses and sins" (Eph. 2:1). Until he does so, we remain dead to God, deaf to the gospel and blind to his glory.

Every believer is "called through grace," out of darkness and into God's marvelous light. Paul's emphasis on grace is not accidental. The Galatians needed to understand the meaning of grace, for only then would they understand the futility of works. We also need to understand what grace is. It is not some supply of religious virtue, extracted from God by our devotions or good deeds. Nor is it God's response to our acts of faith. Grace precedes faith, for we are saved "by grace ... through faith," which is "not of yourselves; it is the gift of God" (Eph. 2:8–10). The work of salvation is planned, initiated, executed and perfected entirely by God's free grace.

Preaching Christ (1:16)

Paul tells us that **"It pleased God ... to reveal His Son in me, that I might preach Him among the Gentiles"** (1:15–16). This does not, I think, mean that God revealed his Son *to* Paul, in conversion. Rather, the reference here is to the gospel of Christ revealed to men *through* his servant. This revelation, as we have seen, was given to Paul directly by God. It was then declared, or revealed, to others through his preaching.

Notice especially that the purpose and effect of Paul's preaching was to make Christ known. When he preached to the Gentiles, he preached Christ—no more, no less.[2] Christ was the sole subject of his preaching, as Paul makes plain, not only here, but also in several of his other epistles (e.g., 1 Cor. 1:23; Eph. 3:8; Col. 1:28). The gospel is Christ; Christ is the gospel. If only the Galatians could grasp this fundamental truth, they would be immune to the ravages of false teaching. If "Christ is all and in all" (Col. 3:11), then what need is there of extras and additions to the gospel? What need is there for rituals, circumcisions, or works of the law? None, for Christ is our sufficiency, in time and in eternity.

This emphasis on Christ is sadly lacking from many of our pulpits today. Even sincere, Bible-believing ministers sometimes lose sight of this central imperative. They preach morality, activism, law, doctrine for doctrine's sake, fellowship, love, heaven, and much else that is good. Without Christ, however, it is all empty, the ministry barren, the labor vain. Unless Christ is at the heart of every sermon, whatever the ostensible theme, no spiritual good will be done.

Paul's movements (1:16–24)

In verses 17–24 Paul describes the travels that followed his conversion on the Damascus road. His purpose in providing this account is clear. He wants to demonstrate to the Galatians that he **"did not ... confer with flesh and blood"** (1:16). He did not visit the apostles at Jerusalem until three years after his conversion (1:18). Even when he did go, he saw only Peter and James, and stayed for only fifteen days. Otherwise, he went where none had gone before, preaching the gospel of God's grace in Syria and Cilicia. The churches of Judea certainly heard of him, and were amazed at the news. The former Saul of Tarsus now preached the faith he once had sought to destroy! (1:22–24). They never saw him, however; he remained for them a legend in his time. Thus Paul could demonstrate, from his own history, that he had no opportunity to learn the gospel second-hand. The chronology verifies his claim that his gospel came to him directly, by divine revelation. He learned his message at the feet of Christ himself.

Summary

Paul tells us here of his background in Judaism, his calling to faith in Christ, and his separation to the service of the gospel. All was by God's sovereign grace, and in accordance with his good pleasure and purpose.

God set him apart for the work of revealing Christ, and he revealed Christ by preaching Christ. His message was not learned from man, not even from the other apostles. It was imparted to him directly by divine revelation. The Galatians must therefore heed the apostle, and not turn away from the gospel that he preached. If they did so, they would be rejecting God's word, not man's.

Notes

[1] "Notice how at each stage the initiative and the grace of God are emphasized" (Stott, *Message of Galatians*, p. 32).

[2] "Christ was the subject of his ministry; the things respecting his person ...; the things concerning his office ...; the doctrines of his grace ..." (Gill, *Exposition*, vol. 8, p. 859).

5
The Gospel Shared

Please Read Galatians 2:1–2

This passage introduces us to one of the most significant watersheds in the development of the early church, namely the Council of Jerusalem. This event is recorded at length in Acts 15, and was a special gathering convened to settle the argument between Paul and the Judaizers. Referring, therefore, to this occasion, Paul's narrative continues, **"Then after fourteen years I went up again to Jerusalem with Barnabas, and also took Titus with me"** (2:1).

As we shall see, this was in fact Paul's third visit to Jerusalem, not his second, as might be concluded from a reading of Galatians alone. It was destined to be of the utmost importance to the Gentile church.

Chronology (2:1–2)

Before proceeding further, we must clarify the chronology of Paul's travels, especially his visits to Jerusalem. This is important, if only because the apostle attaches some significance to his lack of contact with the parent church in that city.

To understand the chronology we need to refer to Acts. The conversion of Saul of Tarsus is recorded in Acts 9:1–19. Following these events, we are told, "Immediately he preached the Christ in the synagogues, that He is the Son of God" (Acts 9:20). However, "After many days were past, the Jews plotted to kill him," and Paul (still known as Saul at that time) made a dramatic escape from Damascus by night (Acts 9:20–25).

The next thing we read in Acts is that Paul visited Jerusalem (Acts 9:26–30). There is no mention in Acts, therefore, of Paul's visit to Arabia and return to Damascus, recorded in Galatians 1:17.

It is most likely that this "Arabian interlude" occurred during the period recorded in Acts 9:20–25; that is, the "many days" that Paul spent in Damascus were divided into two periods, between which he went to Arabia. It is traditionally held that God revealed the gospel to him during this time of solitude.[1]

Following his time in Damascus, Paul made his first visit to Jerusalem (Acts 9:26). This visit must be the one referred to in Galatians 1:18, which took place three years after Paul's conversion. In Acts we are told that "Barnabas took him and brought him to the apostles" (Acts 9:27). In the Galatians account, Paul says he saw none of the apostles except Peter and adds that he also saw James, the Lord's brother. There is no contradiction here, since Peter and James may have been the only church leaders available in Jerusalem during the short visit. Nevertheless, Paul's contact with them represented, in a formal sense, an introduction to the apostles as a group.

According to Acts 9:30, Paul had to make a hurried departure from Jerusalem, just as he had from Damascus, to escape a plot against his life. He was taken to the seaport of Caesarea, where he departed for his home town of Tarsus, the chief city of Cilicia, in the south of Asia Minor. This period is referred to in Galatians 1:21, where Paul tells us that he went from Jerusalem "into the regions of Syria and Cilicia." There he remained until Barnabas, impressed by the events at Antioch, sought him out to assist with the work of the gospel in that city (Acts 11:19–26).

Paul's labors at Antioch were interrupted by his second journey to Jerusalem, of which there is no mention in Galatians. The purpose of this visit was to take the gifts raised by the Antioch church to relieve their famine-stricken brethren in Judea (Acts 11:27–30). Paul and Barnabas fulfilled their mission and returned to Antioch, bringing John Mark with them (Acts 12:25).

Paul omits to mention this second visit to Jerusalem when writing to the Galatians. Was he therefore being dishonest? After all, his purpose was to show how little contact he had with the Jerusalem apostles, so that he could not have learned the gospel second-hand from them.

To reason in this way is to misunderstand Paul's argument. It is true that Paul wished to demonstrate his independence of Jerusalem in this matter. But he has already achieved this objective by the end of Galatians 1, where he shows, first, that he had no contact at all with Jerusalem for the first three years of his ministry, and, secondly, that following his first brief visit, he was again completely out of touch with the churches of Judea and their leaders for a considerable time. Having made his point, he moves on to the next important topic, namely the Council of Jerusalem. The intervening relief mission is simply not relevant to the Galatian epistle.

Paul made no further visits to Jerusalem or Judea until fourteen years later, following his first missionary journey. Together with Barnabas, Titus and others, he was then sent to Jerusalem by the church at Antioch (see Acts 15:1–6), to seek a resolution of the controversy to which he now refers in Galatians 2:1–10.

An objection

It is sometimes argued that Galatians 2:1–10 does not refer to the Council of Jerusalem at all, but to the earlier famine-relief visit of Acts 11:27–30. The arguments for this idea are, briefly, as follows:

1. If Paul wrote Galatians after the Council of Jerusalem, he would have used the council's decision and letter explicitly as his main evidence against the Judaizers.

2. Galatians was written precisely because there were no clear guidelines on the subject of Gentile believers and the law. The Council of Jerusalem established such guidelines, so it must have taken place after the epistle was written.

3. Peter and Barnabas would not have been led astray by the Judaizers (2:11–13) *after* the clear-cut outcome of the Council of Jerusalem. Therefore their defection must have occurred before the council, not after it, as would be implied if Galatians 2:1–10 refers to that meeting.

My answers to these objections are as follows:

1. The events described in Galatians 2:1–10 are too important to

be equated with the simple famine-relief visit mentioned, without details, in Acts 11. The Galatians 2 visit involved: Paul being specially guided to go ("by revelation"); the scrutiny of Paul's gospel by the apostles; face-to-face conflict with the Judaizers; the "test case" of Titus; and an agreement of far-reaching importance between Paul and the Jerusalem apostles. All of these things correspond far more closely with the Council of Jerusalem than with a minor relief mission.

2. There was no need for Paul to emphasize the council's letter and guidelines when writing to the Galatians, because they were fully acquainted with them. This indeed may explain Paul's scathing language in this epistle in contrast to his normal patient approach to an erring church (e.g., 1 Cor. 4:21; 10:14–15). Paul does, in fact, summarize the outcome of the Jerusalem Council in Galatians 2:6 by a simple but profound statement. The leaders in Jerusalem, he claims, "added nothing to me." See the comments on this verse below.

3. The defection of Peter and Barnabas described in Galatians 2:11–13 might well have occurred after the council. The issue here was not the one that had precipitated the debate at Jerusalem, namely whether Gentile believers must obey the law. It was merely a matter of not eating with them. This may have seemed to Peter a minor issue, especially as it avoided unpleasant conflicts with certain Jewish believers. It was only Paul who saw the deeper implications of Peter's action, and recognized that it compromised the gospel.

We shall continue, therefore, to identify the events described in Galatians 2:1–10 with the Council of Jerusalem, recorded in Acts 15:1–29. To do so is to agree with the majority of commentators, but to disagree with others.[2]

Sharing the gospel (2:2)

Although Paul and his companions were sent to Jerusalem by the church at Antioch (Acts 15:1–3), we are also told that Paul **"went up by revelation"** (2:2). Such was the importance of this issue that he traveled to see the apostles and elders at Jerusalem under God's direct instructions. Why was so much significance being attached to what might be considered a small, local problem at Antioch? Simply because it was much more than a local issue. The very fundamentals of the gospel were at stake! This is what the Galatians were slow to grasp, and why Paul addresses the issue so vigorously in this epistle. He needs to impress upon them the spiritual realities of the matter.

Arriving at Jerusalem, Paul's first action was to seek a private conference with **"those who were of reputation"** (2:2). These authorities would have included the apostles themselves, and possibly other elders there (see Acts 15:2). Why did Paul seek this private audience? It was, he explains, **"lest by any means I might run, or had run, in vain"** (2:2).

This does not mean that Paul had any doubts about the truth of the gospel he preached! However, he was concerned, even puzzled, at the activities of the Judaizers. We have to bear in mind that they had come from Jerusalem (or at least, from Judea, see Acts 15:1). Had they gone to Antioch on the authority of the apostles? Did the church at Jerusalem know what these men were teaching? Was there something about the gospel that Paul had missed?

Paul was quite sure that his gospel was a complete gospel, revealed to him by the Lord himself. What he could not be sure about was that the Jerusalem apostles were teaching the selfsame gospel. This he had to ascertain once and for all. For if there were two gospels, not one, then surely his preaching, and also his hearers' faith, were vain (empty of meaning). We can compare Paul's position here to the stand he adopted concerning the resurrection: "If Christ is not risen, then our preaching is vain and your faith is also vain" (1 Cor. 15:14). Similarly, Paul was saying, if the Judaizers were right, and believers in Christ were still subject to the law of Moses, then it made nonsense of the gospel he preached. But he did not believe that for one moment.

So, says Paul, **"I communicated to them that gospel which I**

preach among the Gentiles" (2:2). He did not preach the gospel to them, of course. He "communicated," or set it before them. But, equally, this was no mere theological conference. There was an act of communication, of sharing.

We can fall into two, opposite, errors when we consider the communication of Bible truth. The first is to suppose that the gospel cannot be set out in clear propositions. Those who make this mistake have no time for sound doctrine. They are impatient with creedal statements or confessions, dismissive of biblical reasoning and doctrinal distinctions between truth and error. For them, the gospel is subjective, a thing to be experienced, to be "caught," like a common cold, rather than taught.

On the other hand, we can make the opposite mistake of thinking that the gospel consists only of intellectual propositions. Communication of the gospel becomes a theological discussion; its preaching a setting forth of statements about redemption. Such a gospel is lifeless, such preaching barren. It is very easy for those who value doctrine, especially the doctrines of God's free grace, to fall into this mold. Truth is preached, but it is truth without power. Doctrine is presented, but it is doctrine without Christ. When I listen to a sermon, or read an article, I make a point of noting how soon, and how often, Christ is named. If the message does not present Christ, then it is not the gospel, nor is it likely to bless and edify. Whatever the subject, that subject must relate to Christ, for it is the Holy Spirit's sole work to reveal him (John 15:26; 16:14).

We can be sure that when Paul shared the gospel with the apostles at Jerusalem, he told them of God's gracious dealings with him. He would have spent time "describing the conversion of the Gentiles," causing "great joy to all the brethren" (Acts 15:3). He would have marveled with them at the grace of God, exulted in the lordship of Christ, and been awed by the power of the Spirit. There would have been genuine fellowship in Christ, true rejoicing and much glory to God.

Sadly, this kind of sharing of the gospel is uncommon today. Believers are too busy with their private lives, or with their church programs, or with their theological preoccupations, to enjoy (or even desire) this kind of fellowship in Christ. Writing to the Philippians, Paul could say, "I thank my God upon every remembrance of you ... for your fellowship in the gospel from the first day until now" (Phil. 1:3–5). We should be the same.

Summary
The chronology of Paul's travels during this period of his life was probably as follows:
1. Conversion on the road to Damascus.
2. First period in Damascus, preaching Christ.
3. Visit to Arabia, the gospel revealed to him.
4. Second period in Damascus, preaching Christ.
5. His life threatened; he escapes from Damascus.
6. First visit to Jerusalem, three years after his conversion; he sees Peter and James.
7. His life again threatened; he escapes from Jerusalem.
8. Journey to Tarsus in Cilicia (his home town).
9. Preaches in Syria and Cilicia.
10. Barnabas fetches him back to Antioch; he becomes a prophet/teacher in that church (Acts 13:1).
11. Paul's first missionary journey; he plants churches in Galatia (Acts 13–14)
12. He returns to Antioch; dispute arises with Judaizers.
13. He goes to Jerusalem with Barnabas and Titus; he consults the apostles; he participates in the Council of Jerusalem; there is defeat for the Judaizers.

Notes

[1] "We believe that in this period of withdrawal ... the gospel of the grace of God was revealed to him in its fulness" (Stott, *Message of Galatians*, p. 34).

[2] Those who identify Galatians 2:1–10 with the famine visit of Acts 11:27–30 include commentators from Calvin to Longenecker (*Galatians*, p. 46). However, they appear to be in the minority. Ramsey states: "There is practically universal agreement among critics and commentators of every shade of opinion that the visit described as the third in Acts 15 is the one that Paul describes as the second in Gal. 2:1–10. Scholars who agree in regard to scarcely any other point of early Christian history are at one on this" (*St Paul the Traveller*, p. 154).

6
The Gospel Threatened

Please Read Galatians 2:3–5

This passage brings us to the heart of Paul's narrative, the purpose behind his rehearsal of past events. Once again, we shall have to turn to Acts 15 to get the full background. In Galatians Paul refers only to the cause of his dispute with the Judaizers and the outcome of the Council of Jerusalem. He does not describe what transpired during the council itself.

False brethren (2:3–4)
We have already seen the basic nature of the problem. Paul expresses it thus: **"False brethren** [were] **secretly brought in (who came in by stealth to spy out our liberty which we have in Christ Jesus, that they might bring us into bondage)"** (2:4). It is not clear who brought them in. There is perhaps a suggestion that some, highly placed in the church, were deliberately promoting the Judaizing message. To advance their cause, they introduced into the council meeting certain spokesmen who were ostensibly present under a different, more innocent, guise. We do not know for sure, but this would account for Paul's references to secrecy and stealth.[1]

There is no place among believers, gathered in the local church, for stealth. True believers have "renounced the hidden things of shame, not walking in craftiness nor handling the word of God deceitfully." Instead, "by manifestation of the truth" they commend themselves "to every man's conscience in the sight of God" (2 Cor. 4:2). Let us see that human ambition, power struggles and other motives of the flesh do not intrude into our dealings with our fellow-believers. These dealings must be honest, open and conducted under the gaze of God. The church is Christ's body, not our own.

The purpose of these false brethren was to **"spy out"** the believers' liberty in Christ. First, notice they were **"false brethren."** Paul did not regard these men as true Christians, even though they are said, in Acts, to be "some of the sect of the Pharisees who believed" (Acts 15:5). It is possible to believe intellectually in Christ without trusting him alone for salvation. As James points out, "Even the demons believe—and tremble!" (James 2:19).

The expression "spy out" suggests that the false teachers were seeking opportunities to discredit Paul's gospel by misquoting him and making false accusations against him. We see an example of this kind of thing in Romans 3:8, where Paul writes, "Why not say, "Let us do evil that good may come"?—as we are slanderously reported and as some affirm that we say." It is in Satan's interest to misrepresent as libertines those who preach the gospel of liberty in Christ. We shall need to return to this point later, for it is central to the message of Galatians.

The false teaching: mixing faith with works (2:4)
These men were false brethren because they bore false teaching. At this point we need to explore the full extent of this teaching, even though we have outlined it previously by reference to "Judaizers" and "Judaizing." The teaching in question is described in Acts 15:1, 5: "And certain men came down from Judea and taught the brethren, 'Unless you are circumcised according to the custom of Moses, you cannot be saved.' ... Some of the sect of the Pharisees who believed rose up, saying, 'It is necessary to circumcise them, and to command them to keep the law of Moses.' "

At first sight, the essence of their error was to add to the work of Christ. Obviously, they taught that belief in Christ was necessary for salvation, since they themselves "believed." Equally, however, they were saying that belief in Christ was not sufficient of itself. To qualify for salvation, one must also be circumcised and keep the law of Moses.

The Bible teaches that salvation is by faith in Christ alone. To the Romans Paul wrote, "Therefore we conclude that a man is justified by faith apart from the deeds of the law" (Rom. 3:28). This is true whether the "deeds of the law" referred to are religious rituals, such as circumcision, pious offerings or sacrifices, or acts of moral righteousness. Paul continues, "To him who works, the wages are not counted as grace but as debt. But to him who does not work but believes on Him who justifies the ungodly, his faith is accounted for righteousness" (Rom. 4:4–5).

The problem, therefore, is that faith and works cannot be mixed as means to obtain righteousness and acceptance with God. They are mutually exclusive. Salvation is a gift from God; that is, salvation is by grace. It cannot be earned by religious or moral activity because, being sinners by nature, we are incapable of any act which is morally perfect. Even if we *could* perform such acts, our failure to do so *consistently* would be sufficient to condemn us in the eyes of a holy God. To teach, therefore, that faith in Christ must be augmented by works (of whatever kind) is actually to reject faith as the means of salvation.

To see why this should be, we have to understand what faith is. It is not a capacity that resides in fallen human nature. It cannot, therefore, be a response of the natural man to the gospel, as many seem to think. "The natural man does not receive the things of the Spirit of God, for they are foolishness to him; nor can he know them, because they are spiritually discerned" (1 Cor. 2:14). If faith were merely a natural response to the gospel, then faith itself would be a work (since a "work" is anything than can be done by the natural man without the power of God). Genuine faith is the capacity to see (or understand) the invisible realities of God. It is imparted to a man or woman by the Spirit of God as part of the process of regeneration. "By grace you have been saved, through faith, and that not of yourselves; it is the gift of God" (Eph. 2:8).

But doesn't James say, "Faith without works is dead"? (James 2:20). Indeed, he does. This does not mean, however, that faith must be supplemented by works in order to obtain salvation, which was the error taught by the Judaizers. What James means is that genuine faith will produce good works, as a fruit. "I will show you my faith by my works" (James 2:18), he declares. Paul tells us the same thing in Ephesians 2:8–10. Having stated that we are saved by grace, through faith, he continues: "We are His workmanship, created in Christ Jesus for good works, which God prepared beforehand that we should walk in them." Good works, then, are the fruit and evidence of genuine faith; the consequence, not the cause, of saving grace. (Note also the distinction between "good works" and mere "works.")

The false teaching: confusing the covenants (2:4)

I wrote earlier that "at first sight" the essence of the Judaizers' error was to add to the work of Christ. This was, indeed, a serious misrepresentation of the gospel. Nevertheless, their teaching implied an even more fundamental falsehood, and one which Paul pursues throughout Galatians with unremitting zeal. This falsehood I have called "confusing the covenants."

The Judaizers taught that faith in the person and work of Christ was insufficient of itself for salvation; but why did they do so? Did they merely decide to add a few extras, to incorporate some "good ideas" from their Jewish background? Or was there something more basic at fault with their understanding of the gospel?

It seems to me that a movement as strong as theirs—which had support in high places in the church, which nearly seduced such stalwarts as Peter and Barnabas (2:11–13) and which prompted the writing of a significant portion of the New Testament in order to counteract it (I refer to Galatians, parts of Romans, and Hebrews)—such a movement, I say, must have been rooted in something stronger than the desire for a few spiritual "add-ons." There must have been more to it than that.

Surely, the full extent of their heresy lay in the attempt to bring the Gentile believers under the old covenant.[2] To understand this is to understand the epistle to the Galatians, for this is Paul's great fear. The "yoke of bondage" of which he speaks in Galatians 5:1 is not circumcision, nor even certain elements of Moses' law. It is the old covenant in its totality.

Seen in this light, the Judaizers were not so much adding the law of Moses to the work of Christ, as adding the work of Christ to the law of Moses! We do not know, of course, exactly what they thought about the death and resurrection of Christ. The cross of Christ must have meant something to them, but they plainly misunderstood the nature of the atonement. Possibly they saw Christ only as the Jewish Messiah, sent to save those who pleased God by obeying Moses' law. Thus it seemed essential to them to bring the Gentile believers under the old covenant, since this was the only arrangement they could perceive by which men might be saved.

A correct understanding of the atonement is essential, for there are many erroneous ideas. One very common notion is that the death of Christ simply "makes it easier to get to heaven" (as I was once told by a Roman Catholic priest). The Bible, however, teaches that Christ did not die merely to open up possibilities. On the contrary, by his death he "obtained eternal redemption," and became "the Mediator of the new covenant ... that those who are called may receive the promise of the eternal inheritance" (Heb. 9:11–15).

We shall have to clarify the whole question of covenants later, when we come to Galatians 4:21–31. Suffice it to say here that the epistle to the Galatians (and the epistle to the Hebrews, for that matter) teaches that the old and new covenants are distinct and incompatible (in the sense that they cannot coexist). Of course, the old covenant did foreshadow the new in many ways. To give but one example, the high priest of the old covenant pictured Christ's priestly ministry under the new. But that does not alter the fact that Christ's priesthood *abolishes* that of Aaron and his sons. The Judaizers had failed to understand that there *was* a new covenant in force. The same error is perpetuated in those churches today which retain a sacerdotal (sacrificing) priesthood. Clinging to the old covenant, they implicitly deny the new.

Only in this way can we understand the vehemence of Paul's

words, and his obvious belief that the very nature of the gospel was under threat. **"We did not yield submission** [to the Judaizers] **even for an hour, that the truth of the gospel might continue with you"** (2:5). If Paul's opponents were right, the gospel he preached would be totally undermined, for the reality of the new covenant would be swept aside.

Titus—proof of the new order (2:3)

Returning to Galatians 2:3, it is now possible to see why Paul attaches so much importance to Titus, a Gentile believer who had gone with him to the Council at Jerusalem. He points out that the Jerusalem apostles accepted Titus as a Christian without requiring him to be circumcised. In Paul's eyes this was clear proof that salvation is found in Christ, wholly outside of the Mosaic covenant. If this were not so, then the apostles would have required Titus to be circumcised, to bring him under the old covenant, before he could be accepted as a true believer.[3]

Paul did not seek the abolition of circumcision. In fact he used it in the case of Timothy, another Gentile believer, to avoid unnecessary offense to the Jews (Acts 16:3). As far as the gospel was concerned, circumcision was a matter of indifference. "In Christ Jesus neither circumcision nor uncircumcision avails anything, but faith working through love" (5:6). However, if a Gentile believer submits to circumcision *as a means of placing himself under the old covenant*, then "He is a debtor to keep the whole law ... [has] become estranged from Christ ... [has] fallen from grace" (5:3–4).

Summary

The teaching of the Judaizers threatened the gospel at its foundations. Paul's opponents were not just adding human works to the work of Christ as means of salvation, though that was serious enough. They were denying the very existence of the new covenant in Christ.

Seeing only the old covenant of works, they believed that salvation could only be found under that covenant. Hence it was logical for them to demand that Gentile believers be brought within the Mosaic covenant, by circumcision and obedience to its requirements.

This, Paul tells us, is to deny Christ and sweep aside the gospel of God's grace. Those who embrace this teaching, therefore, are estranged from Christ and fallen from grace. The apostle will not yield an inch to such teaching.

Notes

[1] "The interlopers mingled among the true believers with the purpose of *spying*, that is, discovering the strategic situation of those whom they opposed—their strong and their weak points—specifically their *liberty* ..." (Hendriksen, *Galatians and Ephesians*, p. 80)

[2] "It was the intention of the Judaizers to bring all Gentile converts under the yoke of the law, but it was Paul alone who saw that the adoption of this error would reduce Christ's 'free men' to a condition of abject slavery" (Wilson, *Galatians*, p. 34).

[3] "The very point which characterized [Paul's] gospel was gained, that point being the free admission of the Gentiles into the church; for even in Jerusalem the circumcision of Titus was successfully resisted ..." (Eadie, *Galatians*, on Gal. 2:3).

7
The Gospel to the Gentiles

Please Read Galatians 2:6–10

Paul now reports, in brief, the outcome of the Council of Jerusalem. The full details are given in Acts 15:6–31 but here Paul restricts himself to making two main points. Firstly, and negatively, he says the leaders of the church at Jerusalem **"added nothing to me"** (2:6). Secondly, and positively, they **"perceived the grace that had been given"** to Paul and Barnabas, and commended them to preach the gospel to the Gentiles.

Pillars of the church (2:6–9)
The letter to the Gentile churches from the Council of Jerusalem was sent by "the apostles, the elders and the brethren" of the Jerusalem church (Acts 15:23). It was therefore a missive from the whole church, not from the apostles. It is important to make this clear, for some would argue that the apostles held jurisdiction over churches everywhere, and thus over the Gentile churches to which the letter was addressed. This is clearly not so. The Council of Jerusalem affords no argument for apostolic rule over local churches. Although the letter was an apostolic edict (Acts 16:4), its purpose was to *remove* constraints, not impose them. Indeed, as far as the exercise of authority was concerned, the Jerusalem apostles adopted a hands-off approach to the Gentile churches, agreeing that Paul and Barnabas **"should go to the Gentiles and they to the circumcised"** (2:9).

There are some who claim that apostles still exist today, having authority over local churches. Since this was not even the case in New Testament times, such claims must be false. On the question of the foundational nature of the apostolic office, and its consequent cessation, the reader is referred elsewhere.[1]

Although the outcome of the Council of Jerusalem was a decision of the church as a whole, under the guidance of the Holy Spirit (Acts 15:22, 28), there were clearly certain men who gave a strong lead. Of these, Paul singles out James (who seems to have chaired the meeting), Cephas (Peter) and John for special mention (2:9). It is probably this same group (among others) who are referred to a little earlier as "those who were of reputation" and **"those who seemed to be something"** (2:2, 6). In verse 6 Paul adds: **"Whatever they were, it makes no difference to me; God shows personal favoritism to no man."** Was he being dismissive of them, or disrespectful? Not at all. He refers to them as men of reputation, and pillars of the church (2:9), which are terms of high regard. Those who lead churches must be respected if they are to labor effectively. "Esteem them very highly in love for their work's sake," Paul instructs the Thessalonians (1 Thess. 5:13).

What Paul is doing here is to remind his readers that the greatest of church leaders are only servants at best, and fallible at that. For example, Peter's inconsistency is recorded in the verses which follow our present passage. There is no room in Christ's church for those who seek their own elevation, who "lord it" over his flock (1 Peter 5:3). We are all unprofitable servants, however accomplished we may be in men's eyes. The opinions and decisions of these "pillars" of the church were only valid in so far as they accorded with the mind of Christ, not because they emanated from famous men. Paul wants his readers to understand this.

We do well to remember it today also. There is a natural tendency in the human heart to elevate and follow men. When Israel sought a king, they preferred a man, whom they could see, to God who was invisible (1 Sam. 8:4–9). We also lionize our leaders, and put our trust in man instead of God. At Corinth this led to disastrous divisions (1 Cor. 1:11–17). God has given leaders to his church for its edification (Eph. 4:11–16), but the church they are to edify is the body of Christ, not their personal fiefdom. Let us respect and love our leaders; but let us follow only Christ as he is revealed in "all the Scriptures" (Luke 24:27).

A clean bill of health (2:6)

These respected leaders, claims Paul, **"added nothing to me."** What does he mean by this expression? It could signify one of two things.

It could mean that the Jerusalem apostles imposed no added requirement upon Paul's Gentile converts. These converts, of whom Titus was a test case, were accepted as true believers without having to submit to circumcision or any other ordinance. Their faith in Christ was sufficient.[2]

The council pronounced as follows: "It seemed good to the Holy Spirit, and to us, to lay upon you no greater burden than these necessary things: that you abstain from things offered to idols, from blood, from things strangled, and from sexual immorality" (Acts 15:28–29).

These "necessary things" were fully acceptable to Paul, being either modes of behavior consistent with any Christian profession, or else things required to avoid unnecessary offense to Jewish brethren.

Alternatively, that they "added nothing" to Paul could refer back to verse 2 of this chapter. There Paul records that he communicated his gospel privately to the church leaders, "lest [he] might run, or had run, in vain." In the event, his understanding of the gospel was fully vindicated. It was in no way deficient, and therefore needed nothing to be added to it. He found that the leaders at Jerusalem could add nothing to his message or his doctrine, nor did they seek to do so.

Whichever meaning we prefer (and both may be implied), it is clear that the Council of Jerusalem gave Paul's gospel a "clean bill of health." Although he had not learned it from the apostles, Paul nevertheless had been preaching the apostolic gospel—no more, no less. Neither the law of Moses nor the more ancient rite of circumcision had any place in that gospel, except as pictures of the work of Christ, who perfectly fulfilled the law (Matt. 5:17–18; Col. 2:16–17), and of the Holy Spirit, who cleanses or "circumcises" the heart of every believer as he applies the work of Christ (Rom. 2:28–29; Col. 2:11).

This needs to be emphasized. The ordinances of the Jewish law, whether expressed "in food, or in drink, or regarding a festival or a new moon or sabbaths ... are a shadow of things to come, but the substance is of Christ" (Col. 2:16-17). It is so typical of the human heart to desire ordinances—rules to live by, rituals and regulations to obey. The natural man gravitates to this religion of works as water runs downhill. Even the believer is commonly tempted to return to works as a means of pleasing God. We are too easily "entangled again with a yoke of bondage" and thereby forfeit "the liberty by which Christ has made us free" (5:1).

The gospel of God's grace proclaims liberty from such ordinances, which can never make us holy. All our holiness is in Christ, who "became for us wisdom ... righteousness, sanctification and redemption" (1 Cor. 1:30). In place of ordinances, the gospel prescribes circumcision of the heart, that we may be free to obey God. As Paul puts it, "In Him you were also circumcised with the circumcision made without hands, by putting off the body of the sins of the flesh, by the circumcision of Christ" (Col. 2:11).

The outcome of this spiritual circumcision is the very righteousness of life that obedience to the law can never bring. Being buried with Christ (Col. 2:12), and raised with Christ (Col. 3:1), the believer has the liberty to "set [his] mind on things above," to "put to death" the sinful tendencies of his old nature and to "put on the new man who is renewed in knowledge according to the image of Him who created him" (Col. 3:2-10).

The gospel committed (2:7-8)

The Jerusalem leaders not only approved what Paul was teaching, but also **"saw that the gospel for the uncircumcised had been committed to [him], as the gospel for the circumcised was to Peter"** (2:7). Paul is not, of course, referring to two different gospels, but merely to two different constituencies, Gentiles and Jews.[3]

It was not the church that had entrusted the gospel to these men, but God himself. **"For He who worked effectively in Peter**

for the apostleship to the circumcised also worked effectively in me toward the Gentiles," declares the apostle (2:8). The proof of their apostleship lay in the work of the Holy Spirit, bringing men and women to repentance and faith through their ministries. As Paul tells the Corinthians, "My speech and my preaching were not with persuasive words of human wisdom, but in demonstration of the Spirit and of power" (1 Cor. 2:4).

There are two things for us to notice here. Firstly, God commits or entrusts the gospel to men. How amazing this is! It defies our comprehension that God should place the treasure of his eternal purposes into such frail hands. "We have this treasure in earthen vessels, that the excellence of the power may be of God and not of us" (2 Cor. 4:7). Although this was especially true of the apostles, it applies equally to gospel preachers today, and even (in one sense) to every believer. The gospel is a solemn trust. We are not to keep it to ourselves, but preach it to all. Until we have done so we are (to use Paul's terminology) in debt to the unevangelized masses around us (Rom. 1:14). It is by this means that it pleases God to call out his elect people.

The second thing to notice is that genuine gospel preaching is accompanied by the power of the Spirit. This must also be true today. We must not excuse powerless preaching by saying that New Testament times were different, somehow easier, for gospel preaching and church-planting. Jesus promised his disciples that he would be with them in power "always, even to the end of the age," and that age has not yet ended (Matt. 28:18–20).

The powerlessness of so much preaching today can be traced to several causes. First of all, our expectations are too low. We have grown accustomed to ineffective preaching, to listless prayer meetings and lifeless worship. Secondly, preaching is too often an academic exercise, lacking passion for Christ and for the lost. But perhaps our greatest problem is that we fail to preach the true gospel at all! We do not preach Christ, and we do not preach salvation through God's grace alone. In the mistaken view that doctrines like election and particular atonement will "put people off," we place the onus for salvation on man, where we should be giving glory to God. Galatians was written to rescue the true gospel from its imitations, and we need its message today as much as ever.

The right hand of fellowship (2:9)
The leaders of the mother church, Paul tells us, **"perceived the grace that had been given to me."** As a result, he continues, **"They gave me and Barnabas the right hand of fellowship, that we should go to the Gentiles and they to the circumcised"** (2:9). Here was a total vindication of Paul's position. They did not merely say, "You go your way and we will go ours," as they might easily have done. Rather, they proffered the right hand, a sign of agreement, approval, and warmth. Nor was this a parting of the ways, even though they and Paul were to labor in different fields. The hand they offered was one of fellowship, denoting a common purpose and mutual dependence.

Notice that their fellowship centered on the gospel that they preached. When Paul wrote to the Philippians, thanking God for their fellowship, he was talking about "fellowship in the gospel" (Phil. 1:3–5). The fellowship between Paul and the Jerusalem apostles was forged from their mutual discovery that they preached the same gospel. How greatly we need to realize this today! Many spurious grounds are advanced for fellowship. Membership of a particular denomination or church group does not create true fellowship. The names "Christian," "Protestant," "evangelical," or even "reformed," are no guarantee of fellowship among those who bear them. No common experience, no ecumenical profession, can beget true fellowship in Christ.

Within a local church, also, the same principle applies. We do not have fellowship with other believers simply because we attend the same church. Social mixing is not fellowship, though it is often treated as if it were. True fellowship in Christ arises from a mutual understanding of the gospel, a mutual love of that truth, and of the Lord it glorifies. Furthermore, as with Paul and the apostles, fellowship involves not just believing the truth, but proclaiming it to others. The only basis for fellowship, therefore, is the one, true gospel, the message of God's free grace in Christ. That is the message for which Paul contends in Galatians.

The place of works (2:10)

The Jerusalem apostles did make one final request of Paul, namely that he should **"remember the poor"** (2:10). This may be a general reminder to the apostle or, more likely, a request that Paul, in his mission to the Gentiles, should not forget the needy Jewish churches. Acts 11:27–30 records one occasion when relief was sent from the Gentile church at Antioch to the brethren in Judea. It is easy to be so taken up with one's own vineyard, that the (possibly much greater) needs of those further afield are forgotten. Paul was innocent of this fault, because his gospel vision was worldwide. Does it surprise us that such a mundane matter as relieving the poor should be introduced into this high-level theological debate? Does it seem a massive anticlimax to the Council of Jerusalem? Even worse, does it introduce an element of righteousness by works?

If we really understand the gospel of free grace, we shall not react in this way. Good works are an integral part of God's plan of salvation, not as a cause of that salvation, but as a necessary consequence. As Paul reminds Titus, "Christ gave Himself for us, that He might redeem us from every lawless deed and purify for Himself His own special people, zealous for good works" (Titus 2:14). The intimate relationship between salvation by grace and good works is seen even more clearly in Ephesians. Here Paul emphasizes that we are saved by grace, which is "the gift of God, not of works, lest anyone should boast. For we are His workmanship, created in Christ Jesus ..." Could grace be stated more clearly? Yet the very same passage continues: "created in Christ Jesus for good works, which God prepared beforehand that we should walk in them" (Eph. 2:8–10). We are "created in Christ," yes, by a work of divine grace unaided by our works; but "created ... for good works," eternally ordained by God along with our salvation!

God's purpose for his elect in this life is that they should "proclaim the praises of Him who called [them] out of darkness into His marvelous light" (1 Peter 2:9). How are they to do so? By the way they live. In Christ's own words, "Let your light so shine before men, that they may see your good works and glorify your Father in heaven" (Matt. 5:16). God's children do not perform good works to earn God's favor, for that they already have in Christ. Enabled by his Holy Spirit, they live righteously, graciously, and generously that God might be glorified in them.

Summary

The outcome of the Council of Jerusalem was to vindicate totally the gospel that Paul preached among the Gentiles. Believers in Christ, whether Jew or Gentile, are justified by their faith and neither the requirements nor the provisions of the old covenant apply to them. Circumcision and "the law of Moses" have no place in the scheme of salvation, except as pictures of the spiritual truth revealed in Christ.

Paul and the leaders of the Jerusalem church agreed to a division of work; Paul was to evangelize the Gentiles and they the Jews. This agreement, however, was no parting of the ways. It was based upon a common gospel, fellowship in Christ, and mutual respect. Above all, it stemmed from the recognition that their diverse ministries were empowered by the selfsame Holy Spirit.

Notes

[1] See Andrews, *The Spirit has Come*, pp. 209–14

[2] "What kind of addition does Paul have in mind? Certainly it is that advocated by both the false brothers at Jerusalem (vv. 3–5) and the Judaizers of Galatia: that Gentile Christians must be circumcised and live a nomistic lifestyle in accordance with the Jewish Torah" (Longenecker, *Galatians*, p. 54).

[3] "This is one and the same gospel ... The distinction made is that between the gospel 'to the Gentile world' and that 'to the Jewish world' " (Hendriksen, *Galatians and Ephesians*, p. 83).

8
The Gospel Defended

Please Read Galatians 2:11–14

Paul now recounts an incident which provides the "launching pad" for a powerful exposition of faith and law (which will be the subject of part II of this commentary). The special interest of this passage lies in two areas: firstly, the great importance Paul attaches to Peter's apparently harmless change of practice; secondly, the way in which, for Paul, this opened up dramatic insights into the very heart and nature of the gospel.

Eating with the Gentiles (2:11–12)
"Peter," we are told, **"had come to Antioch,"** which was of course a Gentile church (2:11). The occasion of this visit is unknown, and it is not recorded in Acts. The chronology of Paul's account, here in Galatians, implies that the visit took place sometime after the Council of Jerusalem.[1] However, this is not necessarily the case, and Paul could be referring back to an earlier event in order to make his point.[2]

For a Jew to eat with Gentiles was deemed a transgression of Moses' law. In fact, the Old Testament is not explicit on this point, but it did debar the uncircumcised from the Passover (Exod. 12:48) and laid down strict dietary rules for Jews (e.g. Lev. 11). Anyone taking a meal in a Gentile home, therefore, was almost certain to fall foul of these regulations, and thus break the law.[3]

Peter was accused of just such a transgression on his return from Caesarea, where the Gentile Cornelius and his household had "received the word of God." We read, "When Peter came up to Jerusalem, those of the circumcision contended with him, saying, 'You went in to uncircumcised men and ate with them!'"

(Acts 11:1–3). Peter replied by recounting his dream of the clean and unclean beasts, and the way in which the Holy Spirit had fallen upon his Gentile audience, even as he preached: "If therefore God gave them the same gift as He gave us when we believed on the Lord Jesus Christ, who was I that I could withstand God?" (Acts 11:4–18). These are strong words. Peter does not deny the accusation that he transgressed Moses' law by eating at Cornelius' home. He simply says that God made him do it, making "no distinction between us and them, purifying their hearts by faith" (Acts 15:9).

At Antioch, prior to the arrival of **"certain men ... from James,"** Peter had maintained his practice of eating with Gentiles (2:12). Some commentators believe that this refers to the communal meals, or "love feasts," held by the early church, when Christians came together to eat. This may be so, of course, but Paul's reference may equally be to ordinary meals in Gentile homes, as when Peter was entertained by Cornelius. It would be very natural for the Antioch believers to extend such hospitality to their distinguished visitor from Jerusalem. In either case, the fact that Jews like Peter ate with Gentile believers was a clear indication that "cleanness" for the Christian was no longer a matter of dietary practice, but of inner cleansing by the blood of Christ.

The fear of man (2:12)

In spite of his past clarity about these matters, Peter now **"withdrew and separated himself"** from his Gentile brethren, **"fearing those who were of the circumcision"** (2:12). These Jews who arrived in Antioch, and were associated in some unspecified way with James, were not necessarily Judaizers. They did not, as far as we know, reprove Peter for his behavior. Their presence, as Jews and men of influence in Jerusalem, was sufficient to make Peter nervous. He evidently decided that discretion was the better part of valor.

Peter may well have justified his action. By reducing his contact with the Gentile believers, he was doing them no harm, while avoiding offense to the Jews. Peter did not see this as part of the battle with the Judaizers, who sought to subject the Gentiles to Moses' law. Withdrawing from the Gentiles would impose nothing upon them, and would keep the Jewish brethren happy. It was a prudent compromise, not a betrayal of the Council of Jerusalem. We cannot be sure, of course, that these actually were Peter's thoughts. They are, however, the kind of considerations that might have swayed the kindly Barnabas to be **"carried away with their hypocrisy"** (2:13).

Behind the logic of self-justification, however, lurked a much more primitive urge, the fear of others.[4] "The fear of man brings a snare, but whoever trusts in the LORD shall be safe" (Prov. 29:25). As this proverb indicates, the fear of man is inconsistent with a trust in God. Nevertheless, just such a fear pervades much that Christians do or leave undone.

An American evangelist and convention speaker, Del Fesenfeld, knowing he was dying of an incurable brain tumor, was able to preach one last time. Addressing a ministers' convention, he chose as his subject "the fear of man." Why? Because, he said, the gospel was languishing because preachers were more afraid of what their congregations would think than they were of God himself. He could think of nothing more important in his dying exhortation than to warn his fellow-preachers of this situation.

I believe he was right. When we pay more attention to the reactions and expectations of men than to the truth of God, we are in trouble. Yet how often our message and our methods in Christian service are dictated by the reactions (real or imagined) of others! As a result, the gospel waters are muddied, their clarity lost, their sparkle diminished, their taste compromised. If needy souls are to be refreshed, we must lead them to the pristine springs of grace in Christ, and that we shall only do if we proclaim that grace fearlessly. The church in Acts understood this, and prayed for "all boldness" in their proclamation of the word (Acts 4:29–31).

The truth of the gospel (2:13–14)

To Peter, withdrawing from the Gentiles may perhaps have seemed a matter of no great consequence. Paul, however, saw things more clearly: "I withstood [Peter] to the face," he tells us, "because he was to be blamed" (2:11). Why did Paul take so strong a line? What of importance was at stake? According to Paul, nothing less than **"the truth of the gospel"** (2:14).

I am sure that today Paul would have been labeled a troublemaker. What arrogance, to pick a public quarrel with the revered Peter! How insensitive to embarrass the church at Antioch in this way! How inflexible to place his personal convictions before the feelings of others! One can almost hear them whispering behind his back, "Of course, no one can work with Paul; he has too many rough edges."

There is a great difference, however, between troublemaking and defending the gospel. Paul himself exhorts us, "If it is possible … live peaceably with all men" (Rom. 12:18). The apostle is moved to criticize his fellow believers only when he sees that the gospel itself is under threat. **"They were not straightforward,"** he says, **"about the truth of the gospel"** (2:14). In what way was Peter's withdrawal from the Gentiles a threat to the gospel?

The answer is as follows. By separating himself from the Gentiles, Peter was declaring that a distinction still existed between Gentile and Jewish believers. This in turn meant that the old (Mosaic) covenant was still in force, for it was this alone that required such separation. But if this were so, then the very existence of the new covenant in Christ was called in question. It would be necessary for Gentiles to embrace the old covenant (characterized by circumcision and the law of Moses) to obtain parity with the Jews and thus merit salvation. Without realizing it, Peter was "voting with his feet" for the Judaizers.

We know, of course, that Peter actually opposed the Judaizers. He himself had declared that "God … made no distinction between us and them" (Acts 15:8–9). That is why Paul rightly calls his action "hypocrisy," which basically means playing a false role.

What Peter did was to lend credence to the Judaizers' claims that salvation could only be obtained within the old covenant. This, declares Paul, undermines the whole gospel of God's free grace in Christ. Public opposition was the only way to correct this insidious belief. By ignoring the Mosaic dietary rules, Peter had previously lived **"in the manner of Gentiles"** (2:14). His return to those Mosaic rules now gave legitimacy to the Judaizers' doctrine. This is why Paul accuses Peter and the other Jews of compelling **"the Gentiles to live as Jews"** (2:14). Peter would not consciously have done any such thing, but his actions confirmed the very error that he had, in the past, so robustly opposed.

A new order in Christ (2:14)

An apparently harmless compromise by Peter was, therefore, a threat to the true gospel. Although it may have seemed a mere ceremonial (even ethnic) distinction, Peter's self-separation from the Gentiles proclaimed the continued validity of the old covenant, characterized by circumcision, the law of Moses, and separation. In distinct contrast, for those who are the "sons of God through faith in Christ Jesus ... there is neither Jew nor Greek ... for you are all one in Christ Jesus" (3:26–29).

In Christ there is a new covenant, bringing a new relationship between Jews and Gentiles, and Paul expounds this truth at length in Ephesians 2:11–22. The Gentiles had once been "aliens from the commonwealth of Israel and strangers from the covenants of promise." Having no part in the old covenant, which was for Jews alone, they had no title to God's mercy. "But now in Christ Jesus," Paul continues, "you who once were far off have been made near by the blood of Christ ... who has made both one, and has broken down the middle wall of division." Christ had abolished the enmity between Jew and Gentile by abolishing the "law of commandments contained in ordinances, so as to create in Himself one new man."

This is very clear. The redemptive work of Christ involves, as an integral part, the overthrow of the old order. It is this abolition of "commandments contained in ordinances" that enables Jew and Gentile to be united in the new order established in Christ. All who are thus united in Christ, whether Jews or Gentiles, are co-heirs of the promises of God. It follows that any perpetuation of the divide between Jew and Gentile is a denial of the new order, a rejection of the gospel. If the old covenant is still in force, argues Paul, then the new covenant has not arrived, for the two covenants cannot coexist.

Summary
By ceasing to eat with the Gentile believers, Peter had, by implication, denied the gospel. How? By suggesting that the separation of Jews from Gentiles, required under the old covenant, remained valid in the church. This in turn meant that the old covenant itself remained in force, denying the very existence of the new covenant in Christ, namely the gospel.

To accept the gospel is to accept the abolition of the old Mosaic order and thus the removal of the barrier between Jew and Gentile. If that barrier remains, then the old covenant is still in force; salvation comes, not through faith in Christ, but through subjection to "commandments contained in ordinances."

Paul saw the gospel "holistically," that is, as a self-consistent whole. To subvert the unity of Jew and Gentile in Christ was to undermine every other aspect of the gospel. By his death and resurrection, Christ has not obtained a list of unconnected blessings for men, such as forgiveness of sins, love from God, peace of mind, and unity with others. His accomplishment is a seamless robe, a cosmic whole, the perfect fulfillment of God's eternal plan.

Notes

[1] "The episode in which Peter was involved may well have occurred during the interval between the Jerusalem Council (Acts 15:1–29) and the beginning of the second missionary journey (15:40ff)" (Hendriksen, *Galatians and Ephesians*, p. 90).

[2] "In our view ... the Antioch episode most likely took place *after* Paul and Barnabas returned to Syrian Antioch from their mission to Cyprus and southern Galatia as recorded by Luke in Acts 13:4–14:25, *during* the time when 'they stayed there [at Antioch] a long time with the disciples' as told us in Acts 14:26–28, and *before* the Jerusalem Council of Acts 15:1–29" (Longenecker, *Galatians*, p. 71).

[3] "The Jews were permitted to get meat from a Gentile meat-market when the animal had not been slaughtered by a non-Israelite, when the meat had not been brought into contact with pagan religious ceremonies, and when the proprietor of the place where the meat was sold guaranteed that he did not handle inferior meat, the kind that had been prohibited for Jewish consumption" (Strack and Billerbeck, cited by Hendriksen, *Galatians and Ephesians*, p. 91).

[4] "The words [of Gal. 2:12] describe forcibly the cautious withdrawal of a timid person who shrinks from observation" (Lightfoot, *Galatians*, p. 112).

Part II

The Nature and Necessity of Faith

9
The Works of the Law

Please Read Galatians 2:15–16

It may seem a little strange to begin part II of this book in the middle of Paul's argument with Peter. Would it not be more logical to finish with this issue before starting on a new theme? Possibly so, but there is good reason for treating the verses to which we now come (2:15–16) as the start of a new debate. It is true that Paul is still addressing Peter and his fellow Jews, but there is a genuine watershed here. Paul himself, as it were, "changes gear," and begins to extend his argument into new areas. Two things characterize this new phase of the epistle: firstly, Paul's scrutiny of "the law"; and secondly, the great concept of justification by faith.

It may come as a surprise that neither the law nor faith have been mentioned anywhere in the epistle before this point (2:16). The word "faith" does occur in Galatians 1:23, but it is used there to mean "the faith," that is, Christianity itself, and is not a reference to personal faith. We have, of necessity, mentioned the law in earlier chapters, when discussing the Judaizers and the Council of Jerusalem. But it is only at this stage in the epistle that Paul himself introduces these two great antagonists, faith and law. In doing so, he brings us face to face with the ultimate issue of justification. What is it and how is it obtained?

Because these themes are central to the epistle, we need to take time to understand them. This means that we shall be moving rather slowly for the next two chapters, which cover only two verses between them. Nevertheless, this will lay a good foundation for our understanding of what follows in Galatians 3.

In this chapter we shall consider what Paul means by "the

law" and "the works of the law." In the following chapter we shall move on to consider what it means to be "justified by faith."

Jews by nature (2:15)

Paul begins this new phase of his argument by drawing an important distinction. What does he mean when he uses the words, **"We who are Jews by nature, and not sinners of the Gentiles"?** (2:15).

This is Paul's way of introducing the subject of the law. "Jews by nature," signifies "Jews born and bred." Paul is talking to Jewish believers, and reminds them that they are Jews both by birth and upbringing. To them, it was second nature to observe and revere the law of Moses. This was their heritage, their culture, their custom, their habit from childhood. He emphasizes this profound psychological attachment to the law, to add weight to the statement that follows: **"Even we have believed in Christ Jesus, that we might be justified by faith in Christ and not by the works of the law; for by the works of the law no flesh shall be justified"** (2:16).

Note the emphasis: "even we"—we Jews, who might be expected to preserve this precious law at all costs, to stake our lives upon it, to defend it to our dying breath! Even we have had to accept that this law cannot save us; that we must, instead, flee to Christ for justification before God.

Paul's point is clear. Against all their cultural instincts, Peter and his fellow Jewish believers had been compelled to abandon all hope of pleasing God by the works of the law, whether moral, civic or religious. Morality could not save them. Being citizens of a theocratic society could not save them. The outward rituals of priesthood and sacrifices could not save them. They were Christians just *because* they had seen this truth, had turned from self-effort and had trusted in Christ alone for forgiveness and justification. "Christ is the end of the law for righteousness to everyone who believes" (Rom. 10:4).

Sinners from among the Gentiles (2:15)

Consider next what Paul means by **"sinners of,"** or "from among," **"the Gentiles."** This expression is important because it holds the key to the interpretation of what follows in verses 17–18, which present all kinds of difficulty unless we understand what Paul is saying here.

Paul uses the word "sinners" in this verse to mean "transgressors of the law of Moses." This must be so, since he says that those who are "Jews by nature" are "not sinners." Now we know that all men are sinners in the primary sense of this word, whether they are Jews or Gentiles (see e.g. Rom. 3:9, 23; Gal. 3:22). In what sense, then, can the Gentiles be called "sinners" when the Jews are not? Clearly, only in regard to the Mosaic law, which the Jews obeyed (albeit, in an external manner) and the Gentiles did not. This law of Moses had been given to the Jews alone, and meant nothing to the Gentiles. Thus the Jews despised the Gentiles, and disparaged them as "sinners," that is, law-breakers or transgressors.

To summarize, therefore, both of these terms, "Jews by nature" and "sinners from among the Gentiles," direct our attention to Moses' law, which the Jews obeyed (after a fashion) and the Gentiles did not. There is a more basic law, written in the consciences of all men, which even the Gentiles obeyed as far as any man is able. Paul refers to this in Romans 2:14: "When Gentiles, who do not have the law, by nature do the things contained in the law, these, although not having the law, are a law to themselves." What the Gentiles did not have was the Mosaic law, and this is what Paul means by "the law," both in Romans 2:14 and Galatians 2:16. Let us consider this further.

The law of Moses

"A man is not justified by the works of the law," declares the apostle (2:16). This is the first mention of "the law" in Galatians, and we must spend a little time finding out what it means. The subject of "the law" is not only central to the Galatian epistle, but also underlies some important modern controversies. Unless we are clear about the nature and purpose of the law, we shall find it very difficult to see where the truth lies in the debates which, even today, eddy around this subject.

One problem is that the word "law" can be used in several different senses. This is true in English, and was equally true in New Testament Greek. Today we use "law" to signify such diverse things as natural law (like the law of gravity), the rules of a game (like the laws of football), and statute law (enacted by Congress or Parliament). Similarly, in the New Testament we find that "the law" can mean:

1. Old Testament Scripture (1 Cor. 14:21), particularly the books of Moses (Matt. 11:13; Acts 13:15);

2. The law of Moses, given on Mount Sinai (Gal. 3:17);

3. Civil law, e.g. regarding marriage (Rom. 7:2);

4. Conscience, innate moral principles (Rom. 2:14);

5. An internal principle or power, such as the law of sin (Rom. 7:23);

6. The law (or principle) of faith (Rom. 3:27);

7. The law of Christ (Gal. 6:2); the law of liberty; the royal law (James 1:25; 2:8, 12).

By far the largest number of references to "law" in the New Testament, however, clearly relate to the law of Moses. This body of law was given to Israel at Mount Sinai through the mediation of Moses, the man of God (Deut. 5:5). The giving of the law is recorded in Exodus, chapters 19–31 and 34:1–28, during which process Moses went up into the mountain to commune with God. However, further instructions, which also form part of the same law, were given to Moses later, in the tabernacle rather than in the mount (Lev. 1:1; Num. 15, 18, 19, 28–30).

The law of Moses consists firstly of the Ten Commandments, which were written "with the finger of God" (Exod. 31:18) on stone tablets. The first set of tablets were broken by Moses in anger, when he saw how the people had sinned during his absence (Exod. 32:19), but these were replaced by a second set, which were preserved in the Ark of the Covenant after completion of the tabernacle (Exod. 34:1, 28; 40:20). The breaking of the first tablets is a clear picture of man's inability to keep these commandments. The preservation of the second set is an equally clear picture of the fact that Jesus Christ, our Ark, kept God's laws perfectly on behalf of his people.

Following the Ten Commandments came a variety of laws recorded in Exodus 20:22–23:33. This section of the law is often called the "civil law," to differentiate it from the Ten Commandments, which are called the "moral law." However, a careful reading of Exodus shows that there really is very little distinction between the two. The laws given in Exodus 20:22 onwards, during Moses' second visit to the mountain, repeat and amplify much that is found in the Ten Commandments.

Thus we find idolatry forbidden in the second commandment and again in Exodus 20:23, which goes on to give positive directions for the worship of God. The prohibition of murder in the sixth commandment is amplified, and penalties prescribed, in Exodus 21:12–21. Theft is the subject of the eighth commandment and of Exodus 22:1–15; immorality features in the seventh commandment and Exodus 22:16–19; false report in the ninth commandment and Exodus 23:1–9; the keeping of sabbaths in the fourth commandment and in Exodus 23:10–13. Nor can it be argued that the Ten Commandments lay down the moral principles, while Exodus 20–23 specify the civic penalties for breaking those principles. For example, the passage in Exodus 23 on the sabbaths simply amplifies the fourth commandment without mentioning any punishment for non-observance. The same is true of false report and the perversion of justice in Exodus 23:1–9.

There is, therefore, an essential unity between the so-called "moral law" and "civil law" (these terms are never, in fact, used in the Bible). The latter is better represented as an amplification of the former than as a different "kind" of commandment. Alternatively, the Ten Commandments can be viewed as a summary of the whole body of law set out in Exodus 20–23.

The law as a covenant

In Exodus 24 we are told that "Moses wrote all the words of the LORD" and that he then "took the book of the covenant and read it in the hearing of the people" (Exod. 24:4, 7). This is important, for it establishes that the law given by God to Moses was a covenant between God and the Israelites. It was not simply a list of rules, but an arrangement, under which the nation agreed to live in obedience to God. The people's response to the reading of the law was to declare, "All the words which the LORD has said, we will do" (Exod. 24:3).

That the law was a covenant is the key to its proper understanding. It means that the law stands or falls as a single entity. With a covenant, you cannot pick out the bits you like and ignore the rest. The parties to an agreement are bound to perform all their obligations under their contract, not just some of them. As Paul himself argues in Galatians 3:15, even a covenant between men, once it is confirmed, cannot be amended by addition or (he implies) subtraction. How much less the law, which was an arrangement between God and man! We shall consider the law as a covenant much more fully later, when Paul introduces a discussion of "the two covenants" in Galatians 4. However, in anticipation of that passage, we note here further evidence that the Bible views the law of Moses as a covenant:

1. When the two broken stone tablets were replaced, God said to Moses, "Behold I make a covenant" (Exod. 34:10). He then rehearsed a number of laws, including several of the Ten Commandments along with certain ceremonial rules, and added, "Write these words, for according to the tenor of these words I have made a covenant with you and with Israel" (Exod. 34:27). Here the covenant appears to be the whole law, exemplified by the random selection of regulations rehearsed in the passage.

2. Immediately following the above quotation, we read, "And He wrote on the tablets the words of the covenant, the Ten Commandments" (Exod. 34:28). Here it is the Ten Commandments

themselves that are referred to as a covenant (see also Deut. 4:13; 9:9–11; Heb. 9:4).

3. The stone tablets were placed in the "ark," a wooden box, overlaid with gold, which had as its lid the golden "mercy seat." This ark was the central feature of the tabernacle (see Deut. 10:1–5; Heb. 9:1–5). The ark is commonly called "the ark of the covenant," and this is because it contained the covenant documents, namely the Ten Commandments.

Another name for the tablets was "the testimony" (Exod. 25:16), and accordingly the ark was also known as the "ark of the testimony." The link between "covenant" and "testimony" is that a covenant document, by its very nature, "testifies" against anyone who breaches the covenant.

These passages seem to leave no room for doubt that the law was a covenant, and that, specifically, the Ten Commandments were the covenant document, written by God himself.[1]

The tabernacle, the priesthood and the sacrifices

God had not yet finished delivering the law. Moses was called up into the mountain a third time, remaining there for a further forty days (Exod. 24:15, 18). This third phase of the giving of the law was somewhat different. It concerned the design and construction of the tabernacle, the institution of the priesthood, the sacrifices and (again) the sabbath. This third aspect of the law is often referred to as the "ceremonial law," because it dealt with religious ceremonies. The most important thing about this part of the law is that it addressed the problem of how a sinful man may approach a holy God. Such an approach required: a meeting-place with God, the tabernacle; a priesthood, to mediate between man and God; sacrifices, to make atonement for human sins; and a sabbath, denoting rest from those sins. In all these respects, this part of the law pictured the person and work of the Christ who was yet to come.

"The law" in Galatians

Paul refers to the law twenty-nine times in this epistle. Most of these references, of course, occur in later passages, to which we shall come in due course. The questions we need to resolve here are these:

1. Does Paul, in this epistle, always use "the law" to refer to the law of Moses?

2. When he does so, does he mean the law of Moses in its entirety?

3. Does he, specifically, ever use "the law" to mean "the civil and ceremonial law" without the "moral law"?

The reply to these questions is as follows. Paul does not always mean the law of Moses when he speaks of "law" in Galatians. There is one place in which "law" may have a general meaning, namely in Galatians 5:23 where, having listed the fruits of the Spirit, Paul declares, "Against such there is no law." Of course, he may mean there is nothing against these things in the law of Moses. More probably, however, he means there is no law of any kind that can condemn such fruitful actions. In another place, Galatians 2:21 (b), he uses "the law" to mean the Pentateuch (the five Old Testament books attributed to Moses). In a third reference he speaks of "the law of Christ" (6:2). Elsewhere, however, it is clear that the apostle is speaking only of the law of Moses. He tells us that the law came 430 years after Abraham; that it was "appointed through angels by the hand of a mediator [i.e. Moses]"; that the circumcised man "is a debtor to keep the whole law" (3:17, 19; 5:3). He speaks of the covenant "from Mount Sinai which gives birth to bondage" (4:24).

Secondly, there is no indication in Galatians that Paul ever thinks of the law as being divided into different parts (moral, civil, ceremonial). He specifically states that any Gentiles who submit to circumcision become obliged to keep the whole law, not just parts of it (5:3). This clearly implies that Paul sees the law as indivisible.[2]

Thirdly, it is also clear that when Paul refers to the law of Moses in Galatians, he specifically includes the Ten Commandments.

Part II The Nature and Necessity of Faith

He says, "All the law is fulfilled in this: 'You shall love your neighbor as yourself'" (5:14). If we compare this with Romans 13:8–10 we see that Paul must be thinking specifically of the Ten Commandments. The passage in Romans states: "He who loves another has fulfilled the law. For the commandments, 'You shall not commit adultery,' 'You shall not murder,' 'You shall not steal,' 'You shall not bear false witness,' 'You shall not covet' ... are all summed up in this saying, namely, 'You shall love your neighbor as yourself.'" Romans 13:8–10, therefore, is simply an amplified version of Galatians 5:14, and shows that Paul specifically includes the Ten Commandments when he talks about "the law."

We can conclude, then, that "the law" in Galatians normally signifies the law of Moses, unless the context indicates some different meaning. Further, there is no evidence that Paul ever thought of the law as being divided into separate parts; he speaks explicitly about "the whole law." Finally, the law includes the Ten Commandments, and never refers merely to the "civil and ceremonial" aspects of Moses' law.[3]

The works of the law (2:16)

We know, declares the apostle, **"that a man is not justified by the works of the law ... for by the works of the law no flesh shall be justified"** (2:16). This may be a quotation from the Psalms: "Enter not into judgment with thy servant; for in thy sight shall no man living be justified" (Ps. 143:2, KJV). David had seen clearly what Paul now restates: even the most diligent servant of God cannot be justified before a holy God by his devotion or his works.

The "works of the law" are, of course, acts of obedience to the things commanded in the law. By such works, says Paul, we can never be justified (that is, made or declared righteous). Is this because the law is somehow faulty? Not at all, replies Paul. "The law is holy, and the commandment holy and just and good" (Rom. 7:12). The problem lies not in the law, but in man's inability to keep it. Obedience to the law cannot justify a man before God, simply because man is not capable of such obedience. The law,

Paul says elsewhere, "was weak [i.e. unable to save] through [i.e. on account of] the flesh" (Rom. 8:3).

The law, in its first aspect ("moral/civil"), shows something of what God requires of humankind. I say "something"; we must not forget that the New Testament often goes beyond the Ten Commandments in indicating what pleases God. To give just one example, in Matthew 5:44 Jesus says, "Love your enemies," a concept not found anywhere in Moses' law. Man's Creator demands man's exclusive love, service, and worship. He also requires that we should honor him by loving our fellow men, for they are made in his image. But man is innately sinful, incapable of such obedience. Try as we may, we fail to meet God's standards. In the majestic simplicity of Toplady's hymn,

Not the labor of my hands
Can fulfill thy law's demands:
Could my zeal no respite know,
Could my tears for ever flow,
All for sin could not atone;
Thou must save, and thou alone.

What the law could not do, therefore, because of the sinfulness of human nature ("the flesh"), God has done, by sending his Son, Jesus Christ, to make atonement for sin (paraphrase of Rom. 8:3). This work of atonement was prefigured in the second aspect of the law of Moses, namely in the tabernacle, the priesthood, and the sacrifices. But it was only prefigured. Even this aspect of the law could not *save*. As the writer to the Hebrews argues, "The law, having a shadow of the good things to come, and not the very image of those things, can never with these same sacrifices ... make those who approach [God] perfect ... for it is impossible by the blood of bulls and goats to take away sin" (Heb. 10:1–4).

Christ is the fulfillment of the law, the reality which the law could only picture. "For by one offering He has perfected forever those who are being sanctified" (Heb. 10:14). A new covenant has been established between God and his redeemed people, a covenant foreseen by Old Testament prophets. "This is the covenant that I will make with them after those days, says the Lord: I will put My laws into their hearts, and in their minds I will write them ... their sins and their lawless deeds I will remember no more" (Heb. 10:16–17; cited from Jer. 31:33–34).

How may we enter this new covenant? Through faith in Christ's atonement. By believing that he has "perfected forever" those that he has set apart ("sanctified") for himself, namely, his elect people. We must consider this further in the following chapter.

Summary

In Galatians "the law" refers to the law of Moses unless the context indicates, explicitly, some other meaning. It refers to the whole Mosaic law, including the Ten Commandments.

The law is presented in Scripture as a covenant between God and Israel. The Ten Commandments, specifically, were the documents of this covenant.

The traditional idea is that the law of Moses is a three-part law—moral, civil, and ceremonial. A clearer representation, however, is that of a two-part law. In the first part (or aspect), we see what a holy God required of his people, and what penalties were applied to those in Israel who broke his commandments. In the second aspect we see the provision God made for the forgiveness and reconciliation of those who sinned. This second aspect prefigured the work of Christ.

Obedience to the law can never make a man righteous in the sight of God. This is not because of any imperfection in the law, but because man, in his innate sinfulness, cannot keep it. He may succeed in part, but God requires perfection.

Notes

[1] For a fuller discussion of the law as a covenant see Reisinger, *Tablets of Stone*, pp. 29–41.

[2] "Paul nowhere draws any distinction in the law between ceremonial and moral precepts. The law for him is one, and it is the law of God. It is owing to accidental circumstances that the ceremonial aspect of it is more prominent in this epistle [Galatians], as the ethical aspect is in Romans. But we shall find the same line of argument repeated in Romans, where it is the moral law which is at stake. And when the Apostle tells us that through the law he has died to the law (Gal. 2:19), or that we have died to the law through the body of Christ (Rom. 7:4), or that we are not under law but under grace (Rom. 6:4), he has not the moral law any less in view than the ceremonial. He means that *nothing* in the Christian life is explained by *anything* statutory, and that everything in it is explained by the inspiring power of that death in which Christ made all our responsibilities to the law His own" (Denney, *Death of Christ*, p. 93).

[3] "Let it be settled, then, that Paul by 'the works of the law' means not ceremonial works, but all the works of the law. Then it will also be settled that all works of the law that are wrought without the Spirit are condemned" (Luther, *Bondage of the Will*, p. 286).

And Poole comments, "*By the works of the law*; by any kind of works done in obedience to the law of Moses, whether ceremonial or moral. For it is manifest, that although this question about justification by works began about circumcision and works done in obedience to the ceremonial law, yet the determination of it extended further. For the apostle, by *the law*, understands that law by which *is the knowledge of sin*, Rom. 3:20" (*Commentary*, p. 646).

10
Justified by Faith

Please Read Galatians 2:16

The second major theme introduced at this point in the epistle is that of justification by faith. **"We have believed in Christ Jesus,"** declares the apostle, **"that we might be justified by faith in Christ and not by the works of the law"** (2:16). We saw in chapter 9 that obedience to the law cannot make a man righteous, as God counts righteousness. Man's innate sinfulness renders him incapable of obeying God's law perfectly; and God's standard of righteousness is perfection, nothing less. How, then, may a man be justified in God's eyes? Paul supplies the answer in this verse. This subject is so important to Galatians (and, indeed, to the Christian gospel) that we shall devote the whole of this chapter to it.

The meaning of justification
What is justification? It is the imputation of Christ's perfect righteousness to those who believe. "We implore you," writes Paul, "be reconciled to God. For He made Him [Christ] who knew no sin to be sin for us, that we might become the righteousness of God *in Him*" (2 Cor. 5:20–21, emphasis added).

The verb "to justify" means "to make or declare righteous." The Bible, however, uses the word only in the second of these senses. Thus Jesus tells us, "Even the tax collectors justified God, having been baptized with the baptism of John" (Luke 7:29). Clearly, they did not *make* God righteous. Their action simply declared that God was a righteous God, who requires repentance from sinful men. In the same way, in justification, God pronounces the sinner righteous on the grounds of Christ's atoning work. Justification is the opposite of condemnation. In condemnation, a man is declared guilty before God on account of his sins and transgressions. In justification, the believer in Christ is declared innocent of all offense against the law of God on account of Christ's perfect obedience to that law. All mankind is guilty before God, for "All have sinned and fall short of the glory of God" (Rom. 3:23). But, continues Paul, all who believe in Christ are "justified freely by His grace through the redemption that is in Christ Jesus" (Rom. 3:24).

In justification, God deems the believing sinner to be righteous and thus acceptable in his sight. Sins are forgiven. Blame and guilt are removed, so that the believer in Christ may both stand and rejoice in the presence of God, instead of fearing and shrinking from his holy presence. This is how Paul expresses this great truth in Romans: "To him who does not work but believes on Him who justifies the ungodly, his faith is accounted for righteousness, just as David also describes the blessedness of the man to whom God imputes righteousness apart from works: 'Blessed are those whose lawless deeds are forgiven, and whose sins are covered; blessed is the man to whom the Lord shall not impute sin' " (Rom. 4:5–8).

On the cross, Christ exchanged his righteousness for our sinfulness. He bore our sins so that we might wear his sinlessness. He endured the Father's wrath so that we might be accepted as sons and daughters of the Father. Therefore, in Christ we have been judged for our sin with an eternal judgment; and in Christ we have been justified with an eternal acceptance. God's people, Paul tells us, have been "predestined ... to adoption as sons by Jesus Christ to Himself, according to the good pleasure of His will, to the praise of the glory of His grace, *by which He has made us accepted in the Beloved*" (Eph. 1:5–6, emphasis added). This is justification.

A righteousness that is not our own

We are, writes the apostle, **"justified by faith in Christ and not by the works of the law"** (2:16). The righteousness acquired by the believer is not obtained by obedience to the law, or by works of any other kind; that is, neither our actions nor our thoughts, and neither our attitudes nor our emotions contribute in any way to the righteousness that justifies a sinner. It follows that this righteousness *cannot be our own*, since it does not stem from anything we are or do. It is the righteousness of Christ that is put to our account. This must be so, for only Christ's perfect righteousness is acceptable to God; never our own imperfect efforts to please him. If we are to be accepted at all, we must be "accepted in the Beloved" (Eph. 1:6). Neither is it the act of believing that justifies, but rather the one in whom we believe. Otherwise we would be justified by the work of "believing."

On earth, Christ lived a perfect life, pleasing to God the Father in thought, word and deed. He perfectly fulfilled the requirements of the law, not only outwardly but from the heart. "You are My beloved Son," said the voice from heaven as Jesus was baptized. "In You I am well pleased" (Luke 3:22). Christ was, of course, perfectly righteous before he came to earth. He shared with his Father the beauty of holiness, the ineffable purity of the Godhead. It was, however, necessary for him to earn a *human* righteousness, by living as a man among men. That is why, at his baptism, Jesus said, "It is fitting for us to fulfill all righteousness" (Matt. 3:15). By identifying himself with mankind, in baptism as in life, he was able to obtain, on our behalf, righteousness *as a man*. It is this righteousness that is imputed to those **"who have believed in Christ Jesus"** (2:16).

There is a further sense in which the believer's righteousness is not his own. The righteousness that justifies a sinner always *remains* Christ's; it is not transferred in some way to the believer. The Roman Catholic Church teaches a doctrine of "infused righteousness." According to this idea, as Berkhof explains it, the actual righteousness of Christ is transferred to believers so that "Justification ... consists in the infusion of new virtues after the pollution of sin has been removed in baptism."[1] Thus, they say, the believer acquires righteousness inherently, *in his own right*, as if it were some essence capable of passing from Christ to ourselves.

This is mistaken. The righteousness of Christ is not a transferable commodity. It remains his righteousness and becomes ours *only by virtue of our union with him*. As Galatians 2:20 puts it, "I have been crucified with Christ; it is no longer I who live, but Christ lives in me."

A new creation
This last point raises a second aspect of justification, namely our union with Christ. Since the righteousness that justifies resides in Christ, it can only benefit us in as much as we are *"found in Him, not having [our] own righteousness, which is from the law, but that which is through faith in Christ"* (Phil. 3:9; emphasis added). Notice again that we partake of Christ's righteousness by being "found in Him."[2]

This union with Christ is no mere figure of speech, but a spiritual reality; so much so that it produces a genuine transformation in the believing sinner, for "If anyone is in Christ, he is a new creation; old things have passed away; behold all things have become new" (2 Cor. 5:17). We must never forget that God does not simply impute righteousness to the ungodly, but also transforms those who are justified. As Paul writes elsewhere, "Whom He justified, these He also glorified" (Rom. 8:30). Theologically, justification and regeneration can be treated as separate subjects, but in reality they always go together. In regeneration (that is, the new birth, a sovereign act of God) there is born within the subject a "new man ... created by God, in righteousness and true holiness" (Eph. 4:24). The believer has been born again, "not of corruptible seed but of incorruptible" (1 Peter 1:23; see also John 3:3–8; 1 John 3:9).

This has great practical implications. Paul writes, "Our old man was crucified with [Christ] ... that we should no longer be slaves of sin" (Rom. 6:6). That is, the believer's "old man," which was the slave of sin, is dead, having been crucified with Christ, and a "new man" has been created within him which *is* righteous on account of his union with Christ. This is why Paul can urge, "Reckon yourselves to be dead indeed to sin, but alive to God in

Christ Jesus our Lord" (Rom. 6:11). When he says "reckon," he does not mean "pretend." He means, "Count on it as a fact."

Of course, the justified believer is still capable of sin. However, this sin is not the work of the "new man." Believers sin because sin still dwells in their human nature ("the flesh"), like some unwelcome guest. As Paul explains, "If I do that which I [as a believer] will not to do, it is no longer I [the new man] who do it, but sin that dwells in me" (Rom. 7:20).

Righteousness practiced
A mistake that is often made is to think of justification as a past event, a legal declaration of righteousness which occurred at the time of conversion, but has no practical impact on the believer's life. When a person "accepts Christ," people say, he is declared righteous, but may remain a "carnal Christian," his life unchanged. What he now needs, they continue, is "sanctification," since this is the process by which the justified sinner is transformed into a saint. Accordingly, he must be taught to live a holy life, being told what he may, and may not, do as a Christian. Far from producing holy living, this teaching often leads to a bondage very similar to that which threatened the Galatians (Gal. 5:1).

The mistake lies in a false antithesis between justification and sanctification. These are, alike, both past events and present realities (or states). To "sanctify" simply means to set apart for God's use and glory. "We have been sanctified," says the writer to the Hebrews, "through the offering of the body of Jesus Christ once for all" (Heb. 10:10). Again he writes, "By one offering He has perfected forever those who are being sanctified" (Heb. 10:14). The term "being sanctified" does not necessarily imply a progressive sanctification, but rather that God is continually adding to his church by sanctifying, or setting apart, new believers. In Scripture, therefore, justification and sanctification are parallel, not sequential. A man cannot be justified first and sanctified later. Sanctification is a necessary accompaniment of justification, for without holiness "no one will see the Lord" (Heb. 12:14). It has been pointed out that although justification means only the imputation of righteousness, the related words "righteous" and "righteousness" in Scripture often carry the connotation of practical goodness.[3]

The "new man" is not a slave to sin, as was the "old man," but a slave to righteousness and to God; we should therefore bear "fruit to holiness" in our practical life (Rom. 6:19–22). This tendency to holy living is opposed by the indwelling sin which still inhabits the believer's body and mind, and which frequently leads to sinful thoughts or actions. Nevertheless, as a consequence of regeneration, the true believer does have an innate tendency to obey God and to practice righteousness, and this tendency will normally dominate his practical life. We have every right to question the reality of those who claim to be Christians but in whose lives the fruits of righteousness are not visible. The question of holy living will occupy us more fully in the third part of this book, where we shall consider "the fruit of the Spirit" (Gal. 5:22). Holiness of life must flow from within, from the indwelling Spirit, not be imposed from without by rules and regulations.

Justified by faith

Having considered what justification is, we now turn to the next issue: how may it be acquired? Paul tells us in Galatians 2:16. Justification is obtained by believing in Christ. It is only by believing that we may appropriate the righteousness of Christ and thereby stand justified in the sight of God. **"We have believed in Christ Jesus,"** says the apostle, **"that we might be justified by faith in Christ"** (2:16). Before we go further, it may be helpful to define what faith *is*, for people are often confused about its nature. There are two elements in faith which need to be kept distinct. One element is "trust" and the other is "knowledge." Historically, different theologians have emphasized one rather than the other, and this has sometimes left a legacy of confusion.[4]

To most people, faith is trust or belief in God, and this is correct as far as it goes. "Abraham believed God and it was accounted to him for righteousness" (3:6). Most people also recognize that mere intellectual belief of the facts about God is not faith. "Even the demons believe and tremble" (James 2:19). For faith to be genuine there must be an element of trust or reliance. This trust must be total, for we cannot at the same time trust God and rely on natural wisdom or human strength. Furthermore, this trust has to have an abiding character; it cannot consist in a transitory belief that God will come to our aid at a time of crisis. And so we could continue.

In thinking of faith as nothing more than trust, therefore, we have to add many qualifications to distinguish real faith from mere belief. Here lies the inadequacy of this definition of faith. The problem stems from the fact that "trust" is a capacity of human nature, whereas biblical faith is not. For instance, we can trust other people, such as our doctor, our financial adviser or our minister. We also trust in the reliability or benign nature of physical and social structures. We trust that the bridge will bear our weight, or that the judicial system will be fair. Indeed, life would be impossible if we did not trust a large number of people and things on a daily basis. Human beings are constituted in such a way that they naturally trust others—witness the trusting attitude of a child toward grown-ups. We are sometimes too gullible, trusting people who betray our trust. But that just emphasizes how trusting we are by nature.

However, although by nature we can trust even deceivers, we are incapable by nature of trusting God! The natural man cannot trust God, simply because he cannot know God or the truth concerning God (see 1 Cor. 2:14). Trust in God, therefore, is quite different from trust in human beings, or in social and physical structures. This is why faith must be distinguished from mere "trust." Faith can only exist when spiritual things can be discerned. That is, faith necessarily involves a *knowledge* of the unseen things of God.

The best and simplest way to express this idea is to say that faith is (or involves) spiritual sight. This faculty of sight is not an attribute of human nature, but is imparted by God as a gift, during the process of regeneration (Eph. 2:8; Acts 16:14). Thus the "natural man" is spiritually blind; he "does not receive the things of the Spirit of God, for they are foolishness to him; nor can he know them, because they are *spiritually discerned*" (1 Cor. 2:14, emphasis added). Man by nature cannot comprehend the gospel, because his mind has been blinded by Satan (2 Cor. 4:3–4).

By contrast, believers "walk by faith, not by sight" (2 Cor. 5:7). This familiar statement can be misunderstood. It does not teach, as many think, that faith is blind. It means that the believer lives *relying on spiritual sight, rather than physical sight and natural discernment*. This is evident from the passage found a few verses earlier in 2 Corinthians 4:18: "We do not look at the things which are seen [i.e. by natural sight], but at the things which are not seen. For the things which are seen are temporary, but the things which are not seen are eternal." Notice that we *look* at these invisible things. How can we look at them? By the exercise of spiritual sight, that is, faith. As Hebrews 11:27 puts it, "He [Moses] endured as seeing Him [Christ] who is invisible." The whole eleventh chapter of Hebrews is summarized in Hebrews 12:1–2, where we are exhorted to "run with endurance the race that is set before us, *looking* unto Jesus, the author and finisher of our faith" (emphasis added).

Once spiritual sight is received, we are able to trust in the spiritual realities which we now see. Because we discern the significance of Christ's death, we are able to trust him to "bear away our sins." Because we see, by faith, the unchanging nature of God, and the eternal scope of his purposes in Christ, we can trust him with our own eternal future. Notice that this knowledge of the spiritual which faith allows is no mere intellectual insight, but rather a spiritual and experimental discernment of the things of God. Faith is spiritual sight which issues in trust in God.

Faith and faithfulness

The words **"justified by faith in Christ"** mean literally, "justified by means of the faith [or faithfulness] of Christ." The same Greek word may be translated "faith" or "faithfulness." Some argue, therefore, that the correct translation is "faithfulness" rather than "faith." This idea gains strength from the fact that Paul actually wrote, "the faith [or faithfulness] *of* Christ," rather than "faith *in* Christ."[5]

Most commentators believe, however, that "faith in Christ" is the correct rendering. They point out that "the faith of Christ" can mean "the faith that pertains to Christ," rather than "the faithfulness exercised by Christ." Certainly, both alternatives express truth. We must exercise faith in Christ if we are to be justified, so we are "justified by faith" (Rom. 5:1). Equally, however, in a causal sense, justification arises from Christ's faithfulness to the law of God and his eternal purpose. To place the emphasis upon Christ's faithfulness, rather than our believing, would be wholly consistent with Paul's argument. That is, justification is the outcome of God's free grace, not of any activity by man.

However we may decide to interpret this verse, this latter point is important. There is always the danger of making "faith" a human work, which would negate Paul's whole argument. Faith in Christ must indeed be exercised if we are to be justified. But justifying faith does not lie within the capacity of human nature. Paul is anxious to emphasize this as he writes to the Ephesians: "By grace you have been saved through faith, and that not of yourselves; it is the gift of God, not of works, lest anyone should boast" (Eph. 2:8–9). Again, Peter declares that the "precious faith" of his readers had been "obtained ... by the righteousness of our God and Savior Jesus Christ" (2 Peter 1:1).

Peter's statement neatly summarizes the relationship between the faith of the believer and the faithfulness of Christ. Our faith is not a faculty of fallen human nature. It is not something we can work up by an effort of willpower, or drag from our subconscious minds. It is nowhere to be found in our natural selves. It has to be "obtained" from an outside source. What is that source? It is the faithfulness of a righteous Savior. The whole of salvation, inclusive of the faith that saves, is God's gift. It can be obtained no other way.

Summary

Justification is the imputation of Christ's righteousness to the believing sinner, by which the sinner is declared righteous in the sight of God. The believing sinner is righteous in God's sight by virtue of his union with Christ.

Justification is always accompanied by regeneration. The sinner becomes a new creation in Christ as, by the indwelling of the Holy Spirit, there is planted within him a "new man ... created according to God, in righteousness and true holiness" (Eph. 4:24). This "righteousness of God" is evidenced in the practical life of the believer, whose new nature (the "new man") results in godly living as the norm (Rom. 8:14).

Justification is God's gift to his elect people, made possible through the faithfulness of Christ. It is obtained by faith, which is itself the gift of God. Faith can be defined as spiritual sight, imparted in regeneration by a gracious and sovereign act of God, which enables the believer to discern spiritual realities and thus to put his trust (for salvation and all other things) in the person and work of Christ.

Notes

[1] Berkhof, *Systematic Theology*, p. 524.

[2] "The first particular benefit that a sinner has by his union with Christ, is justification: for, being united to Christ, he has communion with him in his righteousness."

"Thus the person united to Christ is justified ... From this union with Christ results a communion with him in his unsearchable riches, and consequently in his righteousness ... Thus the righteousness of Christ becomes his: and because it is his by unquestionable title, it is imputed to him; it is reckoned his in the judgement of God, which is always according to truth. And so the believing sinner, having a righteousness which fully answers the demands of the law, is pardoned and accepted as righteous" (Boston, *Human Nature*, pp. 195, 196–7).

[3] "Is Paul's use of the δικαι-cluster of words to be understood as 'transfer terminology' ... or as applicable to 'the day to day conduct of those who had already believed' (so D. G. Dunn, BJRL 65 [1983] 121)?"

"In our judgement, J. A. Ziesler has largely resolved this dilemma in demonstrating that the verb δικαιοω (justify) in Paul's letters is used forensically and relationally, but that the noun δικαιοσυνη [righteousness] and adjective δικαιος [righteous] have also behavioural and ethical nuances—thereby showing that Paul joins forensic and ethical categories in his understanding of righteousness, with the one always involving the other ... the four uses of the verb in [Gal. 2] vv. 16–17 and the noun in v. 21 cannot be treated as simply 'transfer terms' when the issue at both Antioch and Galatia had to do with the lifestyle of those who were already believers in Jesus. So ... we must treat the δικαι-cluster of words as having both forensic and ethical significance, though ... over all such terms stands the relational, participatory concept of being 'in Christ' " (Longenecker, *Galatians*, p. 85).

[4] "While the Roman Catholics stressed the fact that justifying faith is merely assent and has its seat in the understanding, the Reformers generally regarded it as *fiducia* (trust), having its seat in the will. On the relative importance of the elements in faith there have been differences, however, even among

Protestants. Some regard the definition of Calvin as superior to that of the Heidelberg Catechism. Says Calvin: 'We shall now have a full definition of faith if we say that it is a firm and sure knowledge of the divine favour toward us, founded on the truth of a free promise in Christ, and revealed to our minds, and sealed in our hearts, by the Holy Spirit' " (Berkhof, *Systematic Theology*, pp. 406–7).

[5] Longenecker, writing in favour of the rendering "the faithfulness of Christ" in Galatians 2:16, says, "It is the faithfulness and obedience of Christ to the contractual obligation of the Law in His life and in His death, as well as His sacrifice in the incarnation and Calvary experience, that is proclaimed as perfectly executed in the triumphant cry 'It is finished' " (Paul, *Apostle of Liberty*, p. 51).

11
The Law Dismantled

Please Read Galatians 2:17–18

P aul is still discussing justification. He continues his argument as follows: **"If, while we seek to be justified by Christ, we ourselves also are found sinners, is Christ therefore a minister of sin? Certainly not!"** (2:17). At first sight, this verse is difficult to interpret, and many different ideas have been put forward as to its meaning. There is, however, only one interpretation that fits the context which, of course, concerns the believer and the law. We shall first examine this most likely explanation and then, afterwards, mention one or two possible alternatives.

The law and the gospel cannot coexist (2:17)
The key to Galatians 2:17 is found in verse 15, which we have already considered. We saw there that the word "sinners" was used in a rather special way, namely, to describe Gentiles as distinct from Jews. It was clear that, in such a context, "sinners" had to mean "those who break the law of Moses," setting the Gentiles in contrast to the Jews, who were keepers of that law. Of course, the Jews" obedience to the law was an outward and highly imperfect obedience (see Rom. 2:17–24). But the Gentiles made no pretence of law-keeping; to them the law was simply irrelevant.

If we now interpret **"sinners"** in verse 17 in this same manner, the meaning of the verse becomes immediately clear. Let me try to show this by paraphrasing the passage as follows:

In seeking to be justified by Christ, (that is, by faith rather than by works), believers turn their backs upon the law. They find themselves acting like Gentiles, rather than Jews, with respect to the law (compare 2:14). This is a necessary consequence of justification by faith. Therefore the followers of Christ are found to be "sinners," since (like the Gentiles) they ignore the law.

Does this make Christ a promoter of sin? Of course not. To reject the law may make us "sinners" in the eyes of the Jews, but in God's sight we are doing the right thing! Far from promoting sin, Christ is promoting righteousness, since this can only be obtained by abandoning the law and embracing faith.

This interpretation has much to recommend it. It dovetails perfectly into both the context and the development of Paul's argument. It links back to verses 14–16 and builds upon them. No alternative explanation of verse 17 has these qualities. One thing emerges clearly from this verse: the law and the gospel cannot coexist. To seek to be justified by Christ is to become a transgressor of the law. One obvious example of this is that the law requires separation of Jews from Gentiles, whereas the gospel unites them in Christ. As Paul tells the Ephesians, "He Himself is our peace, who has made both one ... having abolished in His flesh the enmity, that is, *the law of commandments contained in ordinances*, so as to create in Himself one new man" (Eph. 2:14–18, emphasis added). A second example is that we cannot continue with the shadows (such as animal sacrifice and human priesthood) once the reality has come, who is Christ. To embrace Christ, we must therefore discard the provisions of Sinai's law, for he is our only offering and our only priest.

Is Paul saying Christ is not to blame for a believer's sin? (2:17)

There are alternative interpretations of Galatians 2:17. We could ignore them, of course, but since we will come across them, we shall look at two such alternatives. The chief purpose of doing this is to show how superior is the explanation given above. Secondly, however, this brief diversion will help introduce other issues which arise later in the epistle.

One alternative explanation is that Paul is saying, "We must not blame the Savior for the misdeeds of the saved." Christians are not perfected in this life, for sin still dwells within them, but this does not invalidate justification by faith. Just because believers commit sin, it does not mean that they are not justified. Nor does it mean that Christ is responsible for making them sin (he is not a "minister of sin").

According to this interpretation, Paul is answering an unspoken criticism of his teaching. The Jews point the finger at those who claim to be justified by faith instead of law-works: "These Christians claim that faith is all they need, but look at their lives! They are far from perfect. The Christ they follow is only teaching them to sin!" Not so, says Paul. Christ teaches us to live righteously. It is only our failure to follow him perfectly that leads to sin. Christ cannot be blamed for that.

The problem with this interpretation is that it introduces, out of the blue, a theme that has nothing to do with the context. The problem of sin in the believer is a real one, and elsewhere Paul devotes close attention to it (see e.g. Rom. 7:13–25). He also addresses certain aspects of this matter later in Galatians (e.g., 5:16–17). However, this is not the subject here in chapter 2. The only sin in view is that of Peter, whose return to Mosaic practice would have been applauded by the Jews, not condemned by them as a fault!

Is he speaking of antinomianism? (2:17)
Another possible interpretation of verse 17 is as follows. The Judaizers complained that justification by faith, apart from the works of the law, promotes lawlessness (or "antinomianism"). If believers do not need to obey the law, they argue, then they will live as they please, ignoring God's commandments. Paul rejects this criticism, for it would make Christ a promoter of sin.

There is no doubt that Paul was accused of antinomianism. He tells us this explicitly in Romans 3:8: "Why not say, 'Let us do evil that good may come'?—as we are slanderously reported and as some affirm that we say" (see also Rom. 6:1, 15). There is a certain logical force in the accusation. The only defense against lawlessness, argue Paul's opponents, is the enforcement of law. Therefore believers must submit to the law if they are to please God. The Judaizers may have passed into history, but similar arguments are commonly urged, or at least implied, today.[1]

Later in Galatians we shall see how Paul responds to this accusation. Simply put, his answer is that God writes his laws in the believer's heart, as he promised (Heb. 10:16–17). Thus the believer is not without law, but the law he obeys is an inward principle, not one imposed outwardly. The inward law, unsurprisingly, enjoins many of the same imperatives as are found in Moses' law, for God is the author of both. Nevertheless, the inward law is essentially moral and spiritual in nature, in contrast to the ritualism and servility of the covenant of Sinai.

Galatians, therefore, *does* concern itself with the antinomian question, but it is not the subject of Galatians 2:17. To introduce the issue at this point makes no sense. Paul is dealing here with the means of justification, nothing else. The believer's rule of life, his motivation to holiness, is simply not under discussion at this stage of the epistle.

The law destroyed (2:18)

Having dealt with the meaning of verse 17, the impetus of Paul's logic carries us forward into verse 18, which reads, **"For if I build again those things which I destroyed, I make myself a transgressor."**

Having stated in the previous verse that to obey Christ is to reject the law, the apostle now draws an unavoidable conclusion. The believer, by believing, has "destroyed" the law.[2] Sin does not reside in breaking Moses' law, as the Judaizers taught. Rather, the opposite is true, for we sin if we try to "build again" the edifice of law-works as a means of pleasing God. Why? Because to reinstate the law is to reject Christ: "You have become estranged from Christ, you who attempt to be justified by law; you have fallen from grace" (5:4).

But is Paul really talking about the law of Moses, in its entirety, when he uses the word "destroyed"? Did not Christ say, "Do not think that I came to destroy the Law or the Prophets. I did not come to destroy but to fulfill"? (Matt. 5:17). There are several questions here, and we must consider them one by one.

1. Does Paul mean that faith destroys the law, as such?

Or is he speaking only about the works of the law, which he rejects as a means of justification?

In so far as the law is a covenant of works, the law and its works cannot be separated. If we are to obey the law of Moses, then the only reason for doing so is to please God. To please God is to be justified in his sight. Paul therefore means that the law is destroyed as a covenant under which men may find the blessing of God. Of this covenant Paul writes, "Cast out the bondwoman [the old covenant] and her son [those who seek justification under that covenant]" (4:25, 30). The Mosaic covenant is rejected and, in that sense, destroyed.

However, when Paul talks of destroying the law, he does not mean the law no longer has any function. Later in the epistle he explains the purpose of the law: it is "our tutor to bring us to Christ, that we might be justified by faith" (3:24). Again, he tells Timothy that "The law is good if one uses it lawfully, knowing this, that the law is not made for a righteous person, but for the lawless ..." (1 Tim. 1:8–9). The proper use of the law, then, is to convict men of their sinfulness and point them to Christ as their only hope. "By the deeds of the law no flesh will be justified in His sight, for *by the law is the knowledge of sin*" (Rom. 3:20, emphasis added; cf. Rom. 7:7–12).

2. Is the whole law rejected?

Are not the moral elements of the law retained as eternally valid?

We have already seen that Paul makes no division of the law. Had he intended to say that only part of the law was destroyed, there were countless opportunities in this epistle to say so. Yet the apostle does not do so. Indeed, he makes it quite plain that the entire covenant "from Mount Sinai ... gives birth to bondage" and is to be "cast out" (4:24, 30). Paul must include the "moral law," since this was foremost among the commandments given on Sinai.

Does this mean that the believer is free to murder, commit adultery, steal, and so on? Of course not. "How shall we who died to sin live any longer in it?" (Rom. 6:2). The believer in Christ will avoid sin, but he will do so, not out of submission to the old covenant, but because he has died and risen again with Christ (Rom. 6:3–7). Christ died, says Paul, "that the righteous requirement of the law might be fulfilled in us who ... walk ... according to the Spirit" (Rom. 8:4). Walking according to the Spirit clearly involves being taught, from the Scriptures, what is pleasing to God. Thus the believer will heed God's revealed will, and scriptural exhortation, in matters of life and conduct, including the moral content of the Ten Commandments. But he will do so as one who is led and enabled by the Holy Spirit, not as a matter of outward conformity to a discarded covenant.

3. How can Paul say the law has been "destroyed" when Jesus says the opposite?

When Jesus refers to "the law and the prophets" in Matthew, he is actually talking about the Old Testament Scriptures, not the law of Moses. However, Moses' law forms part of those Scriptures, so the question remains a fair one. The word "destroy" must be understood in its context in each case. Christ said he came "not to destroy, but to fulfill." But in fulfilling the law, he rendered it redundant. For example, the Mosaic priesthood was swept away, being replaced by Christ's high priesthood (see Heb. 7–9). So, in one sense, fulfillment can be viewed as destruction, since it renders obsolete that which is fulfilled. The purpose of a flower is fulfilled when its petals fall, leaving the seed-pod to ripen. The blossom is destroyed in the very act of fulfillment. So it is with the law.

Summary

If we are to be justified by faith in Christ, we must abandon all reliance on the law. The whole Mosaic "package," in its entirety, was a covenant of works between God and man. Man, however, is incapable of keeping that covenant, and thereby pleasing God.

Justification by Christ "destroys" the law, both by fulfilling it and by replacing it. The law retains one function, namely to bring sinners to a knowledge of their sin and thus direct them to Christ.

Though the believer no longer strives to keep the law, he is not "without law," since he is risen with Christ to "newness of life" and walks "according to the Spirit." As he does so, the righteous requirements of the law are fulfilled in his life.

Notes

[1] "The true preaching of the gospel of salvation by grace alone always leads to the possibility of this charge [antinomianism] being brought against it ... If my preaching and presentation of the gospel of salvation does not expose it to that misunderstanding, then it is not the gospel" (Lloyd-Jones, *Romans*, vol. 3., p. 8).

[2] "The phrase ... 'those things that I annulled/annihilated/destroyed' ... refers to the law as both the basis for justification and a necessary form of life. The aorist tense of the verb ... has in mind a past, once for all act—that time of conversion when one ceased to rely on the Mosaic law for either justification or the supervision of life, but turned to Christ for both acceptance before God and the pattern for living" (Longenecker, *Galatians*, pp. 90–91).

12
United with Christ

Please Read Galatians 2:19–21

What, then, is the relationship between the believer and the law? As Paul reaches the climax of his argument in chapter 2, how does he sum up this matter? He states his conclusions in terms of a new metaphor, that of death: **"For I through the law died to the law that I might live to God"** (2:19). Everything that has been said in the foregoing verses leads up to this conclusion, and all that follows in verses 20–21 is an amplification of it.

Dead to the law (2:19)

Paul depicts the believer's relationship to the law in terms of death. What is this relationship? It is that of a dead man to his surroundings, namely, no relationship at all! The believer has finished with the law, just as truly as a corpse has finished with its former life.[1]

But is this really what Paul is teaching? Many would disagree. For example, the respected commentator William Hendriksen states, "The hue and cry of the present day, to the effect that as Christians 'we have nothing whatever to do with the law' has no Scriptural justification at all. It is, in fact, a dangerous slogan, especially in an era of lawlessness!"[2]

Like Hendriksen, I deplore mindless slogans. But we have to face up to what Paul is saying here. We shall see presently that Paul does not use this analogy of death lightly, for in Romans 7 he develops the idea in its full legal implication. When he writes, **"I ... died to the law,"** does he really mean, "I am dead, not to the law itself, but only to justification by the works of the law, and I remain alive to certain parts of the law as my rule of life"?[3] I think it unlikely. Whatever difficulties it may cause, we must deal honestly with Paul's uncompromising statements, both here and in Romans, concerning the believer and the law. The difficulties can be resolved by patient comparison of one scripture with another, and by understanding what Paul has to say later in the epistle about the Christian's motivation to holy living.[4]

The point to grasp is that the believer's rule of life is the whole Bible, not just part of it. Taught in the Scriptures by the Holy Spirit, and graciously enabled by that same Spirit, the one who is alive in Christ will walk righteously. God's law is written in his heart, so that he obeys from the heart what God requires. "God be thanked," writes Paul to the Romans, "that though you were slaves of sin, yet you obeyed from the heart that form of doctrine to which you were delivered, and having been set free from sin, you became slaves of righteousness" (Rom. 6:17–18). The new "form of doctrine" into whose embrace (and continuing care) we are "delivered" is, of course, the gospel of God's free grace.

Certainly, Moses' law and the law "written in the heart" have some things in common, but they remain two distinct laws. They overlap, but they are not the same. Both teach me, for example, that I must not defraud my neighbor, but only the law of Christ teaches me to go the second mile, and love my enemy. The Sermon on the Mount is sometimes (wrongly, I believe) said to be Christ's exposition of the Ten Commandments. The fact is that the Sermon on the Mount introduces entirely new concepts of morality. To despise a fellow human is akin to murder. To lust in the heart is akin to adultery.

When a building is demolished, the builders may use some of the old material to rebuild on the same site. Some valuable items may be carefully preserved for inclusion in the new edifice. But the old building is nonetheless destroyed, and the construction that replaces it nonetheless new! So it is with the law of Moses and the law of Christ.

Dead to the law and married to Christ (2:19)

Let us return to Paul's claim that he has "died to the law," and try to understand what he means. This metaphor is a favorite with the apostle. He uses it in an expanded form in Romans 7:1–6. This passage is so clear and helpful on this contentious subject, that I am going to quote it in full.

> Or do you not know, brethren (for I speak to those who know the law), that the law has dominion over a man as long as he lives? For the woman who has a husband is bound by the law to her husband as long as he lives. But if the husband dies, she is released from the law of her husband. So then if, while her husband lives, she marries another man, she will be called an adulteress; but if her husband dies, she is free from that law, so that she is no adulteress, though she has married another man. Therefore, my brethren, you also have become dead to the law through the body of Christ, that you may be married to another, even to Him who was raised from the dead, that we should bear fruit to God. For when we were in the flesh [that is, unsaved], the passions of sins which were aroused by the law were at work in our members to bear fruit to death. But now we have been delivered from the law, having died to what we were held by, so that we should serve in the newness of the Spirit and not in the oldness of the letter.
>
> (Rom. 7:1–6)

We should not be confused because Paul's illustration alternates between the law (the husband) being dead and the believer (the wife) being dead. Either way, the law that binds the wife to the husband is destroyed, and this is the point he is making. In Galatians 2:19, it is the believer who dies to the law, as it is in the latter part of our Romans passage (Rom. 7:4).

Paul's metaphor is uncompromising. The believer has not died partially to the law, for death is total. He has not died temporarily to the law, for death is final. His relationship to the law has not undergone some subtle change; it has been terminated. The believer's subjection to the law, his obligation to perform its requirements, has been swept away, "through the body of Christ." What does this mean?

It means two things. Firstly, the believer is freed from the law through the perfect obedience that Christ yielded to that law during his earthly life. Secondly, he is delivered from punishment for his law-breaking through the death of Christ on his behalf. Thus the law can no longer make any demands upon the believer, either in respect of obedience, or in respect of punishment for transgression. Those demands have been fully and finally met by the man Christ Jesus.

Is the believer, then, without law? Not at all. We are not "without law toward God, but under law toward Christ" (1 Cor. 9:21). The context in which Paul makes this statement is his evangelization of the Gentiles, who are "without law" in the sense that they are without Moses' law. To such, says Paul, he himself became "without law," that he might win them for Christ. It is clear, therefore, that the "law toward Christ," to which Paul *did* submit, was something other than the law of Moses. We shall see what it is as we continue in Galatians.

The cause of death (2:19)

Whenever a death occurs, whether by accident, violence or natural cause, society seeks to establish the cause of death. In a similar way, Paul wants us to understand the cause of our dying to the law. **"I ... died to the law,"** he says, **"through the law."** If he had been using his husband-and-wife illustration here, Paul might have said that the husband killed the wife!

At first sight there may seem to be a contradiction between Galatians and Romans over the "cause of death." In Romans 7 we are told that the believer's death to the law occurs "through the body of Christ," but here in Galatians death is attributed to the law itself.

There is, however, no contradiction. Paul is making two wholly distinct points in the respective passages. We have already seen what it means to die to the law "through the body of Christ." Dying to the law "through the law" refers to something quite different, namely, the effect the law has upon an awakened sinner.

Again we find assistance in Romans 7. "I was alive once without the law," Paul recounts, "but when the commandment came, sin revived and I died. And the commandment, which was to bring life, I found to bring death. For sin, taking occasion by the commandment, deceived me, and by it killed me" (Rom. 7:9–11).

What the apostle seems to be saying is as follows: "I once lived without any qualms about the law. I thought I was obeying it perfectly. 'Concerning the righteousness which is in the law [I was] blameless' (Phil. 3:6). But this was because I was spiritually blind. When God began to awaken me spiritually, the commandments of the law—particularly 'You shall not covet' (Rom. 7:7)—came to me with a wholly new force. Confronted by the commandments, my sin and rebellion against God were stirred up, so that I wanted to break his laws all the more. That is, the holy law challenged and stimulated my sinful nature. This conflict, between God's righteous requirements and my rebellious heart, escalated to such an extent that it destroyed me. I lost my will to live. Inwardly, I died, slain by the law I could not, and would not, keep!" The very desperation engendered by the law, however, drove Paul to Christ. The inward death which is despair, gives birth to hope, not through the law but through Christ.

From death to life (2:19)

In Paul's husband-and-wife scenario in Romans 7, the wife remarries after the husband's death. This, explains the apostle, is a picture of the believer's union with Christ. Liberated from the demands of the law, the sinner is "married" to Christ. Of this new union is born "fruit to God" (Rom. 7:4). Galatians has much to say, as we shall see in due course, about fruitfulness toward God. Indeed, fruit-bearing is the only visible evidence that a man or woman has passed from spiritual death to spiritual life. Many who profess to be Christians, even evangelical Christians, bear little fruit. Jesus said, "By this My Father is glorified, that you bear much fruit; so shall you be My disciples" (John 15:8). There is no such thing as a fruitless disciple, a follower of Christ without good works.

This imagery, of a new and fruitful life, is not confined to Romans. It is found here in Galatians also, albeit more briefly expressed. "I ... died to the law," declares Paul, **"that I might live to God"** (2:19). Notice the word "that," meaning "in order that" or "so that." The Scripture is telling us here that we *must* die to the law before we can live spiritually. Our relationship to the law must be dissolved before we can serve God. This further vindicates the contention made earlier that faith and law-righteousness cannot coexist. They are mutually exclusive.

Union with Christ (2:20–21)
1. In death
Having stated the conclusion to which he has come, that we must die to the law if we are to live to God, Paul now elaborates. Death to the law and new life toward God are not given to us in a vacuum. They occur only as a consequence of the believer's union with Christ: **"I have been crucified with Christ; it is no longer I who live, but Christ lives in me; and the life which I now live in the flesh I live by faith in the Son of God, who loved me and gave Himself for me"** (2:20).

Union with Christ! Paul returns to this life-changing truth again and again in his writings. To him it is the very heart of the gospel, and he loves to dwell upon it. "The riches of the glory of this mystery [the gospel]," he tells the Colossians, "is Christ in you, the hope of glory" (Col. 1:27), Christ is in us, and we are in Christ. This union is the essence of God's eternal purpose, and the secret of living to God.[5]

Firstly, we are united with Christ in his death, "crucified with Christ." He did not simply die on our behalf. That is true, but it tells only half the story. The believer actually died *with* Christ. He was in Christ, our substitute, receiving the rightful punishment for his sin, namely, estrangement and separation from God. Let us try to illustrate this.

Picture the scene in a court of criminal law. The offender stands condemned, and sentence is passed. So it is with the sinner before the bar of God's justice. But Christ steps forward. He takes the place of the guilty person in the dock, while the criminal retires to the public gallery. Christ is the substitute, taking upon himself both the guilt and the punishment required by law. The sinner looks on, a spectator but no longer a participant in the courtroom drama. However, although this aptly pictures the idea of substitution, it falls far short of representing the full extent of the atonement. The problem with the illustration is that it leaves the sinner essentially unchanged! He is freed from his guilt, and delivered from judgment, yes. But he is otherwise unaffected.

The atonement, however, provides for more than the mere pardon of the rebel sinner. It secures his transformation. "If anyone is in Christ," writes the apostle, "he is a new creation; old things have passed away; behold, all things have become new" (2 Cor. 5:17). If we restrict the work of Christ on our behalf to that of substitution alone, we are faced with a dilemma. Christ having freed the sinner from judgment, someone must now make him holy! Christ has made him *legally* righteous, but the sinner must now, by some means, become *practically* righteous. How is this to be done? A common opinion is that a man is justified, in a purely legal sense, by Christ's death, but can only be made practically righteous ("sanctified") by obedience to the (moral) law.

But this is not what Paul is teaching here at all. What he is saying is that the believer, being united with Christ in his death, thereby died to sin. As a dead man no longer desires food, so the true believer no longer desires to sin. His appetite for sin has been destroyed, as has sin's power over him. "How shall we who died to sin live any longer in it?... our old man was crucified with [Christ], that the body of sin might be done away with, that we should no longer be slaves of sin. For he who has died has been freed from sin" (Rom. 6:2–8).

Is the believer, therefore, sinless? Yes and no. The "new man which was created according to God, in righteousness and true holiness," is indeed without sin (Eph. 4:24; Col. 3:10). But the "new man" shares our human frame with an old nature (often called "the flesh" or "indwelling sin," Rom. 7:17). This old nature will live on, retaining its sinful tendencies, until our body dies. In this life, therefore, there is continual conflict between the new man and the old nature, and sin results when the latter gains the upper hand. We shall see in due course how the believer's new nature may be victorious in this conflict.

However, none of this changes the basic fact that being "crucified with Christ" is not just picturesque speech. It means that some real change has been wrought in the believer. He has died to sin, and cannot therefore live in sin.[6] Those who sin habitually demonstrate that they have not been crucified with Christ. They are not true believers, whatever they profess.

2. In resurrection
Just as believers are united with Christ in his death, so are they in his resurrection: **"It is no longer I who live, but Christ lives in me"** (2:20). We may compare this statement with the parallel passage in Romans: "We are buried with Him through baptism into death, that just as Christ was raised from the dead by the glory of the Father, even so we also should walk in newness of life. For if we have been united together in the likeness of His death, certainly we also shall be in the likeness of His resurrection" (Rom. 6:4–5).

Baptism, of course, is simply a physical representation of the believer's burial and resurrection. We are concerned here with the spiritual reality which baptism pictures. Paul expresses this reality by saying, "It is no longer I who live." Following regeneration, the believer is "a new creation" (2 Cor. 5:17). A real change has occurred, for "Christ lives in me" by his Holy Spirit. The apostle underscores this teaching in Romans, where he tells us categorically, "If anyone does not have the Spirit of Christ, he is not His" (Rom. 8:9).

Once again, the message of this verse is that a genuine transformation has taken place in the new believer. In Christ, he has died to sin, and thus is free from the demands and power of the law. He has risen with Christ to a new life, in which the empowering principle is the indwelling Spirit. Where there was a natural propensity to do evil, there is now a supernatural tendency to please God.

Does this mean that the believer automatically avoids sin, without any effort on his part? No, this is not the case. Paul goes on to say, **"The life which I now live in the flesh I live by faith in the Son of God, who loved me and gave Himself for me"** (2:20). Life "in the flesh" means here the Christian's day-to-day life (the word "flesh" does not always refer to the old sinful nature). Our practical life, says Paul, has to be lived out in an attitude of faith toward Christ. The indwelling Spirit imparts and maintains this gift of faith, namely the ability to discern spiritual realities (faith is spiritual sight, see 2 Cor. 4:18).

The believer, however, has the responsibility of using this faculty of faith. As he lives his day-to-day life, he must constantly exercise the spiritual sight he has been given. As Hebrews exhorts, "Let us lay aside every weight, and the sin which so easily ensnares us, and let us run with endurance the race that is set before us, looking unto Jesus, the author and finisher of our faith" (Heb. 12:1–2). Note that this charge is the author's natural conclusion from his review in Hebrews 11 of Old Testament examples of faith.

The life of faith, then, is a life lived "looking unto Jesus," trusting in the efficacy of his work and the reality of our union with him, and depending on the inner strength of the Holy Spirit (Eph. 3:16). It stands in irreconcilable contrast to any attempt to please God by law-works.

The grace of God (2:21)

The closing verse of Galatians 2 is a summary of Paul's whole argument: **"I do not set aside the grace of God; for if righteousness comes through the law, then Christ died in vain"** (2:21). To seek righteousness through the law is to "set aside the grace of God," for if we could please God and satisfy his requirements by obeying the law, then Christ's death was totally unnecessary ("Christ died in vain").

To think that we can please God by an outward obedience to law, observing certain rules and regulations, and conforming to a pattern of behavior imposed from without, is utterly mistaken. This is true at conversion, and remains true throughout the Christian's life. "All our righteousnesses are like filthy rags," declares Isaiah, while Jesus adds, "When you have done all those things which you are commanded, say, 'We are unprofitable [useless] servants. We have done what was our duty to do' " (Isa. 64:6; Luke 17:10).

The only ground of our acceptance with God is, and ever remains, the person and work of Christ. We are "accepted in the Beloved," or not at all (Eph. 1:6). This is what Paul means by the grace of God. Thus to think that works of any kind will somehow make us more holy, or increase our acceptance, or enhance our standing, in the sight of God, is to "set aside the grace of God." (Remember also that Paul is still speaking to Peter and other believers, not to the unconverted.)

Furthermore, says Paul, if grace is set aside, so also is the cross of Christ. If my acceptance with God depends in any way upon what I am, or what I do, in my own person, then union with Christ (in death and resurrection) is no longer necessary. Christ has died in vain; that is, his death was not necessary. Christians must beware the danger of resting upon their works, either for justification or for godly living. For, as Paul reminds the Corinthians, "You are in Christ Jesus, who became for us wisdom from God—and righteousness and sanctification and redemption—that, as it is written, 'He who glories, let him glory in the Lord' " (1 Cor. 1:30–31).

Summary
The believer in Christ is united with Christ, both in his death and his resurrection. This union is not merely a poetic idea or allegory; it is a spiritual reality, brought about in the Christian by the indwelling of Christ by the Holy Spirit. This union is the only basis for our acceptance with God, whether at conversion or at any subsequent time.

Thus the atonement is not limited to Christ's substitutionary death for our sins. He died for us, indeed, but we also died with him. United with him in death, we died to sin, and thus to the law. (That is, the demands and penalties of the law no longer apply to those who trust Christ for righteousness.) He rose again for our justification (Rom. 4:25), yes, but we also rose with him, being made new creations in Christ, that we might walk in newness of life.

This new life is imparted and maintained by the Spirit of God indwelling the believer. It is a life lived "looking unto Jesus," that is, by faith in Christ.

Notes

[1] "In Pauline usage, 'to die to' something is to cease to have any further relation to it" (Longenecker, *Galatians*, p. 91).

[2] Hendriksen, *Galatians and Ephesians*, p. 102.

[3] Samuel Bolton expresses clearly the opinion (with which I disagree), that the law is to be the Christian's rule of life: "We cry down the law in respect of justification, but we set it up as a rule of sanctification. The law sends us to the Gospel that we might be justified; and the Gospel sends us to the law again to enquire what is our duty as those who are justified" (Bolton, *True Bounds of Christian Freedom*, p. 71).

[4] "[Through the death of Christ] I am completely delivered from the law. The law has no more to do with me in the matter of justification. And this freedom from law is at once necessary and effectual to my living a truly holy life—a life devoted to God" (Brown, *Exposition of Galatians*, p. 37).

[5] Boston comments on Galatians 2:20: "[The believer] being joined to the Lord, is one spirit with him. Hereby a believer lives in and for Christ, and Christ lives in and for the believer" (*Human Nature*, p. 191).

[6] "There is through grace, kept up in believers a constant and ordinarily prevailing will of doing good, notwithstanding the power and efficacy of indwelling sin to the contrary. This, in their worst condition, distinguisheth them from unbelievers in their best" (Owen, *Temptation and Sin*, p. 160).

13
The Hearing of Faith

Please Read Galatians 3:1–5

Having recounted at length the dispute with Peter and his fellow Jews, Paul turns again to his readers. **"O foolish Galatians!"** he cries, **"Who has bewitched you that you should not obey the truth?"** (3:1). There is a sound of thunder in his words.

The first five verses of Galatians 3 consist of a series of five rhetorical questions. A rhetorical question is a statement disguised as a question. Paul is, in fact, making five important statements about the nature of genuine faith, which he contrasts with a trust in human nature and its works. The rhetorical question format serves a second, but equally useful, purpose. By using questions, the apostle invites his readers to think things out for themselves. Paul is ever the teacher, even when (as here) he is beside himself with indignation.

The Galatians were not unique in failing to think through the implications of their actions. We, like them, are prone to be carried away by enthusiasms, or mesmerized by novel doctrines. Perhaps they thought the Judaizers could give them acceptance into some "inner circle" of Jewish believers. Perhaps they were just overawed by the fact that these men came from Jerusalem, the birthplace of the church. Whatever the reason for their defection, the Galatians failed to recognize where all this was leading them. The purpose of Paul's interrogation was to make them *think* what they were doing.

There are lessons here for all of us. It is vital that Christians be taught to think through what they believe and practice. They must *understand* the gospel, for only then will they be able to recognize distortions and perversions of it. Too many who profess to believe do so on the basis of emotions, experiences, or submission to self-appointed leaders, rather than understanding. Paul tells us that the ascended Christ gave the church apostles and prophets (who together laid the doctrinal foundations in the form of Holy Scripture, see Eph. 2:20), along with evangelists, pastors and teachers. Why? So that "we should no longer be children, tossed to and fro and carried about with every wind of doctrine" (Eph. 4:11–14). Sound biblical teaching, then, is the antidote to the false ideas and deviations which afflict the gospel in every age. Angry as he is, Paul does not neglect his pastoral duty to the Galatians.

Genuine faith obeys the truth (3:1)
We now turn to the first of Paul's rhetorical questions, which is found in verse 1: **"O foolish Galatians, who has bewitched you that you should not obey the truth, before whose eyes Jesus Christ was clearly portrayed among you as crucified?"** The "eyes" with which they saw the crucified Christ are, of course, the eyes of faith, as we saw in chapter 10. Paul brands the Galatians "foolish." The word means "thoughtless" or "unthinking." He also adds that they had been "bewitched." This is not to be taken literally. It only signifies that they were behaving like men bereft of their critical faculties, as if some magician had cast on them a spell of incomprehension.[1]

We must understand that Paul is not just calling them names! Rather, he is putting his finger on their basic problem, namely, a failure to apply their faith-enlightened minds to discern truth from falsehood. They had allowed themselves to be led into error without questioning their teachers. They had neglected to examine the Judaizers' "gospel" and, as a result, had departed from the truth. There is a familiar ring about all this. The temptations to abandon sound doctrine for novelty or excitement; to submit to human ideologies rather than the truth as it is in Christ; to tailor the gospel to suit the tastes of men; to compromise the truth with error for the sake of peace; to abandon the hard work of thinking for oneself and follow false shepherds with persuasive personalities—all these are prevalent today, as they were in Paul's time.

By contrast, true faith is characterized by its submission to the truth; believers, asserts Paul, "obey the truth" (3:1). When Paul speaks of "the truth," he means, of course, the truth of the gospel (2:14). Where is this truth to be found? It is encapsulated in the death of Christ. The atonement is the key to the gospel.

The Galatians really had no excuse. Paul reminds them that when he first evangelized their city, Jesus Christ had been "clearly portrayed among [them] as crucified" (3:1). He expresses the same idea even more clearly in writing to the Corinthians. "I determined not to know anything among you," he recalls, "except Jesus Christ and Him crucified" (1 Cor. 2:2). Does this mean that the apostle limited his message in some way? Not at all. It means that the gospel of God's grace, in its boundless entirety, is contained in the person and work of Jesus Christ.

To understand the cross of Christ is to understand the truth of the gospel.[2] As he preached the gospel to them, Paul had portrayed the Lord's death with such clarity that it was almost as if he had been crucified "among" them, that is, "before [their] eyes" (3:1). This "portrayal" of the cross, we may be assured, was not limited to a rehearsal of the historical facts. He had expounded to them the *meaning* of the cross in a way that left no room for misunderstanding. Otherwise, his present strictures would have been unjustified. Sadly, such clarity concerning the atonement is seldom heard in our pulpits today. How seldom, for example, do we hear the following questions answered in the following way?

Who died upon the cross?

"The Lord of glory" (1 Cor. 2:8). The only begotten Son of God, the Creator and Sustainer of all things (Heb. 1:1–3).

Why did Christ die?

To fulfill the "carefully planned intention and foreknowledge of God," the "eternal purpose which He accomplished in Christ" (Acts 2:23; Eph. 3:11).

For whom did he die?

He died for his elect, the Good Shepherd giving his life for his own sheep which the Father gave to him before time began (John 6:37–39; 10:11, 26–30; Eph. 1:4–7; 2 Tim. 1:9).

What did he accomplish?

He accomplished the sure, final and eternal redemption of his elect (John 10:27–29; Heb. 9:12–15; 10:14).

What are the consequences?

In this life, to redeem for himself a special people to "proclaim the praises of Him who has called [them] out of darkness into His marvelous light" (Titus 2:14; 1 Peter 2:9). In eternity, that Christ might have his spotless bride (Eph. 5:25–27; Rev. 21:2, 9).

What does this imply concerning works?

Since, by his death and resurrection, Christ has "perfected forever those who are being sanctified" (Heb. 10:12–14), our works count for nothing in the sight of God. Indeed, to trust in works for acceptance with God is to reject the righteousness which is by faith in Christ (Rom. 10:1–4).

Is there righteousness outside of Christ?

None (Acts. 4:12; 2 Cor. 5:19–21).

The statement Paul is making is simply this: true faith is submissive to these truths concerning Christ and his atonement. It greets them with joyful recognition, and relies upon them as the sole ground of confidence and hope. True faith has "ceased from … works" as truly as God has ceased from the work of creation (Heb. 4:10). All this is plainly implied by the death of Christ, for "If righteousness comes through the law, then Christ died in vain" (2:21).

Genuine faith receives the Holy Spirit (3:2)

Paul poses his second question in verse 2: **"This only I want to learn from you: Did you receive the Spirit by the works of the law, or by the hearing of faith?"** Clearly the Galatians knew what the apostle was talking about. He addresses them as believers, as those who *had* received the Holy Spirit, for "If anyone does not have the Spirit of Christ, he is not His" (Rom. 8:9–11).

This is the first mention of the Holy Spirit in Galatians. It is by no means the last, for this epistle contains some of the most important teaching on the Holy Spirit in the whole of Scripture.[3] The thing we need to notice at this point is that all true believers, even the error-prone Galatians, are indwelt by the Spirit of God. Later, in Galatians 4, Paul makes it totally clear that being a son (child) of God implies the indwelling of the Spirit of Christ, and vice versa. Any teaching to the contrary, such as the notion that the Holy Spirit is received as a "second blessing" or "baptism" at some time following regeneration, is wholly unscriptural. The Galatians, then, had all received the Spirit of God. What does this imply?

Firstly, it implies that "by one Spirit" they had all been "baptized into one body—whether Jews or Greeks, whether slaves or free" (1 Cor. 12:13). The body referred to is, of course, the church of Jesus Christ. As Gentiles they were no longer outsiders, lacking something that the Jews possessed. They were "no longer strangers and foreigners, but fellow citizens with the saints and members of the household of God" (Eph. 2:19). Having been thus incorporated into the body of Christ, they were full members of his household and on an equal footing with Jewish believers, and all this without recourse to circumcision and Moses' law! This in itself demonstrated the falsehood of the Judaizers' teaching.

Secondly, as 1 Corinthians 12:13 puts it, they had "all been made to drink into one Spirit." What does this mean? Simply, that they had become partakers of the Holy Spirit as a matter of *experience*. Being baptized (spiritually) into the body of Christ could be regarded as an almost legal process, something done *to* the believer by God. But, says Paul, this is accompanied by a "drinking," a tasting, an experimental partaking—something done *in* the believer by God. "God has sent forth the Spirit of His Son into your hearts," explains the apostle, "crying 'Abba, Father!' " (Gal. 4:6; see also Rom. 8:15–16). We shall consider these verses in more detail when we come to Galatians 4, but it is important at this early juncture to realize that the true believer is gloriously *aware* of the presence of the indwelling Holy Spirit.[4]

Thirdly, the indwelling Spirit *leads* the believer, both in his understanding of the gospel and in his personal life (John 16:13–15; Rom. 8:6, 9, 13–14). The Holy Spirit teaches, guides, strengthens and helps the believer, ever pointing him to Christ. This, then, is something of what it means to receive, and be indwelt by, the Spirit of God. But the point at issue is how do we receive the Spirit? By what means does he take up his residence within our hearts?

He does so by a sovereign, creative work of God. "For it is the God who commanded light to shine out of darkness [i.e., in creation] who has shone in our hearts to give the light of the knowledge of the glory of God in the face of Jesus Christ" (2 Cor. 4:6). Nevertheless, from the point of view of human experience, the Holy Spirit is received (says Paul) by faith. In regeneration, God imparts the gift of faith, by which we begin to *see* spiritual realities previously hidden from our eyes. We trust in Christ, for we now discern his person and his work, and by that same faith we *consciously* welcome into our hearts the very Spirit who gave it to us. Since the knowledge of Christ comes to us through the preaching of the gospel, it is natural for Paul to use the term "the hearing of faith" to describe the means by which the Holy Spirit is received. The coming of the Holy Spirit to the believer is, therefore, the cause of faith, but the conscious experience of his coming is the consequence of faith.

By stark contrast, the person who strives to appease God by law-works knows nothing of the Spirit's presence or power, but remains in spiritual darkness. He is blind to the saving work of Christ, deaf to the gospel of God's free grace. Why, then, should the Galatians turn from light to darkness, from faith to works? It made no sense at all.

True faith relies on the Spirit for growth and maturity (3:3)

Verse 3 brings us Paul's third rhetorical question: **"Are you so foolish? Having begun in the Spirit, are you now being made perfect by the flesh?"** There is here, perhaps, an admission that the Galatians did desire to progress in the Christian life. They had a genuine desire to be "made perfect" (or "complete"), but they were going about it in entirely the wrong way. In this respect they resembled the unsaved Jews, having "a zeal for God, but not according to knowledge" (Rom. 10:2).

In this verse, "the flesh" refers to human nature, unaided by the Spirit. This confirms what is perhaps self-evident, that believers still possess such human nature, alongside the indwelling Spirit. There is always the danger, therefore, that believers will revert to former habits, attempting to accomplish spiritual objectives in the strength of human nature, rather than by faith.[5] Thus a Christian businessman, trying to assist his church in outreach, may rely for success upon the advertising methods he uses in his secular work. A minister, who is a gifted orator, may rely upon his natural abilities to affect his hearers, rather than trust in the Spirit of God to do a truly spiritual work in their hearts. Of course, God can and does further his purposes by using men's natural gifts, but only as they rely upon his strength and not upon the gifts themselves. The conflict of flesh and Spirit in the life of the believer is considered at length in Galatians 5:16–25.

To follow the Judaizers in their obedience to Moses' law, is (Paul implies) to depend upon the flesh, not upon the Spirit of God. Indeed, rules and regulations, which impose bondage on those who submit to them, are actually attractive to the flesh. "Let no one judge you in food or in drink, or regarding a festival, or a new moon, or a sabbath," Paul warns the Colossians. "Let no one defraud you of your reward, *taking delight* in false humility and worship of angels ... if you died with Christ from the basic principles of the world, why ... do you subject yourselves to regulations ... according to the commandments and doctrines of men?" (Col. 2:16–23, emphasis added).

By contrast, faith looks to Christ, who accomplishes his work in us through the Spirit. The believer produces the fruit of obedience to God, good works and ethical behavior, through the power of the indwelling Spirit. As we read in Hosea, "Your fruit is found in Me" (Hosea 14:8). Again, we shall see this theme developed later in Galatians 5.

It is essential that we heed Paul's oft-repeated warning. Spiritual "completeness" (including what some call "sanctification") cannot be obtained by obedience to the law, for the law makes its demands upon the flesh, not the Spirit. Another way to express this is to say that the law is an external agency, to which man can only respond in the strength of human nature. The Spirit, on the other hand, is an internal principle, promoting faith and producing spiritual fruit. (It might be a good idea to stop and read 2 Corinthians chapter 3 at this point.)

Without faith it is impossible to please God (3:4)
The fourth rhetorical question appears in verse 4: **"Have you suffered so many things in vain—if indeed it was in vain?"** Like most believers of their day, the Galatians had undergone suffering through persecution. It had proved costly to follow Christ and be known as Christians. Although the nature of the persecution may change, all human cultures and societies treat true believers in the same way, because they do not "belong." We are, says Peter, "strangers and pilgrims" in this world (1 Peter 2:11, KJV).

True as this is, the reverse is not equally true. That is, those who suffer are not *thereby* marked out as the true people of God. Many religious groups have suffered serious persecution, both historically and in our own day, which are not Christian or Bible-based. It would be a serious mistake, implies Paul, for the Galatians to rely upon their sufferings as evidence of their faithfulness to God. If they follow the Judaizers, and reject the true gospel, even their suffering will prove to be "in vain" (that is, without spiritual benefit or reward).

The apostle makes a similar point in writing to the Corinthians: "Though I give my body to be burned but have not love, it profits me nothing" (1 Cor. 13:3). Even the supreme sacrifice avails nothing unless there is first a spiritual relationship with God, namely the indwelling of his Spirit, evidenced by the fruit of the Spirit (in this case, love). Similarly, says Paul, without genuine faith, in Christ alone, all that the Galatians had endured for their religious beliefs would have been suffered to no purpose. However, he does add the words, "if indeed it was in vain." As we have seen before, Paul still regards the Galatians as true believers, in spite of their errors. So here also, he is willing to give them the benefit of the doubt. If they return to the truth, then their suffering will not have been in vain after all.

Only true faith really works (3:5)

Paul's final question is as follows: **"Therefore He who supplies the Spirit to you and works miracles among you, does He do it by the works of the law, or by the hearing of faith?"** (3:5). We must first resolve an ambiguity as to the subject of this sentence: is it God or the apostle? The word "supplies" is a more accurate rendering than the KJV's "ministereth," and though the apostle might be said to "minister" the Spirit, he can hardly be said to "supply" the Spirit to believers. It follows that Paul is here speaking of the direct ministry of God among them.

This ministry took two forms, an outward ministration of miracles, and an inward supply of the Holy Spirit. The latter we have already considered when discussing Galatians 3:2, but the emphasis in verse 5 is slightly different. While verse 2 drew our attention to the fact and experience of receiving the Spirit, this verse points to the actions that follow, namely, the believer's "work of faith" (1 Thess. 1:3). This is implied rather than expressed, but the stress in Galatians 3:5 is undoubtedly upon God's *workings* among them.

True faith issues in works, in fruit, in God-honoring action. As James shrewdly comments, "Show me your faith without your works [if you can!], and I will show you my faith by my works" (James 2:18). This is the entire burden of Hebrews 11, where again and again the writer begins with the words, "By faith ...," and goes on to describe some action, some venture, some achievement, accomplished by the person in question, in reliance upon God. "By faith Noah ... moved with godly fear, prepared an ark"; "By faith Abraham obeyed when he was called"; "By faith Sarah ... received strength to conceive seed," and so on (Heb. 11:7–11).

Now this work of faith is *also* the fruit of the Spirit's indwelling. God "supplies the Spirit ... by the hearing of faith," and those who thus receive the Spirit are thereby empowered to accomplish works.

Here, then, we have the secret, the mechanics if you like, of godly living. As part of the work of regeneration, God the Holy Spirit imparts the gift of faith (which may be thought of as spiritual sight). By the exercise of this faith, the believer receives, or is supplied with, the power of the Spirit. In this power, the believer then accomplishes the "work of faith," acting and living in a way that pleases God. Only faith can function in this manner. The works of the law involve no gift from God, no spiritual sight, no empowering by the Spirit. They depend instead upon the arm of the flesh, the powerless "strength" of human nature.

The second aspect of God's ministry among them, says Paul, was the working of miracles (3:5). The miracles of the New Testament were, with few (if any) exceptions, divine acts of authentication. They point to the authenticity of Christ as God's anointed one, either directly in his own miracles, or indirectly in the signs and wonders wrought by those who testified of Christ (Heb. 2:3–4). Thus Paul could claim that the gospel he preached was authenticated by "the signs of an apostle" (2 Cor. 12:12). Such miracles, therefore, attach only to Christ himself and to those through whom the gospel was first revealed. These historical miracles still serve the same purpose today, that is, to authenticate Christ and the Scriptures which declare his gospel. There is no need for them to be repeated.

The signs and wonders witnessed by the Galatians, therefore, had but one purpose: to confirm their faith in the Christ-centered gospel preached by Paul. In the absence of faith, miracles are meaningless, for they themselves do not persuade unregenerate men to believe. Indeed, in the face of unbelief, such signs may become impossible. Of Christ himself we read, "He did not do many mighty works there because of their unbelief, (Matt. 13:58). In this realm also, therefore, it is only faith that "makes things happen."

This is a general truth. As we have seen, Hebrews 11 recounts the exploits of men and women of faith. Without faith they could have achieved nothing of value in the sight of God. We deceive ourselves if we think we can further the kingdom of God by our labor, our organizing ability, or our zeal. Unless our efforts are exercised in faith, and empowered by the Spirit, we accomplish nothing.

Summary

Paul wants to make the Galatians think about both their faith and their actions. Clear thinking leads to an understanding of the gospel. To understand the gospel, and particularly the atonement, is to be protected against error.

Faith (spiritual sight leading to trust in God) is the bedrock of Christian experience and life. True faith:

- obeys (submits to) the truth of the gospel;
- receives the Holy Spirit;
- relies on the Spirit for growth and maturity;
- pleases God;
- accomplishes, through the Spirit, those "good works, which God prepared beforehand that we should walk in them" (Eph. 2:10).

The works of the law can do none of these things, because such works are the fruit of human effort, carried out in spiritual blindness and in the strength and discernment of sinful human nature ("the flesh").

Notes

[1] "The word translated *bewitched* signifies vitiating the eyes, or spoiling the sight, so as that men cannot discern an obvious object ..." (Poole, *Commentary*, p. 647).

[2] "The phrase 'Christ crucified' was on Paul's lips an abbreviated form of the gospel" (Longenecker, *Galatians*, p. 101).

[3] The centrality of the Holy Spirit to the Galatian epistle has not always been recognized. Thus Longenecker comments, "Much that has been written on Galatians has tended to ignore the central place of the Spirit in Paul's argumentation throughout his Galatian letter. J. B. Lightfoot actually omitted any reference to the Spirit ... in his comments on 3:1–5, and in dealing with 5:13–26 only tells us that ... the statement 'we live by the Spirit' of v.25 speaks of 'an ideal rather than an actual life' ..." (*Galatians*, p. 101).

[4] For an extended treatment of 1 Corinthians 12:13 see Andrews, *The Spirit has Come*, pp. 139–41.

[5] "What Paul wants his converts to see is that the Christian life is one that starts, is maintained, and comes to culmination only through dependence on the activity of God's Spirit ..." (Longenecker, *Galatians*, pp. 103–4).

14
The Faith of Abraham

Please Read Galatians 3:6–9

Having completed the interrogation of his Galatian readers, Paul now turns to Scripture for further proof of his claim that faith alone can justify the sinner. The Old Testament, of course, is full of such testimony. In Hebrews 11 the writer rehearses a multitude of exploits accomplished by men and women of faith throughout human history, from Abel onwards. However, here in Galatians, the apostle singles out Abraham as his example and proof that "The just shall live by faith" (3:11, cited from Hab. 2:4).

Why choose Abraham, rather than Abel, Enoch, Noah, Joseph or Moses? There are three possible reasons:

1. Abraham was an outstanding example of faith. Hebrews 11 devotes more space to him than anyone else.

2. It was to Abraham that the most explicit promises were made concerning the coming of Christ, the seed of Abraham (3:16). Jesus himself declared, "Abraham rejoiced to see My day, and he saw it and was glad" (John 8:56).

3. The Judaizers, like all Jews, were exceedingly proud of their descent from Abraham (see, for example, John 8:33). It was to Abraham that the sign of circumcision had been given, to distinguish his descendants from the heathen that surrounded them. To demonstrate that Abraham was justified by faith, therefore, would be the most telling argument possible against these false teachers.

All three of these reasons may have been in Paul's mind as he wrote the remainder of Galatians 3. It is not till the closing verse of that chapter that he finishes with Abraham's role and testimony, and even then he returns to the life of Abraham and his sons in Galatians 4:21–31. Clearly, Abraham has a great deal to teach us about the nature and objects of genuine faith. Indeed, as we shall see, he also reveals much concerning the nature of the gospel and God's eternal plan. Although Galatians 3:6–29 has this single unifying theme of Abraham, his faith and the promises of God, these verses contain so much teaching that we need to take them slowly. They will, in fact, occupy us throughout the next six chapters of this book.

Abraham's faith (3:6)

As soon as he mentions Abraham, Paul goes straight to the heart of the matter: **"Abraham 'believed God and it was accounted to him for righteousness'"** (3:6). The reference is, of course, to Genesis 15:4–6, where God promised Abraham that "One who will come from your own body shall be your heir." In spite of his advanced years, and the fact that his wife was past the age of childbearing, Abraham "did not waver at the promise of God through unbelief, but was strengthened in faith, giving glory to God ... being fully convinced that what he had promised he was also able to perform" (Rom. 4:20–22). This last quotation reminds us that the whole of Romans 4 is devoted to Abraham's faith. It is therefore a parallel passage to Galatians 3:6–29, and we shall have occasion to turn to it again as we consider these verses.

The first question that arises is this: *in what exactly did Abraham believe?* The gospel teaches that we must believe *in Christ* if we are to be counted righteous. But how could Abraham believe in a Messiah who had not come, and an atonement that was yet to be made? Can it be that Old Testament believers were justified by a general trust in God, having no perceived Christological content?

I do not think so. To accept such an idea would be a profound misunderstanding of imputed righteousness, and would turn faith into a work. Let us be clear. The only righteousness that God accepts is the righteousness of Christ, for that alone is perfect. Imputed righteousness is *Christ's* righteousness put to the sinner's account, none other. If the act of believing were, of itself, a means of justification, then we would be justified by a work. It is not the act of believing that justifies the sinner, but the one in whom he puts his trust.[1] This is evident from Romans 4:6–8, where we are told that "David also describes the blessedness of the man to whom God imputes righteousness apart from works." Paul then quotes Psalm 32:1–2: "Blessed are those whose lawless deeds are forgiven, and whose *sins are covered*; blessed is the man to whom the LORD shall not impute sin" (emphasis added). Now it is evident that men's sins can be "covered" only by the blood of Christ. The Bible knows no other way. But it is those whose sins are thus covered to whom God imputes righteousness. Therefore righteousness can only be imputed on the basis of Christ's atoning work.

Although it is true that Old Testament saints could not see the full import of the gospel (see, for example, Eph. 3:5), their faith never lacked that necessary Christological element. Thus by faith Abel, at the dawn of human history, "offered to God a more excellent sacrifice than Cain, through which he obtained witness that he was righteous" (Heb. 11:4). What was Abel's sacrifice? A lamb, pointing to the "the Lamb of God who takes away the sin of the world" (John 1:29). In Abraham's case we have already cited Jesus' words, that "Abraham rejoiced to see My day, and he saw it and was glad."

When God promised Abraham a son, through whom all the families of the earth would be blessed (Gen. 12:3), Abraham perceived not merely the promise later fulfilled in Isaac, but also a more distant promise (see Heb. 11:10, 13). That promise was Christ, of whom Isaac was a type (born miraculously, sacrificed on Mount Moriah, raised again, figuratively, from the dead—Heb. 11:17–19). Abraham's faith was not in earthly promises, but in the coming Christ.

The sons of Abraham (3:7)

Paul now comes to the key question: *who are Abraham's true descendants?* Are they the Jewish race, descended physically from the patriarch? It was with these physical offspring that God had made his covenant through Moses, namely the law. If, then, Abraham's seed were indeed the Jews as a nation, it follows that the blessings promised to Abraham could only be obtained under the Mosaic covenant. This, or something very like it, would have been the reasoning advanced by the Judaizers.

Paul stems this argument at its source. Was Abraham justified by faith? Then, **"Know that [only] those who are of faith are sons of Abraham"** (3:7). The word "only" has been inserted by the translators for emphasis. Such insertions are sometimes difficult to justify, but in this case the meaning is correctly conveyed. Paul's statement here is forceful. It is not merely a deduction from the preceding verse, but also a strong assertion, evidenced by the command, "Know …"!

Abraham's heirs are not "of blood," but "of faith." In God's eyes, descent is not reckoned genetically or ethnically, but spiritually. Abraham's children are not those who share his genes, but those who share his faith.[2] Abraham is "the father of all those who believe … that righteousness might be imputed to them also" (Rom. 4:11–12; we shall consider the issue of circumcision raised in these verses later). The truth that Paul is teaching here was very difficult for the Jews to accept. Even today many Christians cherish the idea that faith can somehow be passed on physically from parents to children. Not so, says the apostle. Faith is God's gift, imparted to each believer by a sovereign work of God's Spirit. "That which is born of the flesh is flesh, and that which is born of the Spirit is spirit" (John 3:6–8).

The gospel for all nations (3:8)

The promises made to Abraham fall into two categories. First there were the *physical* promises, namely that he would be given a multitude of descendants and a homeland. Secondly there were *spiritual* promises, relating to the coming of Christ. To complicate matters, the physical promises themselves, although literally fulfilled, were also pictures of the spiritual blessings to come. Thus God promised Abraham a physical homeland: "All the land which you see I give to you and your descendants" (see Gen. 13:14–17). But at the same time, we are told, Abraham (and those of like faith) "seek a homeland" and "desire a better, that is, a heavenly country" (Heb. 11:14–16). In an ultimate sense, therefore, *all* the promises that God made to Abraham were spiritual in nature and content. Nor were they spiritual in a vague and general manner. They centered in, and pointed to, Christ. This is why Paul can say, **"The Scripture ... preached the gospel to Abraham beforehand"** (3:8). The gospel of Christ was enshrined in the promises.

It is interesting that the apostle chooses to identify the Scriptures with the words of God himself. It was of course God who spoke directly to Abraham, since the patriarch did not deduce the promises from some preexisting writings. However, the Scriptures *record* the promises thus made, and Paul sees no inconsistency in equating the words that God spoke to Abraham with the written record of those words preserved in the Bible. This is an excellent example of the way the New Testament writers regarded the Old Testament writings as the Word of God. The same reasoning, of course, applies to the New Testament which they themselves produced (see, for example, how Peter accords Paul's writings the status of Scripture—2 Peter 3:15–16).

The particular promise that Paul singles out is as follows: **"In you all the nations shall be blessed"** (3:8). There is good reason, for this promise was made no fewer than three times to Abraham (Gen. 12:3; 18:18; 22:18), once to Isaac (Gen. 26:4) and once to Jacob (Gen. 28:14). There are two things to notice about this recurrent theme.

Firstly, *all* the nations of the earth would be blessed through Abraham's seed. In God's eternal purpose the gospel is to be proclaimed to all nations, and through that gospel he will redeem a people for himself "out of every tribe and tongue and people and nation" (Rev. 5:9). Although this fact brings glory to God in a general sense, it was particularly relevant to the Galatian situation. The Judaizers sought to limit the blessing of the gospel to the Jews and any others who would adopt Judaism through submission to the law of Moses. Paul here demonstrates that this teaching is utterly at variance with the Scripture. Far from limiting the blessings of Abraham to the people of the old covenant, the gospel reveals "that the Gentiles should be fellow heirs, of the same body, and partakers of His promise in Christ" (Eph. 3:6).

Secondly, all the nations of the earth would be *blessed*. This is the emphasis on which Paul chooses to conclude this passage. **"So then,"** he writes, **"those who are of faith are blessed with believing Abraham"** (3:9).

No doubt the Galatians were seeking blessing. They had known something of the blessing of the gospel, and quite rightly desired more. But their very desire for a richer experience of Christ had made them prey to false teachers. "You want a deeper spiritual life?" we can imagine the Judaizers saying. "Then follow us, and we promise you the full gospel, the ultimate union of Christ and the law." They are not alone in offering such blandishments. Many other false teachers have savaged the flock of Christ, offering "something extra" by way of novel doctrines, mystical experiences, miraculous powers, emotional excitement, or material well-being. Only too late do those who heed them discover that their teaching leads, not to spiritual fulfillment, but to bondage. "Stand fast," pleads the apostle, "in the liberty by which Christ has made us free, and do not be entangled again with a yoke of bondage" (Gal. 5:1).

True blessing consists in God's favor upon us and our lives, both in time and eternity. Such blessing, Paul tells the Galatians, is found in Christ, and Christ alone. God can only extend his favor toward sinners as they are found in Christ. Thus it was by faith in him that Abraham was blessed, and by that same faith we also shall be blessed along with him. We have seen that faith is spiritual sight. "Abraham rejoiced to *see* [Christ's] day, and he saw it and was glad" (John 8:56, emphasis added). Even today, we can be blessed in no other way. Like Abraham we must look to Christ by faith. As we do, with the apostle John, we shall behold "His glory, the glory as of the only begotten of the Father, full of grace and truth" (John 1:14). And seeing, we shall be blessed indeed.

Summary
Paul turns to Scripture for further proof of his thesis that justification is by faith and not by the works of the law. Abraham is his chosen example.

Faith is spiritual sight and, accordingly, Abraham obtained righteousness through faith in Christ, whose coming he both foresaw and understood. How did Abraham know these things? The gospel was preached to him through the promises God made to him concerning Christ. These promises contained both physical and spiritual elements, but even the physical promises (which were literally fulfilled) were also pictures of the blessings bestowed by God upon all who share Abraham's faith in Christ.

The true descendants of Abraham, therefore, are not his physical progeny, who are yet subject to Moses' law, but those who inherit his faith in Christ. Failing to understand this, the Judaizers had gone badly astray.

Blessing comes through faith in Christ, and by no other means. We must beware of those who pretend to offer greater blessing through novel doctrines, seeking to supplement the person and work of Christ. Such doctrines lead to bondage, not to blessing.

Notes

[1] Commenting on Galatians 3:6, Eadie says, "He [Abraham] was lifted into acceptance with God ... not on account of his faith, but through its laying hold of the promise. That faith had no merit; for what merit can a creature have in believing the Creator's word?... His faith rested on the promise ... That promise ... included the Messiah ... so that his condition was tantamount to justification by faith in the righteousness of Christ."

[2] "Therefore, even though a man should be a Hebrew of the Hebrews, he is not, in the spiritual sense, a son of Abraham unless he be a true believer. Conversely, if he be a true believer in the Lord Jesus Christ, he is a son of Abraham, whether he be a Gentile or a Jew by race" (Hendriksen, *Galatians and Ephesians*, p. 123).

15
The Curse of the Law

Please Read Galatians 3:10–12

The apostle now proceeds to draw a bleak contrast. He has been speaking of those who are "of faith." He now considers those who are **"of the works of the law."** His verdict is: **"As many as are of the works of the law are under the curse"** (3:10). Our subject in this chapter is what Paul calls "the curse of the law" (3:13). There are three questions that we need to answer concerning this matter:

1. What exactly is "the curse of the law"? In what sense can the law be "a curse"?
2. Who are under this curse?
3. What are the consequences of the curse?

The fourth and all-important question, "How may we escape this curse?" will be the subject of the next chapter.

What is "the curse of the law"? (3:10)

A curse, as that word is used in Scripture, means a pronouncement of ill upon a person or object (just as a blessing means a pronouncement of good). Here Paul quotes Deuteronomy: **"Cursed is everyone who does not continue in all things which are written in the book of the law, to do them"** (3:10). The background to this statement is Moses' address to the Israelites delivered on the threshold of the promised land. In a statement of great solemnity, he presented them with two options: obey and be blessed; or disobey and be cursed. His actual words were as follows: "Behold, I set before you today a blessing and a curse: the blessing, if you obey the commandments of the LORD your God which I command you today; and the curse, if you do not obey the commandments of the LORD your God, but turn aside from the way which I command you today, to go after other gods which you have not known" (Deut. 11:26–30).

To dramatize these options, Moses gave certain instructions to be followed after the people had entered the promised land. Six of the tribes were to stand on Mount Gerizim, representing God's blessing upon obedience, while the remaining six tribes were to occupy Mount Ebal, representing God's curse upon disobedience. A series of curses was then to be pronounced by the Levites to "all the men of Israel" (Deut. 27:14). These curses referred to a variety of transgressions, from idolatry to sexual sins, bribery and murder. However, it is clear that the individual curses were simply examples of a wider principle, for at the end of the list we find the verse cited (generally) by Paul in Galatians 3:10: "Cursed is the one who does not confirm all the words of this law" (Deut. 27:26).

The law, therefore, could bring either a blessing or a curse, depending on whether it was obeyed or transgressed.[1] However, as we saw in an earlier chapter, the existence of two options is, for fallen man, an illusion. Because of his sinful nature, man is incapable of obeying the law. The possibility of blessing, received through obedience to the law, does not arise. In order to earn God's favor, it would be necessary for a man to "continue in all things which are written in the book of the law, to do them" (3:10). It is not sufficient to obey some of the laws all of the time, or all of the laws some of the time. God, by his nature, requires perfection. We would have to obey all of the laws all of the time, and that is beyond the capacity of human nature. "By the works of the law no flesh shall be justified" (2:16).

Since the option of blessing is excluded by the sinfulness of human nature, it follows that only the curse upon disobedience remains. The law, therefore, condemns all men, but reserves its greatest menace for those who seek to be justified by its works! "Every man who becomes circumcised," says Paul, "is a debtor to keep the whole law" (5:3). It was while Bunyan's Pilgrim was on his way to seek help from Mr. Legality that he found the mountain (picturing the Ten Commandments) was about to fall upon him.[2]

Who lie under the curse? (3:10)

Paul answers this question clearly: **"As many as are of the works of the law are under the curse"** (3:10); that is, the curse lies upon all those who practice law-keeping with a view to pleasing God. Such people seek to be justified by the works of the law, and not by Christ. This clearly has its primary application to the Jews of Paul's day, and to those, like the Judaizers, who taught that Christian believers must also keep the law of Moses. These, quite clearly, can be described as being "of the works of the law." We must remember, however, that men generally are morally answerable to law for, says Paul, "The Gentiles, who do not have the law, by nature do the things contained in the law ... [and] show the work of the law written in their hearts" (Rom. 2:14–15).

The "curse of the law" was to come upon Israel if they disobeyed and, specifically, if they went "after other gods" (Deut. 11:28). But this is the basic sin common to all men, as Paul testifies in Romans 1:18–23: "Although they knew God [by natural revelation], they did not glorify Him as God, nor were thankful, but ... changed the glory of the incorruptible God into an image ..." It is not possible, therefore, to distinguish between Jews and Gentiles in respect of their rebellion against God. Indeed, this is the burden of Romans 2–3. "What then? Are we [Jews] better than they [Gentiles]? Not at all. For we have previously charged both Jews and Greeks that they are all under sin" (Rom. 3:9).

Since all men have the law "written in their hearts," and since they reject God as truly as did rebellious Israel, it follows that all mankind lies under the "curse of the law," not just the Jews. Admittedly, the Jews and Judaizers made a conscious effort to obtain justification by law-works, so rejecting the sufficiency of the work of Christ. Yet all unregenerate men are essentially the same, seeking to please God (or merely to appease their consciences) by the things that they do. It is not *only* the Jews who seek "to establish their own righteousness" and "have not submitted to the righteousness of God [in Christ]" (Rom. 10:1–3).

On account of our descent from Adam, then, all human beings are sinners. (This, incidentally, is why it is so important to resist the modern idea that man has evolved from apes, since this would require the evolution of a *population* of humans, not a single individual. If Adam is not the unique father of the human race, then Paul's argument here is fallacious.) As sinners, we are by nature under the dominion of sin. We are its willing slaves, neither wanting nor able to escape its power. God will punish with eternal death those who live thus. Free redemption is our only hope, and this is found in Christ.

What are the consequences of the curse? (3:11–12)

Very simply, the consequence of the curse is that **"No one is justified by the law in the sight of God"** (3:11). Neither the laws of Moses nor the dictates of conscience in those who lack the written law provide a means of pleasing God. Try as we may to live righteously, to obey the law, to heed the promptings of our conscience, we fall short of the perfection that God requires. "All have sinned and fall short of the glory of God" (Rom. 3:23). When the law is viewed in this proper, scriptural light, argues the apostle, it is evident that no one can be justified by keeping it. The holy law serves only to make sin more obvious, as man's behavior is measured against God's requirements. "By the law is the knowledge of sin" (Rom. 3:20). Far from helping us to escape sin's control, the law actually exposes and excites our sin, deepening our guilt before a holy God.

However, Paul is not satisfied to rest his conclusion merely on logic; he adds a further proof of the matter, drawn from Scripture: **"That no one is justified by the law ... is evident, for 'The just shall live by faith' "** (3:11). The quotation is, of course, from Habakkuk: "Behold the proud, his soul is not upright in him; but the just shall live by his faith" (Hab. 2:4). "The proud" in this context were the Chaldean invaders, raised up by God as an instrument of judgment upon rebellious Israel and other nations (see Hab. 1:1–6). Paul's use of the text, however, is apposite, for the Chaldeans thought themselves invincible. They are thus representative of man in his proud self-sufficiency. By contrast, the man of faith relies for justification, not upon himself, but on the grace of God.

So, says Paul, those who are justified in the sight of God (that is, the just) "live" before God by virtue of their faith. This tells us that faith is the basis of their acceptance with God and their escape from divine judgment. There is no other way. Where does this leave those who seek justification through the law? Nowhere, replies the apostle, for **"The law is not of faith"** (3:12).

This is an important statement, for it demonstrates once again that faith and obedience to the law are mutually exclusive. They cannot be mixed. Why? Because, Paul continues, **"The man who does them** [law-works] **shall live by them"** (3:12). Referring back to the source of this statement in Leviticus 18:5, we read, "You shall therefore keep My statutes and My judgments, which if a man does, he shall live by them." What Paul is telling us here is that faith and law-works are based on entirely different principles. If a person were able to keep the commandments of the law, perfectly and consistently, then he would "live" (be spiritually alive and accepted by God) as a result.[3] He would have earned acceptance and would be justified by his works, as Paul argues in Romans 4:4: "To him who works, the wages are not counted as grace but as debt." God would *owe* such a person his justification. "But," continues the apostle, "to him who does not work but believes on Him who justifies the ungodly, his faith is accounted for righteousness" (Rom. 4:5).

Once again, therefore, we see two distinct options: either try to earn God's favor by your works, or else recognize your ungodliness and look by faith to Christ who died, "the just for the unjust, that He might bring us to God" (1 Peter 3:18). We cannot do both at the same time, for there is a mutual contradiction. To claim salvation through our works, we must at the very least establish that we are godly. To claim salvation by grace, through faith, we must admit the very opposite! It is only as we recognize that man is incapable by nature of pleasing God that we will apply for mercy. Faith is the sight that shows us both our sinfulness and the hope of salvation by grace. No man possessing faith can linger with the law, for he sees clearly that it cannot justify, but only condemn.

We return, then, to the question posed at the beginning of this section, "What are the consequences of the curse of the law?" The first consequence is that no man can obtain acceptance with God by law-works.

The second consequence, which follows automatically, is that any attempt to do so leads to bondage, for it entails a fruitless, anguished search for the impossible. Those who make the attempt are crushed beneath a law they cannot keep. Paul develops this point later in Galatians 5:1–6.

The third consequence is also clear: those who persist in seeking salvation through their own works will reap judgment, not deliverance. Those whose only claim upon Christ resides in the works that they have done will hear his declaration: "I never knew you; depart from Me you who practice lawlessness" (Matt. 7:21–23). Tragically, this verse tells us, the attempt to keep the law leads to lawlessness. By contrast, those who come to Christ in repentance and faith, becoming God's children by adoption, produce the "peaceable fruit of righteousness" (Gal. 4:6; Heb.12:11).

Summary

In principle, the law of Moses could bring either a blessing or a curse. That was its nature. Perfect obedience would secure God's blessing, but anything less would result in his curse. However, because human nature is sinful, the blessing could never be obtained by humankind. Only the curse remains.

This curse rests not only upon the Jews, who had the written law, but also on all men who seek acceptance with God through their own works.

Because of the curse, it is impossible to obtain justification through human efforts. That route to salvation is forever barred.

Only faith in the work of Christ avails. Reliance on works and trust in Christ are mutually exclusive, for the one presumes that the natural man can be godly, whereas the other accepts the innate sinfulness of man and looks alone to grace (God's free, unmerited giving). Reliance upon law-works for salvation leads to bondage and rejection by God.

Notes

[1] "Israel had willingly placed herself under the stipulations of the covenant (cf. Exod. 24:3, 7), and in so doing had accepted the threat of being cursed for nonfulfilment ... Coming under a curse was therefore inextricably bound up with receiving the law ..." (Longenecker, *Galatians*, p. 117).

[2] Bunyan, *Pilgrim's Progress*, pp. 22–3.

[3] "The law saith nothing of faith in the Mediator, though faith in God be commanded in the first precept, yet faith in Christ is not commanded by the law as that by which the soul shall live. For that which the law saith is, *Do this and live; The man that doeth* the things contained in the law, *shall live in them*; life, in the law, is promised to those who do the things which it requireth ..." (Poole, *Commentary*, p. 649).

16
The Promise of the Spirit

Please Read Galatians 3:13–14

Against the somber background of the law's curse, Paul now makes a declaration that, though brief, is breathtaking in its scope and implications: **"Christ has redeemed us from the curse of the law, having become a curse for us (for it is written, 'Cursed is everyone who hangs on a tree'), that the blessing of Abraham might come upon the Gentiles in Christ Jesus, that we might receive the promise of the Spirit through faith"** (3:13–14).

We are told here:

1. That Christ has redeemed us from the curse of the law;

2. How he did so (by becoming cursed for us);

3. That as a result, the blessing promised to Abraham is finally fulfilled;

4. That the blessing in question is the coming of the promised Spirit;

5. That this blessing is given "in Christ Jesus";

6. That it is poured out upon the Gentiles as well as the Jews;

7. That it is appropriated by faith.

We shall look at each of these assertions in turn.

Christ has redeemed us from the curse of the law (3:13)

We have seen that the curse of the law lies upon all men, whether Jew or Gentile. The good news is that Christ provides a way of escape from that curse. Does the curse signify that nothing we can do will ever please God? Then Christ has pleased God on our behalf (Luke 3:22). Does the curse leave us bereft of righteousness? Then Christ has become our righteousness (1 Cor. 1:30). Does the curse bring us into bondage? Then Christ will set us free (John

8:30–36). Does the curse condemn us to the wrath of God and a lost eternity? Then there is "now no condemnation to those who are in Christ Jesus" (Rom. 8:1).

Christ, we are told, has **"redeemed us."** The word "redeem" means literally "acquire at (or out of) the forum," and is a direct reference to the practice of freeing slaves through the payment of a purchase price. Christ, then, has "bought us back" from the slave-market of sin. Man is in bondage to the law just because he is in bondage to sin. "Whoever commits sin is a slave of sin," said the Lord Jesus (John 8:34). If we were able to reject sin, to shrug it off, we would have nothing to fear from the law. It is because we cannot escape sin's clutches that we are like slaves, "sold under sin" (Rom. 7:14).

Paul develops this analogy of slavery in Romans 5–7. Men were "made sinners," we are told, through the disobedience of Adam (Rom. 5:19). As long as our "old man" (our Adamic human state) remains alive, we remain slaves of sin (Rom. 6:6). While in this state, we *willingly* present ourselves as servants to sin, to do its bidding (Rom. 6:16–17, 19). The inevitable outcome of such a life is eternal death, for the "wages of sin is death" (Rom. 6:23).

Can the law not help us to escape from this plight? "No," replies Paul. "The law entered that the offense [sin] might abound" (Rom. 5:20). Far from offering relief from sin, the law makes matters worse. Indeed, claims the apostle, "The strength of sin is the law" (1 Cor. 15:56). Paul explains that sin has dominion over a man as long as he is "under [the] law" (Rom. 6:14). Why? The answer is given in Romans 7:9–13: "When the commandment came, sin revived and I died … for sin, taking occasion by the commandment, deceived me, and by it killed me … sin … was producing death in me through what is good [the law], so that sin through the commandment might become exceedingly sinful."

These verses allow us to develop further the meaning of **"the curse of the law."** In the previous chapter we saw that the curse resides in, firstly, man's inability to keep the law and, secondly, the penalty demanded by the law for sin. Now we see a further aspect of that curse, namely the increased power that the law imparts to sin. The law is like a red rag to a bull. The commandments and injunctions of God's Word actually stimulate rebellion in the human heart. "The carnal mind is enmity against God; for it is not subject to the law of God, nor indeed can be. So then, those that are in the flesh cannot please God" (Rom. 8:7–8). Our hope for deliverance from this threefold curse cannot, therefore, reside in human nature (the flesh), but only in Christ's free redemption.

In a moment we shall see how Christ provides such redemption, but first we must take note of one important claim that Paul makes here. He writes, "Christ *has* redeemed us from the curse of the law" (emphasis added). A price was paid, the very life of Christ. "You were not redeemed with corruptible things, like silver or gold ... but with the precious blood of Christ, as of a lamb without blemish and without spot" (1 Peter 1:18; Peter uses a different Greek word for "redeem," meaning "to free by a payment"). If the price has been paid, then the transaction is complete and the slave is free. There is no room for the idea that Christ's death only makes *possible* the salvation of the sinner. The redemption of the elect has been accomplished, not merely facilitated.

How has Christ redeemed us? (3:13)

The method of redemption is now made clear: **"Christ has redeemed us ... having become a curse for us (for it is written, 'Cursed is everyone who hangs on a tree')"** (3:13). Paul cites Deuteronomy, but his reference is, of course, to the crucifixion. This mode of execution was unknown to the Jews of Moses' day, but Paul clearly treats the quotation as prophetic of the death of Christ. "If a man has committed a sin worthy of death, and he is put to death, and you hang him on a tree, his body shall not remain overnight on the tree, but you shall bury him that day so that you do not defile the land which the LORD your God is giving you as an inheritance; for he who is hanged is accursed of God" (Deut. 21:22–23).

Galatians offers us here the clearest possible teaching of substitution.¹ We are the ones who had committed sins worthy of death, not Christ. Moreover, the death that we earned by our lawlessness was not just physical, but eternal. But Christ took our place, "having become a curse for us," and bore "our sins in His own body on the tree" (1 Peter 2:24). As Paul puts it elsewhere, "God ... made Him who knew no sin to be sin for us, that we might become the righteousness of God in Him" (2 Cor. 5:21). The curse and judgment of an offended God fell upon his righteous Son, instead of us. God punished God, as Zechariah prophesied: " 'Awake, O sword, against My Shepherd, against the man who is My Companion,' says the LORD of hosts" (Zech. 13:7).

However, as we saw above, the curse of the law resides not only in the penalty *for* sin, which Christ has suffered on our behalf, but also in the power *of* sin. Has he also delivered us from this? Yes, indeed, for Scripture teaches not only that Christ died for his people, but that they died *with* him.

Paul elaborates in Romans 6: "Knowing this, that our old man was crucified with Him, that the body of sin might be done away with, that we should no longer be slaves of sin. For he who has died has been freed from sin ... we died with Christ" (Rom 6:6–8). The apostle continues, "God be thanked that though you were slaves of sin, yet you obeyed from the heart that form of doctrine to which you were delivered [i.e., the gospel]. And having been set free from sin, you became slaves of righteousness" (Rom. 6:17–18). Very simply, our deliverance from slavery to sin resides in our identification with Christ in his death and resurrection.

The blessing promised to Abraham is finally fulfilled (3:14)

The effect of Christ's atonement is now revealed. The **"blessing of Abraham"** has at last come to fruition. It has **"come upon"** those for whom it was intended. These have now become "partakers" of the long-promised blessing. This blessing comes not only upon Abraham's family, the Jews, but also on the Gentiles and thus on all the nations of the earth.

What is "the blessing of Abraham" (that is, the blessing promised to Abraham)? Paul has not previously answered this question, even though he referred to the blessing earlier, in Galatians 3:8–9. There he made it plain that this blessing is inherited by faith, not by natural descent, but he did not specify its nature and content. Now, however, he declares what actually constitutes the blessing: **"Christ has redeemed us from the curse of the law ... that the blessing of Abraham might come upon the Gentiles ... that we might receive the promise of the Spirit through faith"** (3:13–14).

The blessing of Abraham is the "promise of the Spirit." This does not signify a promise made *by* the Spirit, but rather that *the Spirit himself is* the promised entity. The blessing promised to Abraham, then, is nothing other than the gift of the indwelling Holy Spirit. We shall consider presently what this gift implies. The point to be made here is that this promise had at last been fulfilled, in human experience, *as a result and consequence of Christ's atonement*. This accords with John's observation that, prior to the death of Christ, "The Holy Spirit was not yet given, because Jesus was not yet glorified" (John 7:39). It was the risen, glorified Christ who sent upon his people "the promise of the Father" (John 15:26; Acts 1:4). Note that the Holy Spirit proceeds both from the Father and the Son, for both are said to send the Spirit; for example, compare Luke 24:49, John 14:26 and John 15:26. Historically, this has been a subject of controversy between the Orthodox and Roman Catholic Churches.[2]

God had, and still has, a distinct program in terms of human history. The call to Abraham, the giving of the law, the incarnation of Christ, and the coming of the Holy Spirit are all set in their historical context here in Galatians. We shall see this more clearly as we proceed, but a quick reference to Galatians 3:8; 3:17; 4:4 and 4:6 will demonstrate the point. God's eternal plan is worked out on the stage of world events, and this applies not only to great events such as the incarnation and the death of Christ, but also to the very warp and woof of history (see, e.g., Acts 17:26–27). To live in this era of fulfilled promise is a great privilege. The apostles clearly felt this, and rejoiced in it. It induced in them a sense of awe and wonder. "Behold what manner of love the Father has bestowed on us, that we should be called children of God!" cries John (1 John 3:1; see also Eph. 3:5–11; Heb. 11:39–40). This same sense of privilege and awe should still enliven our worship today, but is often sadly missing. Perhaps the reason is that we do not have the apostles' panoramic concept of redemption, from foreknowledge, through election, to calling, justification and glorification (Rom. 8:29–30).

Although the Holy Spirit was given in fulfillment of the promise only after the Lord Jesus had been glorified, this does not mean that believers before Pentecost did not possess the Spirit at all. They also were filled with the Spirit, empowered by the Spirit and given utterance by the Spirit. What they lacked, however, was the indwelling of the Father and the Son through the Spirit (see John 14:23; Heb. 11:39–40).[3]

The blessing is given in Christ (3:14)

The blessing of Abraham comes upon the Gentiles, we are told, **"in Christ Jesus"** (3:14). It does not come through Moses, but only through Christ. If men are to find this blessing, they must apply to Christ, for he alone is "the way, the truth and the life" (John 14:6). This is particularly important in the Galatian context. If the blessing comes upon the Gentiles directly through Christ, then of course there is no point in seeking it through submission to the law of Moses.[4] Paul is always careful to emphasize that everything believers possess, now and eternally, is theirs in Christ. Was the believer chosen before the foundation of the world? Then he was chosen in Christ (Eph. 1:4). Is he blessed with every spiritual blessing? Then he is blessed only in Christ (Eph. 1:3). Is he accepted by God? Then it is "in the Beloved" that he is so received (Eph. 1:6). Is he endowed with wisdom, righteousness, sanctification and redemption? Then they are his "in Christ Jesus" (1 Cor. 1:30).

It is easy for us to forget this fundamental principle, namely, that God's grace is extended to us only in Christ Jesus. Although

God loved his elect from eternity past, it is the believer's union with his Lord that secures acceptance with God. Believers possess the imputed righteousness of Christ, but only as they are found in him. It is not through works of any kind—not even those "good works, which God prepared beforehand that we should walk in them" (Eph. 2:10). Of course, God is pleased when his children walk in obedience to his Word, but such obedience is never perfect and cannot *of itself* satisfy a holy God. We are accepted, we are loved, we are forgiven and embraced, because we are in Christ, not because we have made some progress along the road of discipleship or self-improvement. Sanctification, like justification, is ours in Christ, or else it is an illusion.

The blessing is poured out upon the Gentiles as well as the Jews (3:14)

He redeemed us **"that the blessing of Abraham might come upon the Gentiles"** (3:14). To the Ephesians Paul writes of "the mystery of Christ ... which in other ages was not made known ... that the Gentiles should be fellow heirs, of the same body, and partakers of His promise in Christ through the gospel" (Eph. 3:2–6).

Not only has the promise been fulfilled. It has come upon the Gentiles as well as the Jews. Paul takes it for granted that the (believing) Jews inherit the promise, and here emphasizes the position of the Gentiles. Why should he do this? He does it to demonstrate that the Galatians are heirs *in their own right*, and have no need to "become" Jews in order to participate in the heritage of faith. In Old Testament times there were distinct benefits in being a Jew, since to the Jews were committed "the oracles of God" (Rom. 3:1–2). But this no longer applies; the promise comes upon all who are "of faith," regardless of their pedigree or nationality. The Galatians' desire to become like Jews, submitting to the law, was therefore wholly misconceived. We too must be careful not to attribute spiritual value to the traditions of men or claims of ecclesiastical antiquity. Only faith inherits the blessing.

The blessing is appropriated by faith (3:14)

Although the blessing was promised to Abraham and his descendants, this is not to be understood in a physical sense. As we have already seen, it is those who share Abraham's faith who are his heirs, not those who share his genes. The law of Moses was given to Abraham's natural family, the Jews. The promise, by contrast, was given to the patriarch's spiritual descendants, namely those, both Jews and Gentiles, who are "of faith." It is therefore utterly misconceived to seek the promise under the covenant made with the Jewish nation at Sinai. It can only be received under a different covenant, one made with Abraham's spiritual offspring. To Paul, the admission of the Gentiles into the church of Jesus Christ was proof positive of this fact. Believing Gentiles were thus the evidence that salvation is by faith and not by law-works. No wonder he views the Judaizers' message as an outright denial of the gospel.

Which comes first, faith or the indwelling of the Spirit? It is clear from Scripture that the unregenerate man is incapable of faith (1 Cor. 2:14). Faith is God's gift, imparted by grace (Eph. 2:8–10). Regeneration and the impartation of faith are alike the work of the Holy Spirit, as is clear from such passages as John 3:1–8 and Acts 16:13–15 (the conversion of Lydia). Clearly, no one can exercise faith without first being wrought upon by the Spirit of God in regenerating power.

In what sense, therefore, do we receive the Spirit "through faith"? We have already answered this question when considering Galatians 3:2. It is by faith that we receive the Holy Spirit *consciously*, welcoming him into our hearts and lives as a permanent resident, according to the promise of Christ (John 4:10–14; 7:37–39). Scripture does not countenance the idea that the indwelling of the Spirit may be postponed by our failure to exercise faith. The Spirit does not await our bidding before he enters, for "Because we are sons *God has sent forth* the Spirit of His son into our hearts crying 'Abba, Father!' " (Gal. 4:6, emphasis added).

Summary

Christ has redeemed his people from the curse of the law, delivering them from both the penalty the law demands for sin and the power it lends to sin. He did this by becoming cursed for us, dying on the cross for our offenses, and rising again for our justification.

As a result, the blessing promised to Abraham was finally fulfilled, namely the coming of the Holy Spirit to indwell those who have been redeemed and cleansed from their sin. The Holy Spirit was sent by the risen and ascended Christ, and could not come before he had been glorified.

This blessing is given "in Christ Jesus," that is, it is ours only through our union with him. The permanent indwelling of the Holy Spirit is received consciously by faith, and is thus the birthright of all who inherit Abraham's faith.

The gift is poured out upon the Gentiles as well as the (believing) Jews, demonstrating that it is bestowed under a different covenant from that enacted at Sinai. This covenant is the covenant of promise, which will engage our attention in the following chapter.

Notes

[1] "It is from this curse that Christ has purchased his people and the price of the purchase was that he himself became a curse. He became so identified with the curse resting upon his people that the whole of it in all its unrelieved intensity became his. That curse he bore and that curse he exhausted" (Murray, *Redemption*, p. 44).

"Christ ... became not only man, *bound* to obedience ... but He became *curse* for us. He made our *doom* His own. He took on Him not only the calling of a man, but our responsibility as sinful men. It is in this that His work as Redeemer lies, for it is in this that the measure, or rather the immensity, of His love is seen" (Denney, *Death of Christ*, p. 92).

[2] Cross, *Oxford Dictionary of Christian Church*, p. 419 (on "Double Procession").

[3] For a fuller discussion see Andrews, *The Spirit has Come*, pp. 53–7.

[4] "His sufferings and death ... by completely satisfying all the demands of the Mosaic law ... have put an honourable termination to that order of things, which, during its continuance, necessarily excluded the great body of the Gentiles from the blessing of Abraham—an order of things that, now the Messiah is come, has completely served its purpose—the consequence is that justification by believing is extended to men of every nation; and ... Jews obtain the promised Spirit through believing the gospel, and not by obedience to the law" (Brown, *Exposition of Galatians*, p. 56).

17
God's Covenant in Christ

Please Read Galatians 3:15–18

We are now introduced to yet another of the great themes of the Galatian epistle, namely the covenants of God. Paul's treatment of this theme begins here in Galatians 3 but is developed further in Galatians 4:21–31, to which we shall come in due course. We shall not exhaust the subject, therefore, in the present chapter. In the passage before us, the apostle begins by drawing an analogy with human covenants, and then proceeds to distinguish between the covenant of promise and the covenant of the law.

What is a covenant? (3:15)
Paul begins by pointing out to his readers that covenants made by God can be illustrated by those made between men: **"Brethren, I speak in the manner of men: Though it is only a man's covenant, yet if it is confirmed, no one annuls or adds to it"** (3:15). God's covenants are not mysterious transactions which lie beyond our comprehension, but are basically of the same nature as those commonly made among men.

What, then, is a covenant? Paul uses a Greek word meaning a "disposition" (e.g. of property by a will) or an "arrangement." It is sometimes used in the New Testament to mean a will or testament, as for example in Hebrews 9:16 which says, "Where there is a testament, there must also of necessity be the death of the testator." However, it is also used in the sense of an "arrangement," meaning a solemn (often legally binding) agreement or undertaking between two (or more) parties.[1]

The word "covenant" can therefore signify one of two, rather different, things. It can mean a will, in which one party, the testator, is active and the other, the beneficiary, is passive, except for the act of receiving the inheritance. The implementation of a will lies entirely in the power of the testator. The beneficiary can do nothing but accept and receive whatever the will provides. I shall refer to this kind of covenant as a "covenant of the first kind." On the other hand, a "covenant of the second kind," by which I mean an agreement or contract, implies the active participation of both parties in fulfilling the terms of the covenant. When God is party to a covenant, of course, the terms are dictated exclusively by him. Nevertheless, a covenant of the second kind still exists if the agreement requires man's obedience, or if man has the power to break the covenant (as was certainly the case with the Mosaic covenant, see Jer. 31:32; Heb. 8:9). Which of these two meanings of "covenant" is intended in any particular scripture will usually be obvious from the context, as in the reference from Hebrews cited earlier. In considering our passage, we shall need to keep this distinction in mind, since Paul, in using the word "covenant," seems to make a deliberate and subtle use of its double meaning, as we shall see.

The apostle points out in this verse that a testament or covenant has to be "confirmed" before it comes into force. In our own day the testator or the covenanting parties usually confirm the document by appending their signatures. However, there are other ways of confirming an agreement. Among diamond dealers, for instance, a handshake is considered to be a legally binding confirmation that a deal has been made. The book of Ruth records a particularly strange tradition: "Now this was the custom in former times in Israel ... to confirm anything: one man took off his sandal and gave it to the other, and this was an attestation in Israel" (Ruth 4:7).

Once the covenant has been confirmed, continues the apostle, it becomes binding on the parties. With a testament, the terms cannot normally be varied, the will of the testator being paramount in law. Neither addition nor subtraction is permitted. With a covenant, neither subscriber is free, unilaterally, to annul the agreement, or withdraw from his obligations under it. Neither do the parties imagine they can ask for changes or additions to the covenant once it has been confirmed. Whatever has been agreed is fixed for the duration of the covenant. The only way to alter its provisions is for the original parties to agree to set aside the covenant in its entirety and negotiate a new agreement.

If human covenants are treated with such respect, how much more binding are those covenants to which God himself is party! This is the essence of Paul's argument here. If mere men honor their undertakings, shall not God honor his? Without question, replies the apostle. The changelessness of God is a primary doctrine of Scripture. "I am the LORD, I do not change; therefore you are not consumed, O sons of Jacob" (Mal. 3:6), declares the Old Testament, while the New assures us that "Jesus Christ is the same yesterday, today and forever" (Heb. 13:8). Because God does not change, his promise to Abraham and his seed cannot change either, being the outworking of his eternal purpose in Christ and rooted in his very nature.

The promises made to Abraham (3:16)

In the previous chapter we saw that the essence of God's promise to Abraham was "the promise of the Spirit." That is, in making the promises, God's ultimate purpose was to adopt to himself a people, a family, who would be his true children through the indwelling of the Spirit of his Son, Jesus Christ. However, this ultimate purpose was only implicit, not explicit, in the promises articulated to Abraham in Genesis. How, then, do the promises that were actually made to him relate to the promise of the Spirit?

The explicit promises made to Abraham contained three elements: firstly, the inheritance of the promised land (Gen. 13:15); secondly, descendants without number (Gen. 13:16); and, thirdly, that in Abraham's seed all nations of the earth would be blessed (Gen. 22:18). These promises clearly had a historical fulfillment in the Jewish nation. They did possess the land in the days of Joshua; they did become a great and numerous people; and Christ was born, historically, of Jewish stock, bringing the blessing of the Christian message to the whole world.

But these historical fulfillments were clearly not the primary purpose of the promises. Their chief intent was spiritual, as Paul argues here in Galatians and indeed elsewhere. The writer to the Hebrews points out that Joshua did not give "rest" to Israel by conquering the promised land, and that there must therefore be a subsequent, and spiritual, fulfillment of the promises (Heb. 4:8–9). Again, in Hebrews 11, he specifically states that Abraham "died in faith, not having received the promises, but having seen them afar off [was] assured of them" (Heb. 11:13). Far from expecting a merely physical fulfillment, Abraham "waited for the city ... whose builder and maker is God," and "desire[d] a better, that is, a heavenly country" (Heb. 11:10, 16).

The key to the spiritual interpretation of the promises lies in the statement which follows, in Galatians 3:16, namely that the promises were made to "Abraham *and to his seed*" (3:16, emphasis added). Let us therefore examine this important assertion, for this will enable us to understand how the promises made in Genesis find their fulfillment in the promise of the Spirit.

The seed is Christ (3:16)

Having asserted that the promises of God were made **"to Abraham and his seed"** (3:16), Paul develops the argument to show that the ultimate recipient of those promises was none other than Christ.

"He does not say, 'And to seeds,' as of many," declares the apostle, **"but as of one, 'And to your Seed,' who is Christ"** (3:16). That is, the promise was given to Abraham as a kind of trust, to be held in trust for his ultimate seed, namely Christ. This is why the sign of circumcision was given (Gen. 17:9–14), as a constant reminder of God's covenant of promise until the promised seed should come. Thus the promise was made, through Abraham, not to the Jews but *to Christ himself*. Seen in this light, what do the promises mean?

Reinterpreted in spiritual terms, they mean:

1. That Christ would gain the promised land of salvation for his people. It is a land obtained by conquest, that is, Christ's conquest of sin, death, and Satan. It is a land of plenty, for in salvation God has blessed us with all spiritual blessings in Christ (Eph. 1:3). It is a land of rest, for those who have ceased from their works have entered into rest (Heb. 4:10).

2. That Christ would beget (in the sense of redeem and regenerate) a numberless multitude. These are born from the dead (Eph. 2:1). They are born of "incorruptible seed, by the word of God" (1 Peter 1:23); that is, they are called through the preaching of the gospel of Christ and are born of the Spirit (John 3:5–6). Ezekiel's vision of revitalization in the valley of dry bones is an excellent parable portraying these truths (Ezek. 37:1–14).

3. That every nation of the earth would be represented among Christ's ransomed people (Rev. 5:9).

Now, those for whom Christ obtains the benefits of redemption and glory are his elect, who enter into these benefits through the processes of regeneration and adoption, which are alike the work of the Holy Spirit. It follows, therefore, that the giving of the Spirit is the effectual fulfillment of the promises made to Christ through Abraham, which is what we needed to establish.

Paul's argument here is that "seed" is to be understood as a singular noun rather than as a collective noun meaning "descendants." However, elsewhere he does take it to mean "descendants," for example in Romans 4:16 where he says, "The promise might be sure to all the seed, not only to those who are of the law, but also to those who are of the faith of Abraham, who is the father of us all." Is Paul contradicting himself, or using rabbinical sophistry in his arguments? Not at all.

The passage from Romans reminds us that there are both primary and secondary meanings to be found in the "promise" scriptures. The primary meaning is that Christ is the true and ultimate heir of the promises. Secondary to that is the fact that all the redeemed are co-heirs with Christ of the promises (Rom. 8:16–17), being "Abraham's seed, and heirs according to the promise," because they share

Abraham's faith. Thirdly, as remarked above, there was a purely historical and material fulfillment of the promises to "those who are of the law," namely the Jewish nation. Whether "seed" is taken to mean Christ, or his redeemed people, or the Jews, must depend upon which of these three meanings is in view.

Paul's purpose, as he writes to the Galatians, is to demonstrate that all the promises of God, culminating in the gift of the Holy Spirit to his people, are centered in Jesus Christ, and cannot be received or enjoyed outside of him.

Do we wish to inherit the promises made to Abraham and his seed? Then we may do so only by sharing *Christ's* inheritance, being "found in Him, not having [our] own righteousness, which is from the law, but that which is through faith in Christ, the righteousness which is from God by faith" (Phil. 3:9).

The two covenants (3:17–18)

It is at this point that Paul throws into relief the profound distinction between the covenant of promise and the covenant of law, anticipating his fuller exposition of this matter in Galatians 4:21–31. **"The law,"** he explains, **"which was four hundred and thirty years later, cannot annul the covenant** [testament] **that was confirmed before by God in Christ, that it should make the promise of no effect. For if the inheritance is of the law, it is no longer of promise; but God gave it to Abraham by promise"** (3:17–18).

Firstly, we see that the covenant of promise has the nature of a testament, since it gives rise to an "inheritance." In referring to this covenant, therefore, Paul employs the first of the two meanings of "covenant." The law of Moses, by contrast, is a covenant of the second kind, namely an agreement between two parties, as we shall see presently when we consider Galatians 3:19–20. As Calvin says, "As the law has regard to men and their works, so the promise concerns the grace of God and faith."[2] There are not only two different covenants, but two different *kinds* of covenant, under consideration in this passage.

Secondly, we see that the covenant of promise "was confirmed before," that is, firstly, it had been ratified, and, secondly, this happened long before the law of Moses was given. Therefore, according to Paul's argument in verse 15, the law of Moses could neither add to, nor subtract from, the covenant of promise. The two covenants are wholly distinct.[3] Thus it was impossible for the law to annul the promise, and the promise stood unchanged by the events at Sinai. Equally, it is wrong to think of the law as a *development* of the promise. Rather, the law was something superimposed, or parallel, which could in no way affect or modify the original covenant of promise. Finally, since the inheritance was given by promise, long before the law of Moses existed, that law could have no part in *transmitting* that inheritance to subsequent generations and, in particular, to the Gentile believers to whom Paul is writing.

The confirmation, or ratification, of the promise was made "by God in Christ." The meaning of this assertion is clarified by the passage in Hebrews 6:13–18, which reads as follows: "When God made a promise to Abraham, because He could swear by no one greater, he swore by Himself, saying, 'Surely blessing I will bless you, and multiplying I will multiply you' … thus God, determining to show more abundantly to the heirs of promise the immutability of His counsel, confirmed it by an oath." Further, by designating Christ as the ultimate heir of the promises, God made his oath "in Christ," that is, in relation to Christ.

Paul states that the law was "four hundred and thirty years later." This is the period of years spent by Israel in Egypt, from the settlement of Jacob and his sons in the time of Joseph, to the Exodus (see, e.g., Exod. 12:40). It cannot therefore be the time between the first promise to Abraham and the giving of the law. The explanation of this apparent discrepancy in Paul's reckoning is probably that Paul is here merely distinguishing between the patriarchal era of Abraham, Isaac and Jacob and the Egyptian exile. The former was the *era* of promise, for the promises originally made to Abraham were repeated to Isaac and Jacob (e.g. Gen. 26:2–4; 28:13–14). With the settlement in Egypt, and Jacob's death seventeen years later (Gen. 47:28), the era of promise came to an end, though the promises themselves lived on, as did the sign of that covenant, circumcision.

Summary

Jesus Christ is the ultimate recipient of God's promises to Abraham, and he receives them on behalf of, and for the benefit of, his elect. These promises, of redemption and future glory, are implemented in the believer by the regenerating work and indwelling of the Holy Spirit, and are thus appropriately summed up in the term "the promise of the Spirit." The fulfillment of these promises is sure, since God has covenanted to bring them about.

There are, however, two covenants: the covenant of promise and the covenant of law. The first has the nature of a testament or will, under which God provides an inheritance to Abraham and his seed. We have called this a "covenant of the first kind." The second covenant, Moses' law, has the nature of an agreement or contract, involving obligations upon two parties, God and Israel. This is a "covenant of the second kind."

The covenant of promise was not only given, but also ratified by God's oath, long before the covenant of law was established. The latter cannot, therefore, annul or supplement the former. They are distinct and separate. Since the inheritance of God's blessing in Christ is provided under the covenant of promise, the covenant of law has no part in the transmission or realization of that inheritance. This is something the Galatians needed to understand.

The promises were given to Abraham in trust for his ultimate seed, namely Christ. It is Christ who possesses the "promised land" for his people, namely the states of redemption and, eventually, glorification in heaven. It is he who "begets" a great multitude which no man can number, by dying for his elect and rising again for their justification. It is he who numbers among his spiritual "seed" members from all the nations of the earth.

All the redeemed participate in the inheritance because they are joint-heirs with Christ of God's eternal kingdom.

Notes

¹ Longenecker points out that although the Greek word διαθηκη, translated "covenant," properly means a "will" or "testament," the Septuagint (Greek) version of the Old Testament consistently uses it to translate the Hebrew word for "covenant," and suggests that this usage may have shaped Paul's own use of the word: "It appears, therefore, that ... Paul has both secular and theological connotations for διαθηκη in mind and that he is working from that of 'testament' or 'will' to that of 'covenant' " (*Galatians*, p. 128).

Brown says, "The word here translated 'covenant' ... is of considerably more comprehensive signification than the term by which it is rendered in our version. The English word *covenant* means 'a bargain,' an agreement between certain parties on certain terms. To this there is a corresponding term in Greek, but that word never occurs in the New Testament, and rarely in the LXX, or in the other Greek versions of the Old Testament. The Hebrew and Greek words rendered 'covenant' signify a 'disposition,' 'arrangement,' and are applicable not only to *covenants* or bargains, properly so called, but to *laws* and *promises*" (*Exposition of Galatians*, p. 57).

² Calvin, *Galatians ... Colossians*, p. 57.

³ "Therefore these two things (as I do often repeat), to wit the law and the promise, must be diligently distinguished. For in time, in place, and in person, and generally in all other circumstances, they are separate as far asunder as heaven and earth ... so that the law may have dominion over the flesh, and the promise may sweetly (and comfortably) reign in the conscience ... But now, if thou confound and mingle these two together and place the law in the conscience, and the promise of liberty in the flesh thou makest a confusion ... so that thou shalt not know what the law, what the promise, what sin, or what righteousness is" (Luther, *Galatians*, p. 291).

18
The Purpose of the Law

Please Read Galatians 3:19–25

Paul's next question is the obvious one: **"What purpose then does the law serve?"** Having just made it abundantly clear that the promises of God are not obtained under the Sinaitical covenant, he feels obliged to enquire whether the law serves any purpose at all. Surely there must be a purpose, since the law was God-given, but if redemption is not by the law, what exactly is its significance? The apostle supplies an answer to these questions in the verses that follow.[1]

What the law could not do (3:19–22)
Paul has previously made much of the law's failure to provide justification, and he extends the theme here. If we are to understand the true purpose of the law, we must first understand what it was *not* intended to achieve.

Having asked, "What is the purpose of the law?" Paul first makes a rather cryptic reference to the manner in which it was given: **"It was appointed through angels by the hand of a mediator. Now a mediator does not mediate for one only, but God is one"** (3:19–20). This statement is not as obscure as it first seems. It is simply a restatement of the distinction between the two covenants. The law was given to Israel through the mediation of Moses, and Paul is pointing out that where there is a mediator, there must also be *two* parties. Thus the law given at Sinai bore the marks of a contract, what we have called a covenant of the second kind, which placed obligations on both God and man. By contrast, "God is one" signifies that God acted *alone* in giving the covenant of promise, this being a covenant of the first kind (a testament). Human obedience is required by Moses' law, and therein lies its weakness. But the covenant of promise is God's gracious gift, requiring nothing of man but acceptance. This distinction is also stated clearly in Romans: "What the law could not do in that it was weak through the flesh, God *did by sending His own Son ...*" (Rom. 8:3, emphasis added).

This throws considerable light on what follows, for it identifies why the law could not achieve the salvation of its adherents. Paul points out that the law is not **"against the promises of God"** (3:21). God is the author of both law and promise, so there can be no antagonism between the two. "The law is holy," writes the apostle elsewhere, "and the commandment holy and just and good" (Rom. 7:12). The problem lies in the nature of the law, namely that being a covenant of the second kind, it requires human obedience if it is to work. God is well able to keep his side of the agreement, but man in his sin is incapable of keeping his. Paul elaborates: **"If there had been a law given which could have offered life, truly righteousness would have been by the law"** (3:21). This shows that there is nothing intrinsically wrong with the idea of salvation by obedience to law. After all, it is Christ's perfect obedience to the law, *as a man*, that constitutes our righteousness before God (Christ's obedience being imputed to the believer). But Jesus Christ is the only man who never sinned, and sinners, by definition, cannot render to God's law the perfect conformity required for salvation.[2]

Thus the law of Moses, which in principle could lead to life, in practice only condemns the sons of Adam. As Paul confesses, "The commandment which was to bring life, I found to bring death" (Rom. 7:10). This is what the apostle means when he adds, **"The Scripture has confined all under sin"** (3:22). "The Scripture" signifies either the law as recorded in Scripture, or the Scriptures as a whole, which reveal man's inability to obey the law of God. Either way, Scripture bears testimony to the fact that the law serves only to establish man's sinful state and guilt before a holy God.

Note that all this is according to the sovereign purpose of God.

It was his intention that none should be justified by law-works, and that all should stand condemned by the law. Why? In order that the promise should prevail! **"The Scripture has confined all under sin, that the promise by faith in Jesus Christ might be given to those who believe"** (3:22). Again, why must the promise prevail over the law? So that "no flesh should glory in His presence" (1 Cor. 1:29). If salvation were by works, then man would glory in those works. But being condemned by the law, and cast upon the mercy of God, those who embrace the promise of God through faith in Christ bring glory to God, since their salvation redounds to "the praise of the glory of His grace" (Eph. 1:6).

What the law did achieve (3:19, 22–25)

All this, of course, was fully known to God before he gave the law at Sinai. Thus, explains Paul, it was never God's purpose that men should be saved through the works of the law; rather, the law **"was added** [to the preexisting promise] **because of transgressions"** (3:19). What does this mean?[3]

"Because of transgressions" signifies several things. Firstly, it indicates that God gave the law to *restrain* transgression among his people, the Jews. Their tendency to revert to the practices and idolatries of the surrounding nations is, of course, legendary in Scripture. Yet it was vital for the outworking of God's purpose that Israel should preserve the knowledge of the true God, and transmit that knowledge to future generations, until Christ came. To them had been entrusted the oracles of God, the "adoption, the glory, the covenants, the giving of the law, the service of God and the promises" (Rom. 3:2; 9:4). All this had to be preserved, and the law undoubtedly prevented this heritage of revelation from being lost. At times, of course, it was all but buried from sight, but there always remained a remnant in Israel who were faithful to Jahweh, the Lord, and who were often instrumental in restoring the nation to his worship.

Secondly, as a corollary of this, the law preserved the knowledge of the character of God. His uniqueness as the only true and living God, his creatorhood, his holiness, his love of truth and hatred of sin, are all clearly expressed in the law. "Because of transgression," therefore, also signifies "over against transgression," that is, by contrast with the iniquity of man, we see in the law God's purity and anger against sin.

Thirdly, as we have seen already, the law convicts mankind of sin, for "By the law is the knowledge of sin" (Rom. 3:20). Paul explains further: "Until the law sin was in the world, but sin is not imputed where there is no law" (Rom. 5:13), so that "the law entered that the offense might abound" (Rom. 5:20). In this sense, "because of transgression" signifies that the law served to bring human sin into focus, and to unmask it for what it is. It caused man's sin to be *expressed* in the form of transgression, since, technically speaking, "transgression" can only occur where there is some rule or standard to be broken.[4]

Fourthly, the law also showed that God has made gracious provision for the sinner to be forgiven, through substitutionary atonement and priestly mediation. All of this prefigured the work of Christ. "Because of transgression" thus also indicates that God has an answer to transgression, although that answer did not lie in the law itself, but in the "Lamb of God" to whom it pointed.

This fourfold function of the law leads us directly to Paul's conclusion. **"Therefore,"** he declares, **"the law was our tutor to bring us to Christ, that we might be justified by faith"** (3:24). The message is clear: the purpose of the law is unveiled. By preserving the Old Testament revelation of the true God and his Messiah, the law pointed the Jews to Christ. By delineating the character of God, his holiness and hatred of sin, the law demonstrated the necessity of forgiveness and reconciliation. By stating unambiguously what God requires of man, the law revealed man's desperate plight under the wrath of a holy God. By prefiguring Christ, in the tabernacle, the priesthood and the sacrifices, the law unveiled God's answer to the problem of sin. As Thomas Boston puts it, "The law lays open the wound, but it is the gospel that heals."[5]

The word "tutor" does not fully convey the Greek

"paidagogos," since in Greek society the latter was normally a slave who acted as a child-minder, disciplinarian, or even bodyguard, rather than a teacher. Paul puts it this way: **"Before faith came, we were kept under guard by the law, kept for the faith that would afterward be revealed"** (3:23). This could mean one of two things: firstly, that the Jews were kept *from* faith by the law; or alternatively that they were kept *for* faith by the law. I believe that the latter is what Paul intends to convey. The law prepared the Jews for the coming of the Christ, keeping alive the knowledge of the living God and of the promised Messiah. It is true that very few of them understood the meaning of the law in this way. (We can hardly be critical, for very few professing Christians today understand the significance of the law as expounded here in Galatians.) Nevertheless, insists the apostle, the purpose of the law was to *prepare* the Jewish people for the coming of Christ and the gospel of salvation by faith, and to lead them to him. The law reveals God in his holiness, man in his sinfulness, and Christ in his atoning sufficiency. In doing so, however, it points the seeker away from itself and its works, and toward the unmerited promise of grace in Christ.

Does the law have a current purpose? (3:19–25)

This passage concludes with the following words: **"But after faith has come, we are no longer under a tutor"** (3:25). Having served its purpose of leading the believing remnant of Jews to Christ, the law became redundant. Paul therefore seems to teach that the law has no ongoing function, at least in the lives of believers. Is this indeed what Paul is saying? Does the law of Moses have no current role?

We note firstly that, in the Greek text of verse 19, the verb is omitted. The text states literally: **"What purpose then the law?"** We cannot therefore rely on the tense of the verb "serve" to clarify the matter. Paul could be saying either that the law *did once* serve a purpose, or that it *does now* serve a purpose. However, the remainder of this passage refers exclusively to a past function for the law, as is evident from verses 23–25. Paul is silent in this passage regarding any current role for Moses' law.

There are several possible reasons for this emphasis on the past. The first and most straightforward is that Paul does not regard the law as having any current function whatever. We have already seen, when considering Galatians 2:17–18 (in chapter 11), that the believer is dead to the law. Certainly, the law and its works can play no role in the believer's justification or standing with God. Furthermore, as we shall see in the final part of this commentary, sanctification (however it is understood) is the work of the Spirit, not of the law.

Alternatively, it may be argued that Paul is overstating his case in order to wean the Galatians away from the Judaizers' pernicious doctrine. He may not have wanted to say anything positive about the law, in case it were seized upon to justify their false teaching. This does seem to be the underlying view of some commentators, who seek to retain the "moral law" as a pattern for Christian life and the basis for practical sanctification. I am unable to accept this argument. For one thing, the epistle to the Romans is at one with Galatians in rejecting any role for the Mosaic covenant in the life of the *believer*, as we have seen previously. (So also is the epistle to the Hebrews.) Paul's rejection of the law is not reserved exclusively for the Galatians; he is wholly consistent on this subject. Again, to suggest that the case is overstated in Galatians casts doubt on the validity of all Scripture. Although our theology must be based upon the Bible as a whole, and obscure passages in one place must be interpreted by reference to other scriptures, it is going altogether too far to suggest that a whole epistle might be deliberately misleading on one of its major themes. Finally, the New Testament teaching on practical holiness is perfectly clear, and relies in no way on the works of the law, as we shall see when we consider Galatians 4, 5 and 6.

A more cogent argument against a total rejection of the law is that Paul is here writing from a strictly historical perspective; that is, he is concerned to explain the function of the law from the time of Moses until the time of Christ. He is not, therefore, specifically addressing any relevance of the law to the Christian era. It is certainly true that the whole passage, from Galatians 3:6–4:7, is set in a historical context (see particularly 3:17, 19, 23; 4:4). Nevertheless, the apostle is not merely giving a history lesson! He is seeking to instruct the Galatians as to the true purpose of Moses' law, and to persuade them that believers are no longer subject to that law, its purpose having been fulfilled in the coming of Christ (3:19, 24–25).

However, this does leave open the possibility that what was true historically may still be true currently. Just as the law prepared the Jews for the coming of the Messiah, so it must be true that the truth contained in the law still points men to Christ. The holiness of God and the demands he makes upon those created in his image remain true for all time, for God is changeless. Man's inability to conform, even outwardly, to the law's demands, is as evident today as it has always been. Similarly, the rich typology set forth in the tabernacle, with its sacrifices and priestly office, continues to illuminate the work of Christ. Yet it remains true that we no longer *need* these symbolic truths now that Christ has been clearly revealed in terms of New Testament revelation. As the writer to the Hebrews says, "In that [God] says 'a new covenant,' He made the first [Mosaic covenant] obsolete. Now what is becoming obsolete and growing old is ready to vanish away" (Heb. 8:13). As a covenant, the law of Moses has been annulled, in its entirety, by the coming of Christ.

The law as Scripture

But what of the law as *Scripture*? Specifically, the law of Moses continues to emphasize God's holy character and man's sinful inability to meet his requirements. In this sense it still warns men of judgment and directs them to Christ as the only hope for salvation. This seems to be the burden of Paul's words to Timothy: "We know that the law is good if one uses it lawfully, knowing this: that the law is not made for a righteous person, but for the lawless and insubordinate, for the ungodly and for sinners, for the unholy and profane ..." (1 Tim. 1:8–10). However, the law is not unique in this, for many other scriptures teach the same clear truths concerning man's sin. For example, in John 16:8–11, it is the Spirit's testimony to Christ and the cross which will convince the world of sin, righteousness, and judgment.

New Testament teaching, indeed, goes beyond the law in defining God's moral demands upon men, as in the Sermon on the Mount, or the "practical" sections of Paul's epistles. Again, the nature and character of God is revealed most clearly in Christ, as Hebrews 1:1–3 states unequivocally. The law, therefore, takes its natural place as part of Scripture. For example, in the area of evangelism, as far as I can tell, the New Testament does not propagate the idea that we must necessarily preach the law to the unconverted, to bring them under conviction, before presenting the gospel. On the contrary, whenever Paul refers to the content of his evangel, he tells us that he preaches "Christ" (see for example Rom. 1:1–4, 9, 16–17; 1 Cor. 1:23; 2:2; 2 Cor. 2:12; 5:18–21; Gal. 1:16; Eph. 3:8; Phil. 1:18; Col. 1:27–28).

As regards sanctification, the law can be accorded no special place today in the life of the believer, that is, no place *over and above* the rest of Scripture. To suggest that the Ten Commandments are in some *special* way the Christian's rule of life does an injustice to the whole body of New Testament teaching on Christian conduct. See, for example, 2 Corinthians 3:3, where the work of grace in the lives of believers is ascribed to "the Spirit of the living God; [written] not in tablets of stone, but in ... the heart." It is true, of course, that the New Testament builds upon the foundation of the commandments. They are retained, not abandoned, as an (but not "the") expression of God's requirements (see, for example, Ephesians 6:2, where Paul cites with approval the fifth commandment). But it has to be repeated that the New Testament both gathers up and goes beyond the commandments in its moral teaching.

It is often said that the Sermon on the Mount is nothing more than an exposition of the Ten Commandments, but this is not the case. The Sermon on the Mount refers to "these commandments" (Matt. 5:19) but the context is the entire Old Testament, not just the Decalogue. Again, only three of the Ten Commandments are referred to in the sermon, either directly or indirectly, whereas it embodies an abundance of moral and spiritual instruction which is nowhere implied in the Decalogue. This specifically New Testament teaching includes such things as reconciliation, the permanence of marriage, a forgiving spirit, love for our enemies, self-effacing charity, prayer, fasting, our attitude to material wealth, confidence in God's providence, the tests of genuine faith, and a life built upon the rock, that is, obedience to Christ's teaching. It cannot be adequate to suggest that Christian morality and holiness of life stem in some special way from the Decalogue.

Summary

The law could not justify the sinner, because it was a covenant of the second kind, requiring man's perfect obedience. This set it apart from the covenant of promise, which was a testament, requiring nothing of man. Since man is incapable by nature of rendering perfect obedience, the law could not save, but only condemn.

The law was given on account of transgression. In this role, the law restrained sin among the Israelites and thus preserved the knowledge of God and his promises until the coming of Christ. The law reflected the character of God and what he requires of man, demonstrating, above all, that fallen man cannot keep his commandments. Finally, in the tabernacle, sacrifices, and priesthood, the law prefigured God's answer to human transgression, namely the person and work of Christ.

This fourfold action of the law reveals its purpose in the plan of God. The law had the effect of guarding Israel from total apostasy and preparing the God-fearing remnant for the coming of Christ. It could not save them, but it did point them to the one who could. By bringing sin into focus, and demonstrating God's anger against sin, the law led them to embrace the gracious covenant of promise, which they did through faith in Christ. As a covenant, therefore, the law of Moses has been annulled. However, it remains as Scripture, and in this capacity, along with all other Scripture, it continues to play a part in convicting men of sin and pointing them to Christ. In the same way, as Scripture, it contains instruction in righteousness and forms part of the overall biblical testimony to what constitutes Christian morality and holiness of life.

Notes

[1] "Though sadly often treated as an addendum to Paul's earlier discussion of legalism, or worse yet ignored, 3:19–25 is the *crux interpretum* for Paul's response to the problems in Galatia. Here Paul lays out a Christian understanding of the purpose and function of the law vis-a-vis the Judaizers' nomistic message" (Longenecker, *Galatians*, p. 137).

[2] "The apostle proceeds to show that the law was not, could not be, against the promise, so it was altogether unfit to serve the purpose of the promise. If the law had been so constituted as that through it guilty men might have obtained life or happiness, there might have been some plausibility in supposing that it should have taken the place of the promise. But since the very reverse of this is the case, its great use is not to take the place of the promise, but to evince the necessity of the promise" (Brown, *Exposition of Galatians*, p. 66).

[3] "The question is this: why, after a promise had been made, did Moses intervene with a new contract, that he who does those things shall live by them, but cursed be he that fulfilleth not these things?" (Calvin, *Galatians ... Colossians*, p. 60).

[4] "Neither the law of nature nor the law of Moses was such a law [as to justify men]. They make no provision for efficacious atonement for past offences, or for that change of character which is necessary to prevent new offences. They show us what is right and what is wrong; and tell us that obedience, if it is perfect in every point of view, will secure reward, and that disobedience will incur punishment. But they do not, they cannot, give life; they do not, they cannot, justify" (Brown, *Exposition of Galatians*, p. 67).

"It is no small matter then to understand rightly what the law is, and what is the true use and office thereof ... we reject not the law and works, as our adversaries do falsely accuse us ... we say that the law is good and profitable, but in his own proper use: which is first to bridle civil transgressions, and then to reveal and to increase spiritual transgressions. Wherefore the law is also a light, which sheweth and revealeth, not the grace of God, not righteousness and life; but sin, death, the wrath and judgement of God ... the law, when it is in his true sense, doth nothing else but reveal sin, engender wrath, accuse and terrify men, so that it bringeth them to the very brink of desperation. This is the proper use of the law, and here it hath an end, and it ought to go no further" (Luther, *Galatians*, pp. 301–2).

[5] "Yet it is the gospel that crowns the work: 'the law makes nothing perfect.' The law lays open the wound, but it is the gospel that heals" (Boston, *Human Nature*, p. 191).

19
All One in Christ

Please Read Galatians 3:26–29

The law having been set aside, the distinction between Jew and Gentile no longer exists. **"You are all one in Christ Jesus,"** declares the apostle. There is no sense, therefore, in the Gentiles hankering after some illusory special status enjoyed by Jewish believers. In Christ they already enjoy a far higher status than the physical descendants of Abraham ever possessed. Thus, in the passage before us, Paul applies the lessons taught (and, it is to be hoped, learned) in the foregoing theological argument.

Sons of God (3:26)

The section of the epistle that we have just finished, from Galatians 3:7 to 3:25, is intensely theological. That passage began with the assertion that "Only those who are of faith are sons of Abraham" (3:7). Now, at its conclusion, Paul crowns that statement with a new, though related, concept. Not only are believers children of Abraham, they **"are all sons of God through faith in Christ Jesus"** (3:26).

This is the first mention in Galatians of the father-child relationship that exists between God and the believer, but it is by no means the last. This relationship lies at the heart of Paul's teaching in the concluding chapters of the epistle, which we shall cover in the third and final part of this commentary. Our present passage is thus a bridge between Paul's dissertation on faith and law, which extends from the end of Galatians 2 through Galatians 3, and his teaching on the Spirit and the believer in Galatians 4–6. The present verses also provide the apostle with an opportunity to apply to his spiritually embattled readers some of the theological truth he has just expounded.

They are "all sons of God," he declares.[1] According to the Judaizers, these Gentile believers could not even be sons of Abraham unless they submitted to circumcision and the law of Moses. Paul has already put them right on this matter in Galatians 3:7. Their trust in Christ, without the law, qualifies them for *that* privilege, since they are true heirs of Abraham by virtue of their faith, regardless of their Gentile birth. But now Paul unveils a far greater truth, a peerless privilege: they are not only sons of Abraham, but sons of God himself!

What leads the apostle to make this statement at this juncture? Very simply, sonship of God is the culmination of the covenant of promise.[2] In Galatians 3:14 we saw that the promise to Abraham was nothing less than the gift of God's Holy Spirit to indwell the believing soul. As we shall see more clearly in part III, to be indwelt by the Spirit of God is to be a child of God — no more, no less. Whereas the Mosaic covenant emphasized man as a creature, owing an obedience to his Maker that he cannot perform, the covenant of promise bestows on the believer the incomparable status of sonship. Contemplating this privilege, the apostle John exclaims, "Behold what manner of love the Father has bestowed on us, that we should be called children of God!" (1 John 3:1).

We shall explore this subject in greater depth shortly. At this point, however, we should pause to ask a question of ourselves: are we, as believers today, sufficiently *conscious* of the privilege which is ours in Christ? It was surely at the root of the Galatians' defection that they had failed to grasp what God had already done for them. What does sonship imply? Briefly expressed, it means:

1. A permanent, loving relationship with God (John 10:27–29);

2. A sharing of the characteristics of God by his indwelling Spirit (2 Peter 1:4);

3. The right of immediate access to God (Rom. 5:1–2);

4. The expectation of blessing from God (Luke 11:11–13; Rom. 8:32);

5. Confidence in the Father's provision (Matt. 6:31–34);

6. As heirs of God, a promise of even greater things to come (1 John 3:2; Rom. 8:16–17).

Here is food and drink for the soul. Here is the ground of love for God. Here is a reason for heartfelt worship. Here lies our confidence in prayer. Here is hope in darkness and joy in adversity. Here is the burial-ground of fears. Here rise the springs of courage, boldness and active service!

This transcendent relationship with God is ours "through faith in Christ Jesus" (3:26)—faith, not works; trusting Christ's work, not our own. Furthermore, the faith by which we trust is not an attribute of human nature, but the gift of God (Eph. 2:8–9). At the risk of repetition, notice again that faith *of itself* does not bestow sonship; it has to be faith *in Christ*. It is only in him that we attain sonship, for we become sons only by virtue of our union with the eternal Son of God: "It is no longer I who live, but Christ lives in me" (2:20).

Putting on Christ (3:27)

The last point, concerning our union with Christ through faith, is developed in verse 27: **"For as many of you as were baptized into Christ have put on Christ."** The word translated "put on" means "clothe." It is also the Greek word from which derives the English "endue." Thus to put on Christ is to clothe oneself in Christ, or to endue oneself with Christ. Note that the verb is active, that is, this enduement is the direct result of our exercising faith. What then does it mean to clothe ourselves with Christ?

Paul is, of course, using a picture. His metaphor conveys something of the richness of the spiritual reality portrayed. Think of a policeman getting up in the morning to go to work. He is an ordinary man, with nothing special to distinguish him from other men; that is, until he dons his uniform. Then, in a significant sense, he becomes a changed man. The uniform makes all the difference. He becomes a symbol of authority. He assumes certain powers not vested in other men. He represents the strength and rule of law and, on that account, evokes respect.

Poor though the analogy may be, it may help us to understand how those who have put on Christ are thereby transformed. "If anyone is in Christ, he is a new creation; old things have passed away; behold, all things have become new" (2 Cor. 5:17). Believers "have put on the new man who is renewed in knowledge according to the image of Him who created him" (Col. 3:10).

Through union with Christ, the image of God in man is renewed, and the true knowledge of God, abandoned by Adam, is regained. Furthermore, having put on Christ, the believer is endued with new authority, the right to be called a child of God (John 1:12). He becomes an ambassador of Christ, a representative of the most high God (2 Cor. 5:20). He assumes new privileges, as we have seen, and new powers, being freed from slavery to sin and set free into "the glorious liberty of the children of God" (Rom. 6:17–18; 8:21).

All this, says the apostle, applies to "as many of you as were baptized into Christ" (3:27). Clearly, Paul is speaking of believers' baptism, since only believers can exercise faith in Christ. There is no place in Paul's thinking for the "baptism" of infants or unbelievers, for his phrase "as many of you" is surely intended to embrace the entire church in each of the Galatian cities. But why does he introduce baptism here at all? The answer is that baptism is an outward expression of inward faith. They had put on Christ, not by the outward rite of baptism, but by the faith to which that baptism testified.[3] Baptism, therefore, symbolizes faith. However, there is probably more to it than that. By referring to their baptism, Paul *reminds* them of the genuine faith by which they first embraced the gospel of free grace in Christ. They were now being led astray, and stood in urgent need of correction. The apostle seeks to do this by taking them back to their spiritual roots.

Such remembrance can be a means of spiritual restoration to us also. Peter judges it "right … to stir you up by reminding you" (2 Peter 1:13), while Paul tells the Philippians, "For me to write the same things to you is not tedious, but for you it is safe" (Phil. 3:1). "I will remember …" is a recurring theme in the Psalms, especially when the writer is passing through difficult times (e.g. Ps. 42:4, 6).

Psalm 77:9–13 is worth quoting at length:

> Has God forgotten to be gracious?...
> And I said, "This is my anguish;
> But I will remember the years of the right hand of the Most High."
> I will remember the works of the LORD;
> Surely I will remember Your wonders of old ...
> Who is so great a God as our God?

The "ministry of memory" is a most valuable weapon in the believer's armory, a potent force in spiritual warfare. Paul is not slow to use it to help the Galatians recover their spiritual equilibrium (see further examples in Galatians 3:1–4; 4:15).

All one in Christ Jesus (3:28)

Having "put on" Christ, continues the apostle, believers find that the barriers that normally divide mankind are broken down. **"There is neither Jew nor Greek, there is neither slave nor free, there is neither male nor female"** (3:28). Paul does not mean, of course, that these categories are abolished. In racial terms, there were still Jews and Greeks. In social terms there were still slaves and freemen. In sexual terms there were still men and women. What he is teaching the Galatians is that those who are united spiritually with Christ are also thereby united with one another. They now have far more in common than in contrast. The divisions within society, which so often seem insuperable, fade into the background as believers are united in Christ.

This is not just theory, but the living experience of all true followers of Christ. Being in union with Christ, they find themselves at one with fellow believers regardless of differences in race, language, culture, age, education and social standing. How does this unity come about? It is "the unity of the Spirit" (Eph. 4:3). It arises from the fact that each believer is indwelt by the same Spirit; is a child of the same heavenly Father; is a member of the one family of God.

There is much talk of "Christian unity" and much is written

about the goal of ecumenism. Conferences are held and declarations made upon the subject. Working parties are set up to promote unity between churches. With an excess of zeal, some even seek to establish "unity" between different religions, setting aside all questions of truth and error. But this is not the kind of unity Paul is talking about when he says, **"You are all one in Christ Jesus"** (3:28). Those who trust Christ do not have to strive for unity; they have it already! They have all "put on" the same Savior. They have all been born into the same family. They are all indwelt by the same Spirit. They all have the same Father.

This true Christian unity, which is found only "in Christ," is precious beyond words. It finds its expression in love for fellow believers, fellowship in the gospel, sharing in suffering, mutual affection, prayer for one another, mutual rejoicing in Christ, working together for the faith of the gospel, and in many other ways. (I have culled these examples from Philippians chapter 1 alone; there is not space to spell out the full ramifications of this unity.) How sad it is, therefore, when Satan is allowed to create disunity among believers! This is most likely to happen when we take our eyes off Christ, for it is only in him that our unity consists.

Even where there is no open disunity, however, believers often fail to experience the positive fruits of unity, such as those listed all too briefly above. The local church becomes a loveless place, fellowship becomes a formality, and a joyless lethargy sets in. The cause is frequently the same—a forgetfulness of the unspeakable privilege that is ours as sons of God. And what is the antidote? The preaching and exaltation of Christ at every opportunity, for our sonship resides in him!

Heirs according to promise (3:29)
In a well-crafted symphony, it is frequently the case that the composer briefly introduces his various musical themes at an early stage, and then proceeds to elaborate them in turn. Whether intentionally or not, there is something of this character in Galatians. The covenant with Abraham, the promise of the Spirit, and the

privilege of sonship are all unveiled in Galatians 3, but still await their full development in later chapters. Another such theme, namely, that believers are **"heirs according to the promise,"** is now delineated. Of course, it has already been mentioned in Galatians 3:18, where reference is made to "the inheritance," but there its significance is somewhat overlaid by the flow of Paul's argument. To emphasize the importance of this idea, therefore, the apostle reiterates it here. It is a theme that he is about to develop in great and glorious detail in the opening verses of Galatians 4.

The point to be emphasized here is that the covenant of promise gives rise to an inheritance. The words "heirs according to the promise" signify firstly that the inheritance is secure, being promised by a changeless God. Nothing can annul the promise; nothing can dilute or alter it. Unlike the law, it depends in no way upon man's obedience. On the contrary, it is "according to grace, so that the promise might be sure to all the seed" (Rom. 4:16). It is only God's free grace that *guarantees* the inheritance.

It is important that we understand this. It is often suggested that the gospel of free grace in Christ is one of several, equally valid, emphases. Some choose to believe the doctrines of grace, while others choose not to, but all are proclaiming the same gospel, we are told. This cannot be true if grace is the only guarantee of the promise, for grace must then be an *indispensable* element of the gospel. Of course, many use the word "grace" loosely, but there can be no misunderstanding of its biblical meaning. It means that God acts alone, in splendid sovereignty, without man's aid, merit or works, in providing an inheritance for those he has chosen in Christ.

Secondly, "according to the promise" means that the inheritance is exactly what was promised. The things promised to Abraham, and through him to Christ, who receives them on our behalf, are the things actually given. Of course, we need to understand that what was promised to Abraham, in terms of a promised land, a multitude of descendants, and the blessing of all nations, has a primary spiritual interpretation, which is realized in

Christ through the coming of the Spirit. This Paul reveals in Galatians 3:14–16, as we have seen. But Paul was not the first to say these things. The Old Testament prophets also understood, as is evident from Jeremiah 31:31–34; Ezekiel 37; Joel 2:28–32, and other places where the promise to Abraham's seed is explicitly presented as the gift of God's Spirit.

Thus the Lord Jesus could with confidence tell his disciples "to wait for the promise of the Father," knowing that they would indeed be "baptized with the Holy Spirit not many days from now" (Acts 1:4–5). The promise of the Spirit was fulfilled at Pentecost, and continues to be bestowed upon all who **"are Christ's"** and therefore **"Abraham's seed"** (3:29).

Summary

This passage is a bridge between the teaching on the covenant of promise, in Galatians 3, and the outworking of that promise in the life of the believer, considered in Galatians 4, 5 and 6. It introduces the great themes of sonship to God, union with Christ ("putting on Christ"), the unity of God's people, and the inheritance that is theirs. Each of these themes is worked out in the chapters that follow, in which also Paul applies their truth to the practical life of the believer and the church.

Notes

[1] "By their union with him, who is the Son of God by nature, they become the sons of God by grace, John 1:12" (Boston, *Human Nature*, p. 200).

[2] "God is no longer our Judge, who through the law has condemned and imprisoned us. God is no longer our Tutor, who through the law restrains and chastises us. God is now our Father, who in Christ has accepted and forgiven us" (Stott, *Message of Galatians*, p. 98).

[3] "All those, then, who by means of their baptism have truly laid aside, in principle, their garment of sin, and have truly been decked with the robe of Christ's righteousness, having thus been buried with him and raised with him, have put on Christ" (Hendriksen, *Galatians and Ephesians*, p. 149).

Part III

The Spirit and the Believer

20
Heirs of God through Christ

Please Read Galatians 4:1–7

There is no sharp break in the epistle corresponding to the beginning of part III of this commentary, any more than there was between parts I and II. Paul wrote Galatians as a letter, straight from the heart, not as a theological treatise with tidy sub-divisions. However, there is genuine value in breaking the epistle down as we have done, since it helps us to follow the progression of the apostle's thoughts, and the development of his great themes.

In this final part of Galatians, Paul returns to many, if not all, of the themes begun in the first three chapters. Indeed, some commentators regard Galatians 4 as little more than repetition and re-emphasis of earlier material. This is a mistake, however, for these concluding chapters provide some of the most important teaching anywhere in the New Testament concerning the believer's privileges and responsibilities. Furthermore, Paul tells us how those privileges are to be enjoyed and those responsibilities fulfilled, namely through the power of the indwelling Holy Spirit. This is why part III of this book is entitled "The Spirit and the believer." Even where the apostle reviews previous topics, he does so from the new perspective of the believer as a son and heir of God.

It is completely logical that Paul should develop this teaching toward the end of the epistle. He has dismissed the law of Moses as a means of finding favor with God. The whole point of the Galatian epistle is to prevent the Gentile believers being caught up in a covenant of works which had been abrogated by the coming of Christ. But as we have seen, this leaves Paul open to the charge of antinomianism, or "lawlessness." Without the guidance and restraint of the moral law, will not Christians live as they please, being utterly careless of God's requirements for holy living? What is Paul's response to this question? His answer in Galatians is the same as in Romans: "Those who live according to the flesh set their minds on the things of the flesh, but those who live according to the Spirit, the things of the Spirit" (Rom. 8:5).

Heirs in bondage (4:1–3)

Those who are Christ's, declares the closing verse of Galatians 3, are heirs according to the promise. This statement prompts Paul to develop in some detail the meaning and implications of the word "heir." We are reminded here that an heir does not necessarily enter immediately into his inheritance. There are circumstances in which the enjoyment of a legacy is delayed on account of the minority of the heir. **"The heir,"** explains Paul, **"as long as he is a child, does not differ at all from a slave, though he is** [potentially] **master of all, but is under guardians and stewards until the time appointed by the father"** (Gal. 4:1). This may refer to a deceased parent whose will puts the inheritance in trust until the child is old enough to handle it responsibly. Equally, however, it may refer to a case where the father has appointed a share of his wealth to his children, to be possessed when they attain a certain age (compare, for example, the parable of the prodigal son, Luke 15:12).

Either way, the child *is* an heir, assured of the inheritance, long before he enters into it, and this is what Paul is teaching. The spiritual application is clear: the heirs of promise were such, long before the promise was actually fulfilled in Christ. In God's eternal purpose both the blessing and those to be blessed were preordained. "God ... has saved us and called us with a holy calling, not according to our works, but according to His own purpose and grace which was given to us in Christ Jesus before time began" (2 Tim. 1:9–10).

It is not immediately clear whether Paul is here speaking generally, referring to believers of all eras, or historically, referring only to the Jewish nation before the coming of Christ. Certainly, the historical interpretation is the obvious one, since Paul equates the **"time appointed by the father"** in his illustration, with the **"fullness of time"** in which Christ came (4:4). On this interpretation, the "child-heirs" represent those God-fearing Jews who lived under the law during the centuries before Christ, but looked forward in faith to his advent (see Heb. 11:39–40).

However, this cannot be Paul's only intention, since he proceeds to apply the illustration to the Galatians themselves in verses 6–7. Again, in verse 8, he refers to the time when the Galatians "did not know God, [and] served those which by nature are not gods." We have to conclude, therefore, that the apostle is "having it both ways," using the historical scenario as an example to establish a more general truth. What is this truth?

Firstly, as we have seen already, the children of promise are heirs *before* they receive their inheritance. In God's eyes they are the elect, chosen in Christ "before the foundation of the world" (Eph. 1:4), even though they are in bondage to sin until converted to Christ (Rom. 6:17–18; Eph. 2:3–5).

Secondly, before their regeneration, the heirs (the elect) are **"in bondage under the elements of the world"** (4:3). What does this mean? The word "elements," or "rudiments," refers to first principles or basic tenets. "The world" refers to mankind in its natural unregenerate condition. It may also embrace those spiritual powers which keep mankind in darkness and spiritual bondage (see 2 Cor. 4:4; 1 John 5:19). Similar terminology is found in Colossians: "Beware lest anyone should cheat you through philosophy and empty deceit, according to the traditions of men, according to the basic principles [elements] of the world, and not according to Christ" (Col. 2:8). A few verses later he tells the Colossians that they had "died with Christ from the basic principles of the world" (Col. 2:20). Thus "the elements of the world" are those basic tenets to which unregenerate men adhere, *especially in matters of philosophy and religion.*

It is evident that Paul includes the law of Moses among these "elements."[1] In Galatians 4:9 he deplores the Galatians' apparent wish to "turn again to the weak and beggarly elements, to which [they] desire again to be in bondage." Under the malign influence of the Judaizers it was, of course, the law to which they were turning. This creates a problem. How can Paul categorize the God-given law in this manner? The answer is that Paul condemns, not the law itself, but *the idea* that man can be justified by observing that law. It is belief in the *efficacy* of law-keeping, or of works generally, to justify or purify the sinner, that constitutes a basic tenet of the world and brings human beings into bondage. A law (any law) is never satisfied. It requires ever-increasing perfection from its devotees. That is always its tendency. Witness the way in which the Mosaic law was elaborated over centuries of rabbinical toil, until the devout Jew had to observe literally thousands of rules and regulations, affecting every area of life.

This applies to any religious law or code, not just to Moses' law. Before their conversion the Galatians, as Gentiles, had been just as much in bondage as the Jews. Both subscribed to some version of the same worldly philosophy, namely that God (or, for that matter, the gods) could be propitiated by acts of worship, devotion or sacrifice. Such acts are doomed to fail because they relate to outward behavior and do not arise from an inner principle of godliness. Even while men seek to propitiate God by religious exercises, they live sinfully, seeing no contradiction between their religious profession and their practical behavior. This is common in our society today, where many professing "Christians" think nothing of such things as lying, cheating, and infidelity.

There are lessons to be learned here even by true believers (remember that Paul was writing to the Galatians as such). Firstly, outward conformity to the mores and practices advocated by a church or denomination does not of itself constitute Christian discipleship. The way we dress, the way we talk, how much television we watch, our taste in music, the books we read, and so much else, is not what pleases or displeases God. "Man looks at the outward appearance, but the LORD looks at the heart" (1 Sam. 16:7). As Paul exhorts the Romans, "Do not be conformed to this world, but be transformed by the renewing of your mind, that you may prove what is that good and acceptable and perfect will of God" (Rom. 12:2). God looks for *inward transformation*, not *outward conformity;* and since our actions flow from our hearts, the fruit of a transformed heart and mind will be evident in Christ-honoring lives (Matt. 12:33–37). This is probably the major theme of the Sermon on the Mount, namely that God demands righteousness in the heart as the only acceptable basis for outwardly moral behavior (see, e.g., Matt. 5:13–16, 28; 7:15–20).

Secondly, there is a real danger that believers may revert to law-keeping in the mistaken belief that this makes them more "spiritual" and thus more acceptable to God. Paul's purpose here is to point out that the very opposite is true. That is, submission to the law begets bondage, and belongs to the "world" from which Christ has delivered his people rather than the kingdom of God.[2]

God sent forth his Son (4:4–5)

The child-heirs do not remain children forever. There is an end to their bondage, an end which is as certain and predictable as a child's coming of age. What brings their "childhood" to an end? The advent of Christ, replies the apostle.

Once again the initial sense in which Paul speaks is historical. The long night of Israel's bondage to the law is scattered by the dawn of Christ. **"When the fullness of the time had come, God sent forth His Son, born of a woman, born under the law, to redeem those who were under the law"** (4:4–5). Who were under the law? Obviously, the Jews. Who were redeemed by Christ? Clearly, those Jews who believed on him and received him as the promised Messiah, the seed of Abraham in whom the promises were fulfilled. What is meant by "the fullness of the time"? Plainly, "the time appointed by the father," that is, the point in human history ordained by God for reasons known only to himself.

It is important to remember that Christianity has its roots in history. Christ's birth, death, resurrection, and ascension were historical events. Pentecost was a historical occasion. The Scriptures are historical documents. This sets Christianity apart from most of the religions and philosophies of the world, which lose nothing if they are removed from their historical context. Liberal theologians almost always seek to separate the Christian message from its historical roots. They do so firstly to avoid the miraculous element associated with such things as the virgin birth and the resurrection. They do so secondly because it is their stock-in-trade to reinterpret the New Testament in terms more acceptable to human wisdom. A gospel rooted in history stubbornly refuses to be reinterpreted. Who was Jesus of Nazareth? He was God incarnate. What did he accomplish? He died on a real cross at a real point in human history, to save his people from their sins. What did the apostles proclaim? They preached Jesus and his literal resurrection! The authentic gospel is inseparable from the historical events which surround its origin.

However, as we have already seen, Paul is not speaking only about history. Christ came, he tells us, **"to redeem those who were under the law, that we might receive the adoption as sons"** (4:5). By writing "we" rather than "they" (which would have been more natural grammatically) Paul deliberately includes his Gentile readers. We may conclude, then, that Paul intends to make a general application of the historical events relating to the coming of Christ. That is, he came not only to redeem the believing remnant of Israel, who had hitherto been under the law, but also the elect from every nation and every age who, until they receive the gospel, remain in bondage to the elements of the world.

Finally, what is the significance of Christ being "born of a woman, born under the law"? (4:4). Some have seen a reference to the virgin birth in the first of these two phrases, and it may well be that Paul was thinking of Isaiah 7:14: "Behold the virgin shall conceive and bear a son, and shall call His name Immanuel." Alternatively, he may be referring back to the primeval promise that the seed of the woman would bruise Satan's head (Gen. 3:15). However, it is more likely that Paul is making a more general statement—namely that Christ, being born of a woman, became fully human, and that, as a Jew, he was subject to the law. In other words, Christ *fully identified with our condition*, in respect both of our humanity and of our obligation to observe the laws of God. It is because Christ identified so fully with our condition, except for sin, that he was able to "redeem those who were under the law" (4:5).

Christ's identification with man is an important doctrine of Scripture. It explains why Jesus submitted to baptism, despite John's protest (Matt. 3:13–15). Hebrews puts it clearly: "Inasmuch then as the children have partaken of flesh and blood, He Himself likewise *shared in the same*, that through death He might destroy him who had the power of death, that is, the devil, and release those who through fear of death were all their lifetime subject to bondage … Therefore in all things He had to be made *like His brethren*, that He might be a merciful and faithful high priest … to make propitiation for the sins of the people" (Heb. 2:14–17, emphasis added). Here "the children" and "His brethren" are the elect. Since they are "flesh and blood," it was necessary for Christ to assume their human nature in order to be in a position to redeem them. He had to be human as they were, to become their substitute and sin-bearer. He had to earn righteousness as a man subject to the law, in order to impute that righteousness to men. Through perfect obedience to the law, he was able to deliver us from its curse.

Adoption as sons (4:5)

"God sent forth His Son," declares the apostle, "to redeem those who were under the law, *that we might receive the adoption as sons*" (4:4–5, emphasis added). Redemption was not an end in itself, but rather the means to a still greater end. The ultimate purpose of redemption is adoption.

This glorious truth is often overlooked. Many think of redemption as the end-point of Christ's atoning work, putting us back where Adam stood before the Fall. But there is far, far more to it than that! It is impossible to over-emphasize what Christ accomplished on the cross, but we must not dwell upon the *act* of atonement to such an extent that we forget its *purpose*! Forgiveness of sins and reconciliation with God are enabling means. They have a further objective, namely that the elect should be made fit to be the adoptive children of God.

"Adoption" means "placing as a son." In Romans Paul uses the word three times, but in each case it means something different. In Romans 8:15, as here in Galatians, it signifies the spiritual adoption of the redeemed sinner: "You received the Spirit of adoption by whom we cry out, 'Abba, Father.' " In Romans 8:23 it refers to the "redemption of our body," that is, the physical resurrection of believers at Christ's return. Finally, in Romans 9:4 it is employed to describe God's choice of the nation of Israel to be the vehicle of his promises.

Adoption, in the sense used in Galatians 4:5, describes the new relationship established between God and the believer in regeneration. It is by adoption that we attain the legal status of sons and heirs. Adoption is the confirmation and guarantee that the inheritance is ours and can never be taken from us. The elect are God's children and heirs from all eternity, but until regeneration this goes unrecognized and unacknowledged, since they are "in bondage under the elements of the world" (4:3). When the sinner is born again he becomes consciously aware that God is his Father, and that he is now God's child. Adoption bestows on the believer both the *experience* of sonship and its *rights and privileges*.

The Spirit in our hearts (4:6)

Although adoption is a legal concept, this does not exhaust its meaning. The believer's sonship is the culmination of the covenant of promise, and in chapter 19 we listed some of the privileges which attach to this new status. Now Paul delves more deeply into the experiential nature of this glorious relationship. **"Because you are sons,"** he continues, **"God has sent forth the Spirit of His**

Son into your hearts, crying out, 'Abba, Father!' "(4:6; see also Rom. 8:15 cited above).

Notice, firstly, that the Holy Spirit is here described as the Spirit of Christ. It follows that the believer's sonship consists in his relationship to Christ. We are sons only because Christ is God's Son and dwells in us by his Spirit. Once again we see how every benefit we possess is ours in Christ.

Secondly, there is a sense in which believers are sons *before* the Spirit is sent forth into their hearts.[3] He does not say, "You are sons because God has given you his Spirit," but rather, "God has given you his Spirit because you are [already] sons." This is entirely consistent, of course, with the description of the elect as "heirs" even while they are in bondage to the elements of the world. That is, sonship was a status *reserved* for the elect from the moment they were chosen in Christ "before the foundation of the world" (Eph. 1:4). From that point onwards, they were "predestined to *adoption as sons* by Jesus Christ to Himself, according to the good pleasure of His will" (Eph. 1:5, emphasis added).

The word "predestined" is often treated with suspicion, and even fear, by Christians. They feel it implies a harsh and mechanistic God. To some, the very idea of predestination represents an "unacceptable face" of the New Testament, and they are embarrassed to find it there. Never should the word be mentioned by the preacher, for it will put people off the gospel forever! However, such fear and reticence are totally misplaced. They stem from a failure to understand what Paul is teaching here and elsewhere (Rom. 8:29–30). In the Greek, the word "predestine" means to define, determine or appoint, beforehand. In election, God chose those whom he purposed to redeem. In predestination he *defined beforehand what that redemption would mean*. What was this design? That the elect should be "conformed to the image of His Son, that He might be the firstborn among many brethren" (Rom. 8:29). What does this mean for God? It brings to him "the riches of the glory of His inheritance in the saints" (Eph. 1:18). What does it mean for the elect? It means that "We shall be like Him, for we shall see Him as He is" (1 John 3:2).

Thirdly, verse 6 tells us that adoption involves the entry and indwelling of the Holy Spirit. At a time of his sovereign choosing, God calls and regenerates the elect sinner. In the process of regeneration, and as an integral part of it, he "sends forth" the Spirit of Christ into the believing heart, actualizing in the elect the Father-child relationship that was previously potential or dormant. By the indwelling Spirit we cry "Abba, Father!," in conscious recognition of this relationship. Before regeneration, the sinner was a child and heir in God's eternal purpose. After regeneration, he is a child and heir in a joyful, conscious and experimental relationship.[4]

"*Abba*" is the Aramaic word for "father." Being composed of simple sounds, such as a baby might utter, the word is akin to our "dada"; that is, a form of address that the youngest of children might use. Paul thus implies a degree of intimacy between God and his children that the word "father" alone cannot convey. Otherwise there would be no point in using a foreign word in writing to the Galatians and the Romans, who probably did not speak Aramaic. Jesus himself addressed the Father by this word (Mark 14:36), which further emphasizes the status conferred on the believer in Christ.

Fourthly, Paul emphasizes that the indwelling Spirit *bears witness* to the believer's status: "You have received the Spirit of adoption by whom we cry out, 'Abba, Father.' The Spirit Himself bears witness with our spirit that we are the children of God" (Rom. 8:15–16). This inner testimony of the Spirit is the primary ground of assurance for the believer. John elaborates the matter in his first epistle: "By this we know that He [Christ] abides in us, by the Spirit whom He has given us" (1 John 3:24); and again, "By this we know that we abide in Him, and He in us, because He has given us of His Spirit" (1 John 4:13); and again, "He who believes in the Son of God has the witness in himself" (1 John 5:10). Of course, John also stresses the necessity of visible fruit in the life, from which it is possible to infer the believer's spiritual state (see, e.g., 1 John 3:10; 4:7, 15; 5:2). John's message seems to be that true assurance stems from the Spirit's witness in the heart, but that this inner witness must be confirmed by the practical fruits of love and righteousness in the believer's life.

Heirs of God through Christ (4:7)

Paul reaches his conclusion: **"Therefore you are no longer a slave but a son, and if a son, then an heir of God through Christ"** (4:7). Similarly in Romans he argues, "If children, then heirs—heirs of God and joint-heirs with Christ" (Rom. 8:17). Notice how the apostle switches to the singular, "a son," to emphasize that each and every believer enjoys these privileges in his own right. Since each believer is already an heir, there is nothing extra to be gained by subscribing to the law.

What does it mean, to be an heir of God? It lies beyond our comprehension. Heaven as our possession? Yes. Praise as our language? Surely. Glory as our dress? Indeed. Joy and peace beyond imagination? Of course. "In Your presence is fullness of joy; at Your right hand are pleasures forevermore" (Ps. 16:11). Yet, "Eye has not seen, nor ear heard, nor have entered into the heart of man, the things which God has prepared for those who love Him" (1 Cor. 2:9). It is true that Paul continues, "But God has revealed them to us through His Spirit" (1 Cor. 2:10), but the full extent of this revelation is by way of anticipation. The vacation getaway brochure may reveal much in anticipation, but when we reach our destination the real-life experience is something altogether different. So it is for the heirs of God. "Now we see in a mirror, dimly, but then face to face. Now I know in part, but then I shall know just as I am also known" (1 Cor. 13:12).

Finally, but also of the highest importance, the elect are heirs of God "through Christ" (4:7), and "joint-heirs with Christ" (Rom. 8:17). The promises were made, through Abraham, to Christ, and it is only as we are found in him that we partake of the inheritance. It is *Christ's* inheritance, and he graciously shares it with his people, for they are his bride (Eph. 5:25–27; Rev. 21:2, 9–27).

Summary

The elect are God's children and heirs from eternity past, but until the time of their regeneration they remain in bondage to the beliefs and powers which control the world ("the elements of the world"). For God-fearing Jews, that period of bondage and preparation was terminated by the coming of Christ. For the elect generally, it is terminated at God's appointed time by the regenerating work of the Holy Spirit.

Being born of a woman, Christ became one of us. Being born under the law, he kept that law perfectly. He was therefore fully qualified to become our substitute and to redeem his people from the curse and condemnation of the law. This work of redemption was a means to an end, namely the adoption of the elect as God's children and heirs. This adoption is both effected and experienced through the indwelling of the Holy Spirit.

The inheritance that believers receive is beyond our present comprehension. It is obtained only in and through Jesus Christ.

Notes

[1] "Now, by the elements here referred to, I understand the whole system of external observances under the law ..." (Brown, *Exposition of Galatians*, p. 79).

[2] "We cannot come to Christ to be justified until we have first been to Moses to be condemned. But once we have gone to Moses, and acknowledged our sin, guilt and condemnation, we must not stay here. We must let Moses send us to Christ" (Stott, *Message of Galatians*, p. 102).

[3] "Adoption by God precedes the testimony of adoption given by the Holy Spirit. But the effect is the sign of the cause. And you dare to call God your Father only by the instigation and incitement of the Spirit of Christ. Therefore it is certain that you are the sons of God. This means ... that the Spirit is the earnest and pledge of our adoption ..." (Calvin, *Galatians ... Ephesians*, p. 75).

[4] "The Holy Ghost is sent by the Word into the hearts of believers ... when by the hearing of the spoken Word, we receive an inward fervency and light, whereby we are changed and become new creatures; whereby also we receive a new judgement, new feelings and motions. This change and this new judgement is no work of reason or of the power of man, but is the gift and the operation of the Holy Ghost, which cometh with the Word preached, which purifieth our hearts by faith, and bringeth forth in us spiritual motions" (Luther, *Galatians*, p. 360).

21
The Apostle's Concern

Please Read Galatians 4:8–11

From the profundities of the gospel, Paul returns to the dismal condition of his readers. This alternation, between the exposition of God's grace and the exposure of the Galatians' errors, is a particular feature of the epistle. The apostle is driven repeatedly to contrast the Galatians' actual spiritual condition with their "high calling in Christ." There is pastoral wisdom in this approach. While Paul is quick to point out their spiritual failure, he does not do so in a purely negative manner. He also woos them with the glories of God's great purpose in Christ and underscores their privileges as believers in him. Nothing is more likely to wean them from error than a clear sight of the truth.

Paul is frustrated by their lack of understanding, but he is motivated by more than frustration. He has a genuine desire to restore these people to the right path, and to full enjoyment of their standing in Christ. By pointing out the contrast between what they are and what they ought to be, he seeks to awaken them to the spiritual poverty and danger of their situation.

To reinforce his message, the apostle once again employs "the ministry of memory"; that is, he reminds the Galatians of their former state without Christ, and of the manner of their conversion.

Idolatry (4:8)
Paul has already explained that, like all men, the elect begin their lives in bondage to "the elements of the world" (4:3). For the Jews that bondage lay in the belief that the law could make them righteous. For the Gentiles, however, the bondage was of a different kind. **"When you did not know God,"** writes the apostle, **"you**

served those which by nature are not gods" (4:8); that is, before they heard the gospel of Christ, the Galatians had been idol-worshippers, serving their non-gods in slavish fear. From this spiritual slavery they had, like the Thessalonians, "turned to God from idols to serve the living and true God" (1 Thess. 1:9).

Idolatry can be defined as the worship of anything other than the one true God, who reveals himself in Christ. Now, as then, idolatry is universal among mankind. It takes many forms. It may consist of an attempt to reduce God to our own dimensions, portraying him as one whom we can see and touch and comprehend. Such an idol is a god of convenience, fashioned by our own tastes, confirming our prejudices and excusing our sins. This is surely why we are forbidden to make images of God (Deut. 4:16). Alternatively, idolatry may lie in the worship of nature, ancient pantheism dressed in modern garb. Such idolatry is resurgent today, whether in the New Age movement, or in the reverence shown toward evolution as the imagined cause of all creation. The Jews were warned against the worship of the heavens (Deut. 4:19). The Gentiles were condemned for worshipping and serving the creation rather than the Creator (Rom. 1:25).

Yet idolatry is not restricted to such obvious forms. Since the true God reveals himself only in Christ, any system which does not hold Christ central to its worship and teaching is also false religion or idolatry. This includes much that passes for Christianity, but which centers on man rather than Christ. Those who elevate men as dignitaries in the church; who make human "priests" or "saints" the intermediaries between man and God; whose prime purpose is to satisfy man's desire for "health, wealth and happiness"; who preach novel experiences rather than Christ; who claim that man's choice, not God's, is the final arbiter of salvation—these alike are guilty of idolatry, for they teach a false idea of God.

By definition, the idolater does "not know God" (4:8). He may *think* that he knows God, and therein lies the tragedy. Those to whom Christ will say, "I never knew you; depart from Me you who practice lawlessness!" will claim to have rendered him outstanding service (Matt. 7:22–23).

The knowledge of God (4:9)

It is the knowledge of God, therefore, that distinguishes true religion from false. **"But now,"** says Paul, **"you have known God, or rather are known by God"** (4:9). How may we know God? The Lord Jesus Christ provides the answer: "No one comes to the Father except through Me … He who has seen Me has seen the Father … I am in the Father and the Father in Me" (John 14:6–10). "The knowledge of the glory of God" is found only "in the face of Jesus Christ" (2 Cor. 4:6). To know Christ is to know the Father and to possess eternal life (John 17:3).

How, then, may we know Christ? Clearly, it is not enough to know *about* Christ. The scriptures cited above refer to an intimate, personal knowledge of the Son of God. Such knowledge is not the fruit of human enquiry or religious contemplation. It comes from above in a creative work of God's Spirit. To complete the quotation from 2 Corinthians 4:6, "It is the God who commanded light to shine out of darkness [in creation] who has shone in our hearts to give the light of the knowledge of the glory of God in the face of Jesus Christ." This is why Paul seems to correct himself in Galatians 4:9: "You have known God," he says, *"or rather are known by God."* It is God himself who "knows" his elect, and makes himself known to them in a creative act of regeneration and self-revelation. The initiative is God's, not ours, for by nature we are dead in trespasses and sins.[1]

Until we are made alive by the Spirit in regeneration we cannot know God. It is the Holy Spirit, "sent forth" into our hearts, who tells us we are no longer slaves, but sons (4:6–7; Rom. 8:15–17). It is the Spirit who leads us into all truth (John 16:13) and causes "Christ to dwell in [our] hearts through faith" (Eph. 3:16–17). It is because we "have an anointing from the Holy One" that we "know all things" (1 John 2:20). This Spirit-taught knowledge is more than knowledge about God; it is the knowledge *of* God and of his ways. By the law is the knowledge of sin; by the Spirit the knowledge of God!

Thus Paul emphasizes the profound transformation that his readers underwent at their conversion to Christ. They once served idols, in ignorance and fear. Now, through Jesus Christ, they know the living and true God; they have "put on the new man who is renewed *in knowledge* according to the image of [God]" (Col. 3:10, emphasis added). With repentant Ephraim they can sing, "What have I to do anymore with idols?" (Hosea 14:8). As the anonymous poet puts it:

What has stripped the seeming beauty
From the idols of the earth?
Not a sense of right or duty,
But the sight of peerless worth.
Not the crushing of those idols,
With its bitter void and smart,
But the beaming of his beauty,
The unveiling of his heart ...
What have we to do with idols
Who have companied with him?

Bondage renewed (4:9–10)

Paul stands amazed. Having known God, he cries, **"How is it that you turn again to the weak and beggarly elements, to which you desire again to be in bondage?"** (4:9). They were not, of course, reverting to their former idols, but rather seeking to embrace the law of Moses. Yet, declares Paul, to do this would be to return to the selfsame bondage from which Christ had once delivered them.

It was difficult for the Galatians to grasp the fact that submission to the law was tantamount to a return to idolatry. There seems such a world of difference between the two. Yet both idolatry and legalism, asserts Paul, belong to the same philosophical genre; they both represent "the elements of the world" (4:3) from which Christ has set his people free. We saw earlier that these "elements" refer to the basic tenets which underpin the religions and philosophies of unregenerate men. Religious beliefs and practices vary enormously in outward form, but they all have a common thread, namely the idea that man can earn favor with God by his works. Not only *can* he earn such merit, they maintain, but he *must* do so, and therein lies the bondage that man-made religions engender.

There are many today who, like the Galatians, fail to discern the difference between true Christian faith and the efforts of the flesh. Paul had earlier reprimanded his readers asking, "Having begun in the Spirit, are you now being made perfect by the flesh?" (3:3). Law imposed from without appeals only to the flesh and is inimical to spiritual life, "for the letter kills, but the Spirit gives life" (2 Cor. 3:6). Only God's laws, written in the heart of the believer by the indwelling Spirit, can bring forth true holiness of life. (Even that, of course, gives us no standing before God, for our obedience is never perfect; our acceptance continues to reside in Christ alone.)

Paul gives examples of the legalistic bondage of the law: **"You observe days and months and seasons and years"** (4:10). These references are clearly to the Jewish calendar, including the various feast days and sabbaths.[2] Why does Paul condemn these practices, which the Galatians no doubt felt were harmless rituals providing spiritual benefit? Indeed, does not the apostle elsewhere seem to regard such observances as a matter of indifference? "One person esteems one day above another; another esteems every day alike. Let each be fully convinced in his own mind" (Rom. 14:5).

The answer to this apparent inconsistency lies in the attitude we adopt toward these things. Romans 14 makes it clear that both observers and non-observers were acting "to the Lord," that is, they sought to praise and honor Christ in whatever they did (Rom. 14:6). The Galatians' problem was that they had taken their eyes off Christ, and were looking elsewhere for their righteousness and sanctification (see, e.g., Gal. 3:1). Whereas in Romans 14 both those who observed days and those who did not were acting in faith toward God, the Galatians had been persuaded that works (such as the observance of sabbaths) were necessary to *augment* faith. This is why Paul condemns their observances as dangerous legalism, for "Without faith it is impossible to please [God]" (Heb. 11:6).

Paul's fear (4:11)

The Galatians' spiritual condition alarmed the apostle: **"I am afraid for you, lest I have labored for you in vain"** (Gal. 4:11). Although, generally, Paul writes to them as to true believers, there are certain points in the epistle at which he voices doubts on this score (e.g. 5:3–4). Had he labored in vain in bringing them the gospel? Were they "stony ground" believers, receiving the word with joy, but unable to endure in the truth? (Matt. 13:20–21). Were they on the pathway to apostasy?

The doctrine of apostasy is very clear in Scripture. There will be those who appear to believe and trust in Christ, who nevertheless fall away subsequently, rejecting the gospel which they once professed.[3] "They went out from us," explains John, speaking of such apostates, "but they were not of us; for if they had been of us, they would have continued with us; but they went out that they might be made manifest, that none of them were of us" (1 John 2:19). In this passage, John clarifies some important points. Those who had separated from the apostolic gospel had never truly been Christ's. Their profession was spurious, and this was eventually revealed by their defection. There is no support in the New Testament for the idea that true believers, having once been saved, can then be lost again. The biblical doctrines of election, particular redemption and the perseverance of the saints stand as bulwarks against any such notion. What we are taught, however, is that true believers may be so engulfed in error that their fellow Christians cannot be certain as to their spiritual state. It becomes impossible to tell whether they are the Lord's or not, and we are compelled to suspend judgment as to their true standing.

It is both scriptural and necessary to warn any such persons of the danger of apostasy. As long as we cannot tell whether they are in Christ or not, the possibility exists that they are not. This is the burden of those two difficult passages in Hebrews, namely Hebrews 6:4–8 and 10:26–31, where dire consequences are predicted for those who "fall away" and "sin willfully after [they] have received the knowledge of the truth." In both passages the writer hopes, and even believes, that his readers are not apostates (see Heb. 6:9; 10:35–36); nevertheless the warning is genuine, and aimed to bring about an immediate return to faith in Christ alone. This is Paul's objective here in Galatians 4:11. By voicing his fears, he alerts the Galatians to the spiritual danger from which he seeks to deliver them.

Summary
Through the gospel, the Galatians had been delivered from bondage to idol-worship. They had come to know God, personally and intimately, in the person of Christ. This knowledge of God had been given to them on God's initiative, by the regenerating work and indwelling of the Holy Spirit.

Since they had received this knowledge, it seemed incredible that they should desire to return to their old beliefs. Yet this was exactly what they were doing in embracing the law of Moses. Legalism and idolatry alike represent the "elements of this world," namely, a reliance on works for justification and holiness.

No matter how it is dressed up, such reliance is a rejection of Christ and his grace. Those who are caught up in legalism, therefore, stand in danger of apostasy. If they are truly Christ's, they cannot, eventually, fall away. But as long as they dabble with works-religion no man can tell whether they are true believers or not. A warning of apostasy is therefore both scriptural and appropriate.

Notes

[1] "When Paul says, 'but now that you have come to know God or rather to be known by God' he is clearly stressing the fact that 'We love him because he first loved us' ... there is, accordingly, a renewed emphasis on God's sovereignty in the effectuation of man's salvation. And that was exactly the lesson which the Galatians needed, and which, in a sense, we all need" (Hendriksen, *Galatians and Ephesians*, pp. 164–5).

[2] "While not, as yet, submitting to circumcision, Gentile Christians of Galatia seem to have begun to observe the weekly Jewish sabbaths, the annual Jewish festivals and the Jewish high holy days—all, as they evidently were led to believe by the Judaizers, as a means of bringing their Christian faith to completion" (Longenecker, *Galatians*, pp. 182–3).

[3] "The writer of Hebrews observes that the disobedient Israelites died in the desert because of unbelief. By analogy, the possibility that individuals who have professed the name of Christ will fall away is real (Matt. 7:21–23)" (Kistemaker, *Exposition of Hebrews*, p. 163).

22
The Apostle's Plea

Please Read Galatians 4:12–20

There now follows a poignant personal plea by the apostle. Such is his concern for the Galatian church that he leaves no avenue unexplored in his attempt to retrieve them. He has scolded them for their folly; he has explained patiently the difference between law and faith; he has shown them the panorama of God's redemptive purpose in Christ; he has stirred up memories of former times, when they had embraced the true gospel. Now he makes an impassioned personal appeal.

There is, perhaps, too little passion in our preaching today. We tend to be too clinical, too unaware of the spiritual dangers that beset God's people, and too reluctant to open our hearts, lest we be hurt in the process. There are many teachers, but few true pastors. Paul, however, holds nothing back. He is not afraid to become personally involved.

Life without the law (4:12)

"**Brethren,**" pleads the apostle, "**I urge you to become as** "**I** *am*, **for I** *am* **as you** *are*" (4:12). The italicized words are not present in the original, having been inserted by the translators to provide the sense. In this case, however, the added words may actually confuse the meaning of the verse. A better rendering is given by Hendriksen: "I urge you to become as I am, for I became as you were [that is, without law]." We cannot be dogmatic, but Paul seems to be saying something along the following lines:

I plead with you to become like me, one who has died to the law of Moses so that I might live to Christ (2:19). Follow me, not the Judaizers. Look to Christ, not to Moses, for your acceptance with God. Remember that when I came among you preaching the gospel of Christ, I became like you Gentiles, setting aside the law. "For though I am free from all men, I have made myself a servant to all, that I might win the more ... To those who are without law [I became] as without law ... that I might win those who are without law ... that I might by all means save some" (1 Cor. 9:19–23). Why, then, should it be too much to ask, that you now reject this fruitless pursuit of righteousness through the law, and follow my example?[1]

In making this plea, Paul puts his reputation on the line. In effect, he tells the Galatians that they must choose between himself and the Judaizers. This takes pastoral courage, for what happens if they make the wrong choice? Yet Paul is so clear about the importance of this issue that he is willing to burn his boats and compel the Galatians to make an irrevocable choice.

To encourage the correct choice, however, he adds, **"You have not injured me at all"** (4:12). This statement has given rise to endless speculation as to its interpretation. Many regard it as having nothing to do with the earlier part of the verse. Paul is so distressed, they suggest, that his thoughts become disjointed at this point in the epistle. I cannot agree with this view. The apostle has exhibited distress and frustration earlier in Galatians without losing his train of thought. To seek a better understanding of this admittedly obscure statement, let us again paraphrase what Paul may be saying here:

When, for your sake, I became like you Gentiles, setting aside the law of Moses in order to win you to Christ, did that do me any harm? Not at all. You were not the cause of any injury to me, for I have no need of the law for righteousness or godly living. As a follower of Christ, I have the law of God written in my heart (Heb. 10:16) and outward conformity to Moses is redundant, having neither value nor significance (Phil. 3:4–9). Likewise, you will suffer no harm if you jettison this foolish notion that the law will do you good. Quite the reverse, for harm will come from it.

This interpretation has the advantage of continuity of thought, and of cogency. Paul's plea does not trail off into meaningless words. Rather it is reinforced by his firm declaration that the law has no power over the one who rests from his works in Christ (Heb. 4:10).

Received as an angel of God (4:13–16)

Paul's plea continues with further personal references. He reminds his readers of the manner in which he came to them, and the way he was received. His words are calculated at least to stir their consciences and are meant to create a healthy sense of guilt over their current defection from his teaching. **"You know,"** he says, **"that because of physical infirmity I preached the gospel to you at the first"** (4:13). Here again there are differences of interpretation, since the wording in the original suggests that Paul's infirmity, whatever it may have been, was the *reason* why he went to their cities in the first place. However, there is nothing in Acts to suggest that sickness affected Paul's movements when he was evangelizing these regions of Asia Minor. He probably means nothing more here than that he preached to them while suffering some affliction.[2] He tells the Corinthians, "I was with you in weakness …," and there can be no doubt that most of his missionary labors were carried out in (and in spite of) significant physical suffering (see, e.g., 2 Cor. 4:7–15; 11:22–28; 12:7–10).

In any case, the point that Paul is making lies in verse 14 rather than verse 13. **"And my trial which was in my flesh,"** he continues, **"you did not despise or reject, but you received me as an angel of God, even as Christ Jesus"** (4:14). We do not know the nature of Paul's affliction. Perhaps it was partial blindness, as many have suggested. This idea gains support from the following verse, where Paul exclaims, **"I bear you witness that, if possible, you would have plucked out your own eyes and given them to me"** (4:15). It would also explain Galatians 6:11: "See with what large letters I have written to you with my own hand!" along with the fact that Paul normally used an amanuensis to write his letters (see further comment on 6:11). However, most commentators regard this as mere speculation.[3]

Whatever the nature of Paul's disability, it must have been self-evident. It was also of a kind that would normally have evoked rejection and loathing, otherwise he would not have commented on the fact that they "did not despise or reject" it (4:14). It was common in biblical times for physical disabilities to be regarded as punishments from God (or the gods); see for example Job 4:7–9 and John 9:2. In light of this, why was Paul so well received? Clearly, because he came preaching the gospel "in demonstration of the Spirit and of power" (1 Cor. 2:4). Under such a Spirit-filled ministry they were simply oblivious to his physical weakness. They received the word with such joy and blessedness that all such concerns were swept away in the rapture of their new-found love for Christ. Paul reminds them in verse 15 of **"the blessing [they] enjoyed"** at that time.

Far from rejecting the apostle, they welcomed him as a messenger (an angel) of God. So closely did they identify the preacher with the Savior he proclaimed, that they received him "as Christ Jesus" himself (4:14). Their thankfulness to Christ was one with their gratitude to his servant for bringing them the gospel. They would have done anything for Paul, including giving him their "own eyes." As they looked at Paul, they did not see an infirm stranger, but only the messenger of Christ.

This passage reminds us that when the gospel is preached in power, "by the Holy Spirit sent down from heaven" (1 Peter 1:12), those who proclaim it are obscured by the glory of Christ. This is the exact opposite of much modern expectation, where success is commonly measured by the fame and prominence of the messenger, whether he be pastor or evangelist. Lip-service is rendered to the Baptist's dictum, "He [Christ] must increase, but I must decrease" (John 3:30), but there are few who are so self-effacing in practice.

Paul's purpose, of course, is not to revive his fan-club! It is rather to restore the Galatians to the truth. Why, then, does he dwell upon the way they received him at the beginning? Because the apostle was inseparably identified with the gospel that he preached. He invites them to remember the blessing they had once received by heeding his message. Should they not now, again, pay attention to his words, that they might again be blessed?

Zeal, good and bad (4:16–18)

The Judaizers, always lurking in the background of the epistle, now come to the fore once again. They misrepresented Paul as the Galatians' enemy, accusing him of depriving them of the full enjoyment of religion. Yet this alleged deprivation was, in fact, for their good, since to embrace Moses' law was error, not truth. **"Have I therefore become your enemy because I tell you the truth?"** (4:16), asks Paul. It is a rhetorical question, and by it he unmasks the futility of the Judaizers' accusation.

It is one of Satan's chief devices to call black white, and white black; to represent truth as error, and error as truth. Thus those who believe and preach the truth are often branded heretics, and have been throughout the history of the church. Paul's rejection of the Mosaic law was condemned in his own day as a license to sin (Rom. 3:7–8; 6:1, 15), and those who follow him today are often mistakenly branded "antinomians," even though like Paul they advocate holy living through the fruit of the Spirit (Gal. 5:22–25). Similarly, those who preach a Christ-centered gospel are considered narrow, and those who proclaim God's electing grace are viewed with suspicion for denying man his "free will" in the matter of salvation. However, Paul cannot compromise his message. He intends to speak the truth, regardless of how it is received.

There is a further lesson for us in the apostle's boldness. It is all too easy to conceal the truth when we sense it is unwelcome to our hearers. Will people be upset by the mention of "election" or "predestination"? Then perhaps we should wrap up the truth about God's sovereign grace in obscure words and coded language to avoid offense. Does some clear biblical doctrine rebuke certain members of a congregation? Then perhaps the minister should soft-pedal the subject to avoid trouble. Never, Paul replies, for truth is paramount. Of course, truth must be presented graciously. We are to speak the truth *in love*, not with the purpose of provoking or offending others (Eph. 4:15). But we *must* speak the truth if we are to minister to men's souls.

The zeal of the Judaizers knew no bounds. Not only did they brand Paul as the enemy, but they actively wooed the Galatians. **"They zealously court you,"** observes the apostle, **"but for no good"** (4:17). We are not told exactly what enticements the Judaizers offered to the Gentile believers, but they obviously took pains to sell their wares. Again we see a parallel with much that passes for Christianity today. Men are invited to come to Christ for innumerable benefits: for health, for miraculous healing, for material gain, for human happiness, for excitement, for power. Yet the real gospel speaks rather of mercy, grace, forgiveness, redemption, holiness and glory. It promotes the praise of God, not the appetites and ambitions of men. "No good," therefore, can come from following these false shepherds who pervert the gospel. Instead their enticements, attractive though they seem at first, lead to bondage and eternal loss.

Paul continues his indictment of the Judaizers: **"They want to exclude** [isolate] **you, that you may be zealous for them"** (4:17). Their purpose is to isolate the Galatians so that these believers will become their own disciples, looking to them alone for guidance and teaching. In particular, they seek to cut off all communication between the Galatians and Paul, who is represented as the arch enemy. It is a common ploy for those who seek a following, and desire the preeminence, to take steps to isolate their would-be disciples from outside influence.[4] Contact with other believers and churches is discouraged; people are taught to be suspicious of outsiders, who are accused of all manner of heresy; legalistic obedience is instilled to ensure dependence upon the leaders. Such deliberate isolation can be seen today, not only in various sects where it is rife, but even in certain churches and congregations. Those who encourage it claim to be protecting the flock against error, but their real motive is revealed here by the apostle. They desire a following, that believers "may be zealous for them [their leaders]" (Gal. 4:17). Peter warns Christian leaders against becoming "lords over those entrusted to you" (1 Peter 5:3). Those who lead are not to be lords, but examples and servants to the flock, for they are merely under-shepherds serving the Chief Shepherd.

By contrast, a robust Christianity requires no protective isolation. Believers who are properly taught in the Word of God can themselves discern truth from error, spiritual food from spiritual poison. Those who "walk according to the Spirit" fulfill the "righteous requirement of the law" (Rom. 8:4–5) and need no confinement.

Although the Judaizers' zeal was treacherous, and the Galatians' zeal for them misguided, there is nothing intrinsically wrong with being zealous. Indeed, zeal is to be commended provided it is exercised in the cause of truth and not error. **"It is good to be zealous** [or zealously courted] **in a good thing always, and not only when I am present with you,"** writes Paul (4:18). Although the apostle is stating a general principle, he seems to be referring specifically to the things that had excited their zeal when he was "present with [them]." What were these things? Clearly, the truths of the gospel!

A major problem in the church today is misplaced zeal. Much energy is expended on social activities, church programs, famine relief, Christian education, church growth, political activism, and so on, but zeal for gospel *truth* is sadly lacking. Almost any beliefs are tolerated in the "broad church" of evangelicalism, as long as they are sincerely held. Those who feel passionately about the doctrine of the grace of God in Christ are viewed with puzzled incomprehension by much of the professing church. As zeal for "the gospel of the glory of God" (2 Cor. 4:4) has ebbed away, so with it has vanished all sense of excitement with that gospel, and all perception of the glory of our God. Preaching has become dull, and prayer lifeless. Let us redirect our zeal, seeking "first the kingdom of God and His righteousness," for then all other things will fall into their rightful place (Matt. 6:33).

Christ formed in you (4:19–20)

Paul's personal appeal draws to its close. **"My little children,"** he yearns, **"for whom I labor in birth again until Christ is formed in you, I would like to be present with you now and to change my tone"** (4:19–20).

To the apostle, all those who had come to faith in Christ through his ministry were his "children." He calls Timothy his "true son in the faith" (1 Tim. 1:2). Paul does not mean that he was in some way responsible for the regeneration of his hearers, for believers are Christ's children, born of his Spirit (Heb. 2:13; John 3:6). He does, however, see himself as a spiritual parent in two senses: he was *instrumental* in their conversion, and *responsible* for their nurture. In the preceding verses (4:8–15) he has already dwelt upon his instrumentality, as the one who brought the gospel to them. Now he longs to be present with them to discharge more effectively his parental responsibility. If he could be there, how promptly he would deal with those who threatened their spiritual safety! How firmly he would discipline them, not with the commandments of men, but by instruction in the truth! How graciously he would nurture them with the food of the Word! How quickly he would change his tone of disapproval to one of commendation!

In the sovereign will of God, of course, Paul was unable to go to them. He had to write instead. For Paul this seemed "second best," but it gave to us the epistle to the Galatians! How often God turns the problems and frustrations of this life to his own glory, fulfilling his purposes through our weakness, not our strength! (2 Cor. 12:10).

There was more to Paul's letter than just advice. He "labor[s] in birth again until Christ is formed in [them]" (4:19). This strong figurative language does not contradict what was said above about regeneration being a sovereign work of God's Spirit. It simply reflects the agony of prayer and longing that filled the apostle's heart. Of the Philippians he could say with joy, "I have you in my heart" (Phil. 1:7). The same was true of the Galatians, who caused him pain rather than comfort. We can say two things about this pain. Firstly, Paul did not avoid it. Good pastor as he was, he was prepared to know both pain and joy in his care for Christ's flock. Secondly, he viewed his pain as productive and purposeful. His suffering was not the pain of the terminally ill, but of the mother in labor. By the will of God, it would issue in a joyful outcome, for Christ would be formed in them.

He had once before labored to this end, when he had first preached the gospel in Galatia. Now he must "labor in birth again" (4:19) to turn them back from error. But his purpose is always the same, namely that Christ should be "formed" in them. The difference between Paul and the Judaizers could not be more plain. They sought disciples for themselves; Paul sought to espouse the Galatians to Christ. There is a question here for all Christian leaders and pastors.[5] What is our ambition for our churches and members? Is it to build up a loyal following for ourselves, or to build up believers in Christ? Is it to see growth in numbers, or growth "in grace and the knowledge of our Lord and Savior Jesus Christ"? (2 Peter 3:18).

Paul's desire is clear. Christ must be "formed" in the believer. Having received the Spirit of God's Son, Christians should "walk in the Spirit" (5:25); that is, they should bring forth, both in their spiritual understanding and practical living, the evident fruit of Christ's indwelling by the Spirit. They should both know the truth, and live it out. The apostle anticipates a happy outcome, but he cannot be sure. He ends on a somber note of warning. **"I have doubts about you,"** he writes (4:20). It is not sufficient that Paul has done all that he can, in this epistle, to correct their thinking. It is necessary for them to make a positive response. Until they do so, their spiritual state remains open to doubt. By voicing his continued unease, he also gives notice that he has more to say on the dangers of the law.

Summary
Up to this point in the epistle, Paul has employed censure, personal testimony, reason, scriptural arguments and, above all, the glorious truths of the gospel of Christ. Now he launches an impassioned personal appeal for the Galatians to return to the path of truth.

Once again he refers back to the circumstances of their conversion and the manner in which they received him. Far from being their enemy, as the Judaizers suggest, Paul is, and always was, the messenger of God to them. They should follow him in his rejection of the law, not the Judaizers in their bondage to it.

Unlike the Judaizers, who sought a personal following, Paul desired the glory of God, seeking that Christ should be "formed" in his readers' hearts by the indwelling Spirit. Until such evidence of grace becomes apparent, Paul remains in doubt of their spiritual standing.

Notes

[1] Fausset, writing on Galatians 4:12, says, " 'I am become as ye are'—viz, in not observing legal ordinances. 'My having laid them aside among Gentiles shows that I regard them as not at all contributing to justification or sanctification. Do you regard them in the same light and act accordingly?' " (*Galatians*).

[2] "In favour of the idea that the infirmity of which Paul speaks was not the *cause* of the apostle's preaching [to the Galatians] but rather the accompanying circumstance it might be stated that not only Luke (see Acts 13:50; 14:5, 6, 19) makes some remarks about the physical afflictions ... which Paul had to endure while working in Galatia, but so does also Paul himself, many years later" (Hendriksen, *Galatians and Ephesians*, p. 170).

[3] See, for example, Hendriksen, *Galatians and Ephesians*, p. 171.

[4] "When Christianity is seen as freedom in Christ (which it is), Christians are not in subservience to their human teachers, because their ambition is to become mature in Christ. But when Christianity is turned into a bondage to rules and regulations, its victims are inevitably in subjection, tied to the apron strings of their teachers ..." (Stott, *Message of Galatians*, p. 116).

[5] "Yet it is not what he [the minister] can do by himself or apart from God, but what God does through him that is described here. If ministers wish to be something, let them labour to form Christ, not themselves" (Calvin, *Galatians ... Colossians*, p. 83).

23
The Two Covenants

Please Read Galatians 4:21–24

Paul now launches into a new and powerful exposition of the covenants of God. Using Abraham's two sons, Ishmael and Isaac, to illustrate his argument, the apostle drives home the lesson that there are two distinct covenants (of works and of promise), operating by two different principles (the flesh and the Spirit), and leading to two distinct results (bondage and liberty). Although this is an area of much theological debate, Paul's message is clear. The two covenants are distinct, opposed, and mutually exclusive.

Heeding Scripture (4:21)
"Tell me," begins the apostle, **"you who desire to be under the law, do you not hear the law?"** (4:21). Paul is using "the law" here in two different senses. His meaning is, "You who desire to be under the law of Moses, do you not hear (or heed) the Mosaic scriptures?" Of course, there is no sleight of hand intended. Paul is simply pointing out that the Sinaitical law forms part of a larger body of Scripture from the hand of Moses, namely the Pentateuch. Had the Galatians seen Moses' law in the context of *all* Moses' writings, implies Paul, they would have rejected the Judaizers' advances.

This is an enduring principle. We must always interpret particular scriptures in light of their larger context. Failure to do this lies at the root of all error and most heresy. We can prove almost anything from the Bible if we are sufficiently selective; sects like the Jehovah's Witnesses are living proof of this. However, it is not only sects which are guilty in this respect; evangelicals are capable of the same mistake. I remember hearing a well-known preacher speak on the text, "This is your hour" (Luke 22:53). He preached an impassioned sermon on the need to grasp any "hour of opportunity" that God might extend to us, whether to believe or to respond in some other way. Of course, the full citation is, "This is your hour and [that of] the power of darkness," and refers to the apparent triumph of Satan at the arrest of Jesus by the chief priests. Such distortions of Scripture are not uncommon, though they are usually less blatant. Too often, we use Scripture merely as a peg on which to hang our prejudices.

This is a temptation to us all, whether we are teachers or hearers of the Word of God. It is prevalent in the treatment of the Old Testament, where many are vague about the principles of interpretation they should employ. The answer Paul gives us here is that all Scripture must be interpreted Christologically, that is, in relation to Christ. Are Sarah and Hagar just Old Testament characters? No, declares the apostle; they are also living parables, demonstrating the futility of works and the efficacy of grace. There is considerable conflict among theologians as to whether the Old Testament should be interpreted in a purely historical manner, or Christologically. For Bible-believers, however, there can be no debate. The New Testament writers, together with Jesus himself, *always* see the Old Testament as testifying to Christ (Luke 24:27; John 5:39; Heb. 1:5–14; and innumerable other places). Even those of us who subscribe to a Christological interpretation can be inconsistent in applying the principle. For example, we speak of the "Messianic psalms," meaning those that refer explicitly to Christ, but by doing so we may overlook the fact that *all* the psalms relate in some way to him. Fanciful spiritualization of the Old Testament must be avoided, but its testimony to Christ must never be obscured.

This was the Galatians' problem. Eager to submit to the law, as narrowly interpreted and applied by the Judaizers, they failed to set the law in the wider context of the books of Moses. Thus they missed the essence of Moses' message, namely the promise of God in Christ. If only they had heeded Scripture they would not have fallen prey to false teachers.

Abraham's two sons (4:22–23)

Paul begins his allegory: **"It is written that Abraham had two sons: the one by a bondwoman, the other by a freewoman. But he who was of the bondwoman was born according to the flesh, and he of the freewoman through promise"** (4:22–23).

Abraham had sons by two women: the bondwoman Hagar, and his wife Sarah. Paul uses their contrasting status to underscore his message. Hagar was a slave, subject to bondage, while Sarah was a freewoman. So those who are in bondage to the law are the spiritual descendants of the slave-girl, while those who enjoy liberty in Christ are children of the free wife. Hagar and her son possessed nothing of their own and were devoid of all privilege in Abraham's household, though they dwelt there. Sarah and her son, on the other hand, possessed all things, by virtue of their relationship to Abraham. So those who seek to be justified by the law, though it be God's law, are mere slaves and cannot inherit God's blessing. But those who come to God in faith, without the deeds of the law, inherit all things through their relationship to Christ.

Abraham and his wife Sarah were childless, and accepted this situation as God's sovereign will. "See now," said Sarah, "the LORD has restrained me from bearing children" (Gen. 16:2). This state of affairs seemed to contradict God's promise that Abraham would father a child of his own to be his heir (Gen. 13:16; 15:4–6). Nevertheless, in spite of all appearances, Abraham believed the promise, and his faith was counted for righteousness (Gen. 15:6; Rom. 4:18–22).

Why was it, then, that Sarah and Abraham devised the plan of having a child by Sarah's slave? Very simply, their faith wavered. As the years passed and they grew older, God's promise seemed less and less realistic. They succumbed to human reasoning; that is, the wisdom of the flesh. This may be what Paul means when he says that Hagar's son, Ishmael, was born "according to the flesh" (4:23), although he could also just mean "naturally" as opposed to "supernaturally." If the reference to "the flesh" is pejorative, this is not because of any implied immorality (for a slave to bear children for her mistress was not in those days considered illegal—cf. Jacob's family in Genesis 30:1–13). It refers rather to the fleshly (natural) wisdom which flew in the face of God's promise. It made sense to the natural mind to give God a helping hand in providing a posterity for Abraham. The promise was not abandoned in their thinking, just distorted; Hagar's child *would* be Abraham's seed and, legally speaking, Sarah's also.

The flaw in such reasoning, of course, was the belief that their scheme could somehow secure the fulfillment of God's promise. This was the Judaizers' error, and the same mistake is made today by those who think that man can contribute to his own salvation, whether by conforming to some law, by good works, by decisions or by "commitment" to Christ. The lesson is clear: any attempt to replace the pure promise of God (salvation by God's free grace) by human endeavor or design is doomed to failure. Why? Because "Those who are in the flesh cannot please God" (Rom. 8:8). Human wisdom is inimical to the promise, and God has rejected it outright (Rom. 8:6; 1 Cor. 1:19–21).

By contrast, Isaac was born "through promise" (Gal. 4:23). This does not just mean that God had promised Abraham and Sarah a child of their own. It means also that the child could never have been conceived in a purely natural manner, since Sarah and Abraham were simply too old (see Rom. 4:19). Had a natural conception been possible, there would have been no need for faith, and thus no imputed righteousness (Rom. 4:20–22). Isaac's miraculous birth is a type (a biblically authenticated picture) of Christ's incarnation, though of course the miracle of the virgin birth was of a different order. Nevertheless, Isaac was the seed of promise, and in that respect he pictures Christ (Gal. 3:16–18). Furthermore, the contrasting births of Ishmael and Isaac illustrate profound truths concerning the regeneration of the believer. Isaac, Paul tells us, "was born according to the Spirit" (4:29). Jesus said, "That which is born of the flesh is flesh, and that which is born of the Spirit is spirit" (John 3:6). As Isaac was miraculously born, so also must a man or woman be "born again" by a sovereign work of God's Spirit if he or she is to become an heir of God.

Two covenants (4:24)

Paul continues: **"... which things are symbolic. For these** [two women] **are the two covenants: the one from Mount Sinai which gives birth to bondage, which is Hagar"** (4:24). In using this terminology, he does not mean "merely symbolic," as if the story of Hagar just happens to illustrate his point. Under the guidance of the Holy Spirit, Paul is telling us that the Old Testament story is replete with Messianic truth. Hendriksen translates the opening clause of verse 24 as follows: "Now things of this nature were spoken with another meaning in mind."[1] In other words, the *very purpose* of the Genesis passage was to convey the spiritual truth that Paul is about to disclose. What is this truth?

Paul tells us that there are two covenants, one being the Sinaitical covenant represented by Hagar, and the other the covenant of promise,[2] represented by Sarah. Obviously, the apostle believes that there *are* two covenants, and regards these covenants as: firstly, distinct; secondly, opposed; and thirdly, mutually exclusive. Since these implications are by no means generally accepted, we must look at them more closely. Before we do so, however, it will be helpful to review briefly what the Bible has to say generally about the covenants of God.

Covenants in Scripture

Many reformed theologians consider that there is but one divine covenant, namely "the covenant of grace." Although the Bible never uses this expression, it is a useful concept. This term encompasses all God's dealings with man and refers to an eternal disposition in favor of the elect, in which man plays no part except as the recipient of divine favor. There is much value in this teaching, since it emphasizes the unity of God's "purpose and grace which was given to us in Christ Jesus before time began" (2 Tim.

1:9). This unity of gracious purpose is fundamental to a right understanding of God's dealings with man, and to the correct interpretation of Scripture. Nevertheless, Scripture records not one, but a plurality of covenants, either implied or explicit. These can be listed as follows. (Terms in inverted commas are theological expressions not actually found in Scripture.)

1. The "covenant of redemption"

This is the eternal agreement between the Father and the Son by which the Father gave to the Son, and the Son agreed to redeem, an elect people, namely the flock and church of Jesus Christ.[3]

2. The "covenant of grace"

This is an eternal disposition by God in favor of the elect by which he redeems them from sin, regenerates them, and adopts them, on the grounds of his everlasting love and the merits of Christ alone. It is generally agreed that these first two covenants are, in fact, different aspects of the same eternal plan of redemption.[4]

To some, the "covenant of grace" covers not only the elect, but also persons who may be non-elect, such as the infant children of believers. Berkhof remarks, "Even unregenerate and unconverted persons may be in the covenant."[5] However, he also concedes that "The idea that the covenant is fully realized only in the elect is a perfectly Scriptural idea, as appears, for instance, from Jer. 31:31–34; Heb. 8:8–12. Moreover, it is also entirely in line with the relation in which the covenant of grace stands to the covenant of redemption. If in the latter Christ becomes Surety only for the elect, then the real substance of the former must be limited to them also."[6]

The dichotomy revealed here between the "Scriptural idea" of a covenant limited to the elect, and the different concept of a broader covenant embracing all who are nominally God's people (e.g. the whole Jewish nation and the unregenerate children of believers) leads to a confusion that is not present in Scripture. As Paul tells us plainly, "They are not all Israel that are of Israel" (Rom. 9:6), and elsewhere, "Israel [as a whole] has not obtained what it seeks; but the elect have obtained it, and the rest were hardened" (Rom. 11:7).

3. The "covenant with Adam"

This refers to God's promise that the seed of the woman—that is, Christ—would bruise Satan's head (Gen. 3:15). It is thus an anticipation of the covenant of promise made explicitly with Abraham, since they both looked forward to Christ, through whom salvation would appear. This promise to Adam and Eve prefigures the death of Christ and his triumph over sin and Satan.

4. The covenant with Noah

This encompasses God's promise to Noah, to his descendants, and to all created life, that "Never again shall there be a flood to destroy the earth" (Gen. 9:9, 11). This covenant can only be linked to the covenant of grace in a general way, namely that God, by implication, undertook to restore rather than destroy his creation (compare Rom. 8:21).

5. The covenant with Abraham, Isaac and Jacob

Here the covenant of promise has its full expression, as we have already seen in considering Galatians 3:14–29. Though the full light of the gospel was still obscure, Abraham understood that these promises related to a coming Christ and a heavenly kingdom, not just to his earthly heir and heritage.

6. The covenant with David

Under this covenant (2 Sam. 23:5), Christ was promised as the son of David and the heir to his throne. His resurrection and sovereign rule were also foretold (Acts 2:30; Ps. 132:11). Clearly, this represents a continuation and elaboration of the covenant of promise, and can be regarded as part of that covenant.

7. The "covenant of works"

This embodies the idea that man may, in principle at least, obtain salvation through perfect obedience to the laws of God. This covenant was in force between God and man prior to the fall of Adam, but many believe that it has been inoperative since that time.[7] On this view, the Sinaitical covenant was not a covenant of works except in the mistaken perception of the Jews; it was simply the Old Testament "administration" or "dispensation" of the covenant of grace. There could be a problem of definition here. If by a "covenant of works" we mean a covenant that fallen man is *able* to keep, or one by which God actually intended to justify sinners, then, indeed, Sinai was not a covenant of works. If, on the other hand, a covenant of works is one under which God's promises are *conditional* upon human obedience, then Moses' covenant is a covenant of works.[8]

8. The covenant of Sinai

Also referred to as the "first covenant" (Heb. 8:13; 9:15), this was reviewed in chapter 9 and will be considered further below. This covenant has a dual character. On one hand it made demands upon Israel that they were unable to satisfy ("By the law is the knowledge of sin"), while on the other hand it reveals Christ under the figures of tabernacle, priesthood and sacrifices. It was "our tutor to bring us to Christ" (Gal. 3:24) and thus, quite evidently, is not without gracious dimensions. This is sometimes expressed by saying that the law was given in a "context of grace"; that is, it was given to a redeemed people and is full of "types" (pictures) of Christ.

Nevertheless, in my view, the Sinaitical covenant was, by its very nature, a covenant of works. There are many Scriptures that represent Moses' law as a covenant of works, not only in the perception of the Jews but in reality. "The commandment, which was to bring life," laments the apostle, "I found to bring death" (Rom. 7:10). Paul seems here to make a very plain statement: the law had the theoretical potential to bring spiritual life; that is, to justify men in God's sight. After all, Jesus Christ satisfied the law perfectly during his life on earth as a man, and thereby obtained righteousness for his people.

Again, Paul quotes Leviticus 18:5 as definitive of law-righteousness: "You shall therefore keep My statutes and My judgments, which if a man does, he shall live by them" (see Rom. 10:5). A similar statement is made in Deuteronomy 6:25: "Then it will be righteousness for us, if we are careful to observe all these commandments before the LORD our God, as he has commanded us." Again, in Deuteronomy 26:13–15 we read, "Then you shall say before the LORD your God, 'I have removed the holy tithe from my house, and also have given them to the Levite, the stranger, the fatherless and the widow, according to all Your commandments which You have commanded me; I have not transgressed Your commandments, nor have I forgotten them … [therefore] Look down from Your holy habitation, from heaven, and bless Your people Israel.' "

And what of Israel's acceptance of the terms of the covenant? "Then [Moses] took the book of the covenant and read in the hearing of the people. And they said, 'All that the LORD has said we will do, and be obedient' " (Exod. 24:7). Similar passages are to be found throughout Deuteronomy and elsewhere. We see here all the elements of a covenant of works. God's requirements are set out and man freely accepts them. In theory, at least, conformity is a genuine option. Rewards are to be claimed for obedience, and punishments expected for transgression.

Finally, only a covenant of works can be broken by man. Yet this is just what happened with the law of Moses. "The house of Israel and the house of Judah have broken My covenant which I made with their fathers," says God through Jeremiah (Jer. 11:10; see also Deut. 31:16; Lev. 26:15; Jer. 31:32).

In light of these Scriptures, the covenant made at Sinai emerges as a covenant of works. Of course, man's sinfulness prevents him from keeping the law, so that he can never, in fact, be justified by its works. But this is no reason why God should not, justly, *require* man to obey, or make divine blessing conditional on such obedience. As Paul remarks, "If there had been a law given which could have offered life, truly righteousness would have been by the law [of Moses]" (Gal. 3:21).

9. The new covenant

Also known as a "better covenant" (Heb. 8:6) and "the everlasting covenant" (Heb. 13:20), the establishment of this covenant was explicitly prophesied by Jeremiah (Jer. 31:31–37). It is the ultimate redemptive covenant, made in the blood of Christ (Matt. 26:28). The new covenant is "not of the letter but of the Spirit; for the letter kills, but the Spirit gives life" (2 Cor. 3:6). The writer to the Hebrews devotes much space to the contrast between the covenant of Sinai and the new covenant of which Christ himself is mediator (Heb. 8:1–9:15; 10:16–23; 12:18–24; 13:20).

Having reviewed the various covenants as they appear in Scripture, let us now return to Paul's teaching on the two covenants represented by Sarah and Hagar.

The two covenants are distinct (4:24)

Paul declares, **"These are the two covenants"** (Gal. 4:24). He implies that there are ultimately *only* two covenants—no more and no less. What we found in the previous section is consistent with this teaching. The first of these covenants is *the covenant of promise*, which runs as a golden thread throughout biblical history. It was a covenant made with Adam, with Noah, with Abraham, Isaac and Jacob, and with David. Since this covenant can be equated with God's redemptive purpose in Christ, it finds its fulfillment in the *new covenant*, so that these covenants (promise and new) can be regarded as one and the same with the covenants of grace and redemption.

This covenant of promise is distinguished by two things. Firstly, *it requires nothing from man for its fulfillment*. At no point in God's dealings with the patriarchs did he make his promised blessings conditional on any human act. Of course the promises, once made, were received by faith, and that faith was counted for righteousness. But the promises themselves were absolute, declaring as they did the unchangeable purpose of God. Their reception by faith was *a sequel, not a condition* of their ratification. The same is true of the new covenant, for under it salvation is bestowed on him who "does not work but believes on Him who justifies the ungodly" (Rom. 4:5).

The second distinguishing mark of the new covenant is *its spiritual nature*; it is fulfilled not by the endeavor of man but by the indwelling of the Spirit. That is why Paul describes the substance of the covenant of promise as "the promise of the Spirit" (3:14) and why also, perhaps, he returns to the subject of the covenants in this section of the epistle.

By contrast, the other covenant of which Paul speaks, in the Sarah-Hagar allegory, is a covenant of works. Under this covenant God makes known what he requires of man (whether through the written law or conscience or natural revelation) and man seeks (and even promises) to satisfy those requirements, so as to attain to righteousness and the blessing of God (see e.g. Rom. 10:2–5; Deut. 6:25). In the covenant with Abraham, it was God who made the promises; in the covenant of works it is man who makes them! Accordingly, God's blessings under such a covenant are conditional upon obedience, and he justly condemns and punishes those who fail to satisfy its demands (see Deut. 8:19–20). The Mosaic covenant, Paul implies, is just such a covenant of works. Nor can it be claimed that this was simply a Judaistic misinterpretation of the law. Paul tells us that it is the covenant of Sinai *as such* that brings men into bondage, and *only a covenant of works can do that*.

But does not the law of Moses point to Christ? Is it not at one with the covenant of promise in this respect at least? Are not its ceremonies pregnant with the promise of redemption in Christ? Yes, indeed. Nevertheless it remains a covenant of works, which points to Christ by pointing *away from itself*. Both covenants direct us to Christ, but they do so in completely different ways.

Part III The Spirit and the Believer

Summary

There are ultimately only two covenants, the one of works and the other of promise. They are distinguished by the fact that the covenant of promise (also known as the covenant of grace and the new covenant) requires nothing of man but to receive it, whereas the covenant of works requires human obedience for its fulfillment. Although the covenant of Sinai prefigures Christ, and is our tutor to bring us to him, it is nevertheless a covenant of works. It makes explicit demands for obedience, extracts specific promises from its adherents, and prescribes comprehensive rewards and punishments. That it is, indeed, a covenant of works is demonstrated by the fact that it brings men into bondage, and this by its own nature, not because men misunderstand its purpose.

By contrast, the covenant of promise, which is the new covenant made in the blood of Christ, imparts the blessings of salvation by free grace. It demands nothing of men for its fulfillment. It brings liberty, not bondage, and is mediated by Christ through his Spirit imparted to those who believe.

Notes

[1] Hendriksen, *Galatians and Ephesians*, p. 179.

[2] "An understanding of the Bible is impossible without an understanding of the two covenants ... God established the old covenant through Moses and the new covenant through Christ, whose blood ratified it. The old (Mosaic) covenant was based on law; but the new (Christian) covenant, foreshadowed through Abraham and foretold through Jeremiah, is based on promises. In the law God laid the responsibility on men and said 'thou shalt ..., thou shalt not ...,' but in the promise God keeps the responsibility Himself and says 'I will ..., I will ...' " (Stott, *Message of Galatians*, p. 124).

[3] "The covenant of redemption may be defined as the agreement between the Father, giving the Son as Head and Redeemer of the elect, and the Son, voluntarily taking the place of those whom the Father has given Him" (Berkhof, *Systematic Theology*, p. 271).

[4] "Though this distinction (between the covenant of redemption and the covenant of grace) is favoured by Scripture statements, it does not follow that there are two separate and independent covenants antithetic to the covenant of works. The covenant of grace and redemption are two modes or phases of the one evangelical covenant of mercy" (Shedd, *Dogmatic Theology*, p. 360).

[5] Berkhof, *Systematic Theology*, p. 288.

[6] Berkhof, *Systematic Theology*, p. 276.

[7] Writing of the covenant of works in man's state of innocence, Boston says, "God made man habitually righteous; man was to make himself actually righteous; the former was the stock God put into his hand; the latter, the improvement he should have made of it" (*Human Nature*, pp. 9–10).

[8] "Through the coming of Christ it [the law of Moses] received its full accomplishment, and came to an end; the ceremonial law was utterly abolished, and the moral law *ceased to be a covenant of works*, though it continues as a rule of walk and conversation; and the whole Mosaic economy was no more" (Gill, *Exposition*, vol. 9, p. 20, emphasis added).

Poole implies that, until faith comes, the law is a covenant of works; "... being dead to the law, as a covenant of works ..." (*Commentary*, p. 647).

24
The Two Jerusalems

Please Read Galatians 4:25–31

Continuing his allegory, Paul now explores the differences between the two covenants. The allegory is complex, featuring three "layers" of meaning. Sarah and Hagar not only represent the two covenants, but "correspond" to the two Jerusalems, which cities also have adherents or "children." The two Jerusalems, in turn, represent the church and corporate Judaism respectively.

Some commentators believe that Paul is here responding to the Judaizers "in kind." His opponents, they suggest, had been the first to introduce this allegory into the argument.[1] According to this idea, the Judaizers accused the Gentile converts of being like Ishmael, excluded from the inheritance, while the Jewish believers were true sons, like Isaac. To share the inheritance, therefore, the Gentiles must become Jews through circumcision and law-keeping. In reply, Paul reverses the allegory, showing that the distinction is not racial, between Jew and Gentile, but spiritual, between those born of the flesh (Ishmael) and those born of the Spirit (Isaac). Either way, whether Paul uses the story on his own initiative or by way of response, he uses it with great effect.

The two Jerusalems (4:25–27)

We have already seen how Paul identifies Hagar and Sarah, respectively, with the two covenants. Now, however, he identifies them also with the two Jerusalems: **"For this Hagar is Mount Sinai in Arabia and corresponds to Jerusalem which now is, and is in bondage with her children"** (4:25). Thus Hagar "is" Sinai (that is, she represents the covenant made there), but at the same time "corresponds to" the present Jerusalem. What does this double identification signify?

Paul is telling us here that the covenant of Sinai gives birth to a people or nation, namely those who are subject to it. "The Jerusalem that now is" refers not primarily to a geographical location, or even a political centre, but rather to the religious system of Judaism that was based there. Thus the Jews of Paul's day were "the children" of this Jerusalem, because they were a people subject to the law of Moses, and "Jerusalem" represented their corporate identity. Take away the covenant, and Jerusalem, in this sense, would cease to exist. Thus Paul uses Hagar as a simultaneous picture of the Sinaitical covenant and the Judaistic "nation." He does so to emphasize the interdependence of covenant and people. The people are in bondage to the covenant.

In a similar way, Sarah pictures both the covenant of promise and the **"Jerusalem above [which] is free ... the mother of us all"** (4:26). The covenant of promise also gives birth to a people, but *this* nation, by contrast, is free! Their corporate identity is the heavenly Jerusalem, that is, the church of Jesus Christ. This picture of the church is, of course, used with great effect in Revelation: "I, John, saw the holy city, new Jerusalem, coming down out of heaven from God, prepared as a bride adorned for her husband ... the bride, the Lamb's wife ... the holy Jerusalem descending out of heaven from God, having the glory of God" (Rev. 21:2–11). As with Hagar, the double identification emphasizes that covenant and people are inseparable. The church only exists because of God's eternal covenant in Christ. She is "the mother of us all" in the sense that the church embraces believing Jews and Gentiles alike. "For as many as were baptized into Christ have put on Christ. There is neither Jew nor Greek, slave nor free, there is neither male nor female; for you are all one in Christ Jesus" (Gal. 3:27–28).

The fact that the two covenants give birth to two distinct nations is central to Paul's argument. It is impossible, argues the apostle, to belong to both of these nations at the same time. We cannot simultaneously be under the law and under grace. We are either children of the earthly Jerusalem, in bondage to a fruitless religion of works; or we are children of the heavenly Jerusalem, and enjoy the glorious liberty of the children of God. We are either slaves like Ishmael, or heirs like Isaac.[2]

The two covenants are opposed (4:25–29)

The covenants are opposed in two ways. Firstly, they lead to different outcomes, namely bondage on the one hand and freedom on the other. Secondly, Sinai's adherents persecute the **"children of promise."**

Concerning bondage, Paul writes, **"For these are the two covenants: the one from Mount Sinai which gives birth to bondage, which is Hagar—for this Hagar is Mount Sinai in Arabia and corresponds to Jerusalem which now is, and is in bondage with her children"** (4:24–25). How are men brought into bondage by the law? By the endless and futile search for obedience to that law: endless, because it is a task from which a man can never rest; futile, because everything man does is tainted by sin and cannot therefore satisfy God. It is because Moses' covenant requires men to *work* for God's blessing that it brings them into bondage. The Jewish nation as a whole ("Jerusalem which now is"), and the Judaizers in particular, were subject to this bondage through their pursuit of the law, asserts the apostle. But they are not alone! Every religion that teaches its adherents to perform deeds, of whatever kind, in order to obtain salvation, is likewise a prison. This is true, even if the work required is to "believe," or "trust," or "commit," or "surrender." As long as these things are undertaken in the strength of human nature, and not in the enabling power of the Spirit, they are just as truly "works" as are penances and pilgrimages. The false idea that salvation can be obtained by such works is rightly called "legalism."

However, there is another kind of bondage to the law that can be experienced even by true believers, who understand that they can be justified only by faith. This occurs when Christians seek holiness or "sanctification" by the deeds of the law, and has been called "nomism" (after the Greek word for "law"[3]). Many commentators see Galatians as addressed only to the problem of legalism, but there is persuasive evidence in the epistle that Paul is also worried about nomism. If Paul's concern is limited to legalism (which denies men salvation through Christ), why does he write such an epistle to people whom he treats throughout as already being saved? (see 3:1–3; 3:26–29; 4:6–9; 5:7–10; 5:13). Does he consider that they could lose their salvation by turning back to legalism? That would be contrary to Paul's gospel of grace. Does he fear that they may not be true believers after all? Yes, to some extent, he considers the possibility of apostasy (e.g. 3:4; 5:2–4), but this is only hinted at. The overwhelming evidence is that Paul regarded them as true believers who were being confused and led astray by false doctrine. There *was* a danger of apostasy, but there was a greater danger of true believers being entangled with a yoke of bondage.

This danger is present today when the law is urged upon believers as the primary pattern for Christian living. Of course, believers should live to please God, and in so doing will strive to avoid the sins condemned in the law. This is both their privilege and duty. But some so emphasize the believer's duties to God that they forget the work of God in the believing heart. The word "duty" occurs only twice in the English translation of the New Testament, the Greek for which it stands usually being translated by the milder term "ought." The New Testament emphasis is not upon duty for its own sake, but (as we shall see) upon the conquest of sin through the liberating and empowering work of the Holy Spirit. The fruit of true Christian obedience is seen in those who are led by the Spirit of God.

By contrast, **"The Jerusalem above is free, which is the mother of us all … now we brethren, as Isaac was, are children of promise"** (4:26, 28). The heavenly Jerusalem referred to here is the church of Jesus Christ, as we have already seen from the book of Revelation. This city is founded on the covenant of promise, which has its fulfillment in the new covenant made in the blood of Christ. The inhabitants of this city are therefore "children of promise," being born spiritually in accordance with the covenant of promise in Christ. They are free from the law, no longer subject to its requirements or its penalties. Are they, then, a lawless people, having no law? Not at all. They are under a new law, even the rule and law of Christ (1 Cor. 9:21; Gal. 6:2). As we have seen before, the law of Christ is an altogether more demanding law than that of Moses. Yet believers can keep it, because it is written in their hearts and because they are enabled by the indwelling Holy Spirit (Jer. 31:31–33). Their obedience is not perfect, for they are still sinners. But they do not rest on the perfection of their law-keeping for either salvation or holiness. Christ is their redemption and their sanctification, and his blood keeps on cleansing them from all sin (1 Cor. 1:30; 1 John 1:7–9).

The phrase, "the mother of us all," reminds the apostle of a passage from Isaiah, which he proceeds to quote: **"Rejoice, O barren, you who do not bear! Break forth and shout, you who do not travail! For the desolate has many more children than she who has a husband"** (4:27, citing Isa. 54:1). Sarah's inability to bear children pictures the inability of man to bring himself to life spiritually. If men were left to themselves, none would be saved. But what is impossible with man is possible with God. "Where sin abounded, grace abounded much more" (Rom. 5:20). Through his grace in Christ, God has generated a multitude of children, reborn miraculously by the Spirit, where by nature there would have been none. What a reason for rejoicing!

How, then, can we summarize what Paul is telling us in this passage?

We are children of one family or another; we cannot be children of both. We may be Hagar's children, born and raised in slavery, our mother wedded to the law. Or we may be Sarah's children, freeborn, our mother (the church) wedded to Christ. If we are under Moses, then we are in bondage. But if we are under the new covenant, then we are joined to Christ; he has made us free, and we are free indeed (John 8:36). We shall see in the next chapter exactly what this freedom entails, but one thing is clear.

The two covenants are diametrically opposed; one leads to slavery and the other to liberty.

Finally, the covenants are opposed in a second sense: **"As he who was born according to the flesh then persecuted him who was born according to the Spirit, even so it is now"** (4:29). We read nothing in Scripture, of course, about Ishmael *personally* persecuting Isaac. However, there are several places in the New Testament where the inspired writer expands upon Old Testament events by providing new information, and this may be a further example. Alternatively, Paul may be speaking of subsequent conflicts between Jews and Ishmaelites.

But why does he introduce this subject of persecution at all? It is surely to emphasize that the two covenants are opposed and irreconcilable. The adherents of the works covenant instinctively recognize this fact, and express it, "even … now," by persecuting the "children of promise." They feel threatened by the doctrine of promise and seek to suppress it. It was for just this reason that Paul himself, as Saul of Tarsus, persecuted the followers of Christ until he met the Lord on the Damascus road, so he knew what he was talking about. Now, ironically, it was Paul himself who suffered persecution at the hand of the Jews.

The two covenants are mutually exclusive (4:30–31)

"Nevertheless," asks the apostle, **"what does the Scripture say? 'Cast out the bondwoman and her son, for the son of the bondwoman shall not be heir with the son of the freewoman' "** (4:30). Neither we nor the Jews of Moses' time could obtain the inheritance of God's free grace through the covenant of Sinai. As long as we are bound by that covenant we are excluded from the covenant of promise. Not only is Isaac the preferred heir, he is the *only* heir. Ishmael cannot be co-heir of the promise together with Isaac; he must be utterly rejected.

The law had no power to deliver the sinner from his sin, or from the wrath of God. The sacrifices had no potency to cleanse the conscience, even though they prefigured Calvary. Only

Christ's blood can "purge [the] conscience from dead works to serve the living God" (Heb. 9:14). Believers, therefore, cannot be hybrids, living simultaneously as children of the bondwoman and the freewoman. **"Brethren,"** declares Paul, **"we are not children of the bondwoman but of the free"** (4:31).

The Judaizers' attempt to marry the law and the gospel was, therefore, doomed to failure. They presented the law as being an advance upon the gospel preached by Paul. Not only must God's people believe in Christ, they taught, but they must also be brought under the covenant of Sinai if they are to be saved. Not so, thunders the apostle. Law and grace are such mutually exclusive principles that the former must be "cast out" (along with those who teach it!) if the latter is to be received. Salvation and liberty of soul are to be had neither through legalism nor nomism (law observance), but by free grace alone.

Summary

The two covenants give rise to two constituencies (two peoples). The "children" of the old Jerusalem are those who remain in bondage to the old covenant, made at Sinai. This bondage can take the form of legalism, namely the idea that man can be justified by the works of that law. But (among believers) it can also take the form of nomism, in which the law of Moses is seen as necessary in some manner for a believer's sanctification or holiness.

By contrast, the "children" of the heavenly Jerusalem (the church of Jesus Christ) are free. They have been delivered from the power and penalty of sin, and thus from the clutches of the law. They are no longer in bondage to the requirements and sanctions of the law. But they are not without law, being subject to the rule and law of Christ, which is written in their hearts. They are enabled to keep this new law by the indwelling Spirit.

Thus Paul establishes that the two covenants, and their respective constituencies, are opposed and mutually exclusive. We can belong only to one "Jerusalem," not both. Any attempt to merge law and gospel into a single system is doomed to failure.

Notes

[1] Longenecker, *Galatians*, pp. 199–200.

[2] "This, then, is the allegory. Abraham had two sons ..., born of two mothers, who represent two covenants and two Jerusalems. Hagar the slave stands for the old covenant, and her son Ishmael symbolizes the church of the earthly Jerusalem. Sarah the free woman stands for the new covenant, and her son Isaac symbolizes the church of the heavenly Jerusalem. Although superficially similar, because both were sons of Abraham, the two boys were fundamentally different. In the same way, Paul is arguing, it is not enough to claim Abraham as our father. The crucial question concerns who our mother is" (Stott, *Message of Galatians*, p. 126).

[3] "Paul's Galatian letter, it must always be remembered, is not concerned just with "legalism," even though sadly it is often understood only in those terms. Rather, Galatians is principally concerned with "nomism" or whether Gentiles who believe in Christ must also be subject to the directives of the Mosaic law" (Longenecker, *Galatians*, p. 219).

25
Freedom in Christ

Please Read Galatians 5:1–6

Galatians is full of exhortations, but none is more powerful than the passage before us. As, layer upon layer, Paul builds his case for grace over against works, the appeal to his readers grows more urgent. The reason is clear: those who attempt to be justified by the law **"have become estranged from Christ"** and have **"fallen from grace"** (5:4). The Judaizers' message was not just a deviation from the gospel; it was an outright denial of it.

Once again, in these verses, Paul reminds his readers that true Christianity is spiritual, and that a life pleasing to God can be lived only by those who are led by the indwelling Spirit.

Liberty through Christ (5:1)

"Stand fast therefore in the liberty by which Christ has made us free," exhorts the apostle (5:1). Notice first how we come by this liberty. It is the result of Christ's work, not our own. It is Christ who has "made us free," and our continuing liberty rests on him as truly as does our first deliverance. It is often said that freedom is not fully appreciated by those who possess it, and this was clearly the case with the Galatians. It can also be true of ourselves, and is another reason for keeping the person and work of Christ at the forefront of all our thinking. What, then, is this liberty? What freedoms are enjoyed by those who trust only in Christ? They are manifold.

1. We are free from the curse of the law

This is Paul's starting-point. Because of man's sin, the law brings bondage in this life and condemnation in the day of judgment. It cannot justify us in the sight of God, "for by the law is the knowledge of sin" (Rom. 3:20). All this we have already seen.[1]

2. We are free from the curse of Adam

"Through one man sin entered the world, and death through sin, and thus death spread to all men, because all have sinned." So Paul writes in Romans 5:12. When Adam rebelled against the rule of God, he immediately became mortal, subject to "the bondage of corruption" (Rom. 8:21). But Christ has delivered his people from this bondage: "Those who receive abundance of grace and of the gift of righteousness will reign in life through the one, Jesus Christ" (Rom. 5:17). Paul appears to be speaking both of spiritual life and physical resurrection in this passage. He refers explicitly to bodily resurrection in Romans 8:21–23: "The creation itself also will be delivered from the bondage of corruption into *the glorious liberty of the children of God*" (emphasis added). He adds, "We also who have the firstfruits of the Spirit ... [are] eagerly waiting for the adoption, the redemption of our body" (see also 2 Cor. 5:1–5; 1 Cor. 15:20–58).

3. We are free from spiritual death

The curse upon Adam was twofold, involving both physical mortality and spiritual death. This curse is, in fact, one with the curse of the law, for Adam also was subject to a covenant of works that he did not keep. On account of his disobedience, Adam and all his descendants became subject to both physical *and* spiritual death. Thus the natural man is "dead in trespasses and sins" (Eph. 2:1), blind to spiritual truth (1 Cor. 2:14), without God and without hope (Eph. 2:12). But those who trust Christ have been "made ... alive together with Christ ... and raised up together, and made [to] sit together in the heavenly places in Christ Jesus" (Eph. 2:5–6). We have been "born again, not of corruptible seed but incorruptible, through the word of God which lives and abides forever ... the word which by the gospel was preached to you" (1 Peter 1:23–25). This is our most fundamental freedom, namely the freedom *to live* spiritually. Nothing can compare with this liberty, and nothing can replace it.

4. We are free from the fear of death

Hebrews tells us that Jesus Christ became man, "that through death He might destroy him who had the power of death, that is, the devil, and release those who through fear of death were all their lifetime subject to bondage" (Heb. 2:14–15). Death itself is the ultimate prison, but long before the event, death casts its shadow over life. How does the fear of death bring us into bondage?

Firstly, it imposes *a sense of futility* upon all our achievements. "I looked on all the works that my hands had done," wrote Solomon, "and on the labor in which I had toiled; and indeed all was vanity and grasping for the wind. There was no profit under the sun" (Eccles. 2:11).

Secondly, it confronts us with *the terror of the unknown*. What lies beyond death? Nothing, say some. But mankind has consistently refused to believe this. Ancient burial rites, and the current popularity of books recounting "near-death experiences," testify alike to an enduring belief in life after death. But what kind of life—reward or punishment, heaven or hell?

Christ delivers us from the fear of death, for he has passed through death and returned, triumphant over it. "Death is swallowed up in victory" (1 Cor. 15:54). For the believer, "To live is Christ, and to die is gain" (Phil. 1:21). To be "absent from the body" is to be "present with the Lord" (2 Cor. 5:8). Death is the gateway to glory.

5. We are free from condemnation

"There is therefore now no condemnation to those who are in Christ Jesus, who do not walk according to the flesh, but according to the Spirit" (Rom. 8:1). Why? Because Christ has borne our condemnation, being "made ... sin for us, that we might become the righteousness of God in Him" (2 Cor. 5:21). Through the mystery of the atonement, the elect escape eternal condemnation (though they deserve it along with all men). The ungodly are justified, and clothed with Christ's perfect righteousness. No one, therefore, can bring a charge against God's elect. The only one who has the *right* to accuse them is God, the judge of all men. But he will not do so, since it is he who has justified them through the work of Christ. So Paul teaches in Romans 8:31–34.

6. We are free from the power of sin

"God be thanked," exclaims the apostle, "that though you were slaves of sin, yet ... having been set free from sin, you became slaves of righteousness" (Rom. 6:17–18). He attributes the believer's freedom from sin to the power of grace: "Sin shall not have dominion over you, for you are not under law but under grace" (Rom. 6:14). The law actually enhances the power of sin, since it brings the knowledge of sin, excites sin, and offers no way of escape from sin's domination (Rom. 7:7–13). Grace, on the other hand, causes us to die to sin that we might live to God, so that Paul can exhort with confidence, "Reckon yourselves to be dead indeed to sin, but alive to God in Christ Jesus our Lord" (Rom. 6:1–14).

7. We are free from the authority of Satan

God, says Paul, "has delivered us from the power [authority] of darkness and translated us into the kingdom of the Son of His love" (Col. 1:13). Before conversion, even the elect lived "according to the course of this world, according to the prince of the power of the air, the spirit who now works in the sons of disobedience" (Eph. 2:1); that is, we dwelt in Satan's kingdom and under his thrall. Through grace, however, and the effectual calling of the Holy Spirit, we have been plucked from Satan's grasp and carried away to another kingdom, namely that of Christ. We have a new king, a new country, a new life.

8. We are free to inherit all that Christ has purchased for us, eternally

Earlier, in Galatians 4:5–7, we were told that Christ has redeemed us in order that "we might receive the adoption as sons

... you are no longer a slave but a son, and if a son, then an heir of God through Christ." Having been purchased by the blood of Christ, cleansed from sin, and delivered from the power of sin and Satan, we are at last free to enjoy the inheritance which "God has prepared for those who love Him" (1 Cor. 2:9).

Stand fast in liberty (5:1)
Seeing, then, that believers have been granted this manifold freedom, what are they to do? Certain things are obvious, of course. Christians should both exercise and enjoy their liberty. The democratic right to vote has only recently been won in some countries, while in others it is still denied. How precious must that right appear to such people! Yet in lands where democracy has long existed, many of those who have the vote fail to exercise it. Freedom is a tender plant, and may wither if we fail to cultivate it. So it is in the spiritual realm. Paul finds it necessary to exhort the Romans to *use* their liberty: "Reckon yourselves to be dead indeed to sin, but alive to God in Christ Jesus our Lord ... do not let sin reign in your mortal bodies" (Rom. 6:11–12). In like manner he here exhorts the Galatians to "stand fast ... in the liberty by which Christ has made us free" (5:1).

What a rallying cry is this! "Stand fast" is a term borrowed from the battlefield. Paul exhorts the Corinthians, "Watch, stand fast in the faith, be brave, be strong" (1 Cor. 16:13). We have a battle on our hands today, just as real as Paul's conflict with the Judaizers. Our freedoms in Christ are constantly under attack. They are attacked by legalism and nomism. They are attacked by false doctrine, of whatever kind. They are attacked by sin and unbelief. They are attacked by Satan, the enemy of our souls. How, then, are we to stand fast against these onslaughts? We must use the weapons supplied to us by God. Some of them are mentioned in verses 5–6 of this chapter, namely faith, hope, and love. We possess and employ these weapons "through the Spirit" (5:5). Above all, our faith, our hope and our love are effective in so far as their object is Christ. We shall see later in Galatians 5 how Paul develops this theme of living and walking in the Spirit (5:22). These are the means by which we shall be able to endure the battle and stand fast in liberty.

Under whose yoke? (5:1)

"Do not be entangled again with a yoke of bondage," warns the apostle (5:1). By "yoke of bondage," he clearly means enslavement to the law. The metaphor of a yoke denotes both servitude and toil (compare 1 Tim. 6:1). The bearer is not only enslaved by this yoke, but also condemned to endless striving in his futile search for righteousness. Such a person knows nothing of the rest that is found in Christ. By contrast, the "yoke" of Christ is easy, and his burden light (Matt. 11:30). To be yoked to Christ is to be at rest (Heb. 4:10). It is to die with him, to rise with him, to walk with him, and to reign with him. It is to be cleansed by his blood, led by his Spirit, taught by his Word, strengthened by his power, filled with his love.[2] A bird, released from captivity, is free to soar above the mountains, rove the land, and cross the oceans. There are no limits to its odyssey. So also there is no limit to the liberated soul. It is free to explore the "width and length and depth and height—and to know the love of Christ which passes knowledge"; free to be "filled with all the fullness of God" (Eph. 3:18–19).

Paul says that his readers are not to be entangled "again." The Galatians had once been in bondage to false religion (4:8). Their former creed was not, of course, the hollow shell which was Judaism, but their paganism had been no less a prison. Apart from the gospel of free grace in Christ, all religions enslave their followers to works of one kind or another. To embrace the Judaizers' doctrine would be to return to the selfsame slavery from which they had been delivered by the Spirit through the gospel.[3]

These things are surely written for our learning. Any religious system that bids us earn merit with God by our actions or observances is a contradiction of free grace. The freedom of conscience that believers have in Christ[4] is easily lost when legalism, nomism, and the doctrines of men are introduced into the church. How, then, may we avoid the "yoke of bondage"?

Firstly, we must never lose sight of the person and work of Christ. He must be the central theme of all our preaching and teaching, and the example for all our practice. Secondly, and as a consequence, we must "rightly divide the word of truth" (2 Tim. 2:15), interpreting all Scripture in a Christological manner. What is the purpose of the law? It is our tutor to bring us to Christ. By what rule should we live? We are to walk in the Spirit of Christ, bringing forth his fruit (Gal. 5:22–25). What is the church? It is Christ's body, in which every member has a role to fulfill, with due humility (Rom. 12:3–8). It is Christ's flock, and no man is to lord over it (1 Peter 5:1–4). What is the place of church discipline? To restore the offender to Christ "in a spirit of gentleness" (Gal. 6:1). What is the basic principle of Christian life and conduct? It is "faith [in Christ] working through love" (Gal. 5:6). And so we could continue.

As long as our religion centers upon Christ, both in its doctrine and practice, we shall remain free. Lose that perspective, however, and bondage will ensue. We become slaves if our Christianity becomes focused on mere doctrine, on religious duties, on ethics, on rules and regulations, on humanitarian concerns, on human authorities and personalities, on self-denial, on mysticism, on religious experiences, on church organization and structure, on ecumenism, or on anything but Christ.[5]

Circumcision; profit or debt? (5:2–4)

Paul introduces the language of accountancy as he turns to the subject of circumcision: **"If you become circumcised, Christ will profit you nothing. And I testify again to every man who becomes circumcised that he is a debtor to keep the whole law"** (5:2–3). The Judaizers insisted that circumcision was necessary for salvation (see Acts 15:1). It was not sufficient for Gentiles to believe in Christ; they must also be brought under the Mosaic covenant made by God with his Old Testament people. They must, in effect, become Jews, for only Jews could be saved. The Judaizers certainly taught that a Gentile would profit from circumcision, for he would inherit salvation! Paul has a different opinion. Any who seek spiritual gain through circumcision forfeit the only true profit, namely that which a believer finds in Christ.

The interesting thing is this: circumcision was a sign of the covenant of promise made with Abraham (Gen. 17:9–14), not part of the Sinaitical covenant. Paul has previously argued that the Gentiles are co-heirs of the Abrahamic covenant of promise. Why, then, does he now condemn circumcision?

The answer is firstly that, in Jewish thinking, circumcision had become inextricably linked with the Mosaic covenant. The Judaizers' message was, "Unless you are circumcised *according to the custom of Moses*, you cannot be saved" (Acts 15:1). Notice how they advocated circumcision according to Moses' custom, not Abraham's. In their thinking, Sinai had come to include the covenant with Abraham. The covenant of promise, together with its sign, had been hijacked by the law of Moses! Not so, declares Paul. Sinai was a temporary provision, pending the fulfillment of the promise in Christ (see Gal. 3:15–25). Nevertheless, since circumcision was being seen by the Gentile believers as an initiation into the covenant of works, Paul is obliged to condemn it.

Secondly, of course, circumcision was given to Abraham only until the promise was fulfilled. It was the tangible cord, spanning the centuries, that bound Abraham and the promise to Abraham's seed, Jesus Christ. It kept alive the memory of the promise and guaranteed that it would be fulfilled. But once Christ had come, the cord came to an end. Circumcision had served its historic purpose and was needed no more. The spiritual descendants of Abraham bear an altogether different sign, the mark of faith. This is why, a few verses later, Paul treats circumcision as a matter of indifference, stating, "In Christ Jesus neither circumcision nor uncircumcision avails anything, but faith working through love" (5:6).

Thus although circumcision had actually lost all significance, Paul was obliged to take it seriously as long as it was being employed to initiate Gentile believers into the covenant of works. Used in this way, circumcision placed a man in debt, not profit. "Every man who becomes circumcised ... is a debtor to keep the whole law" (5:3). Such a person, warns Paul, burdens himself with a debt he can never pay, namely, the obligation to observe every precept of the Mosaic law, perfectly and without end. This was a burden, Peter told the Council of Jerusalem, that "neither our fathers nor we were able to bear" (Acts 15:10).

But this is not all. To submit to the law (by being circumcised) implied an attempt to find *justification* through the law, instead of through faith in Christ. Anyone who does this, thunders Paul, has become **"estranged from Christ ...** [and has] **fallen from grace"** (5:4). We have to realize, of course, that the Galatians and their false mentors did not see it this way. As far as they were concerned, submission to the law was wholly consistent with faith in Christ. Again, therefore, Paul has to drive home the truth that those who seek righteousness (or even *additional* righteousness) through law-keeping cannot have righteousness through Christ. The two approaches are mutually exclusive. To embrace law-righteousness is to become a stranger to Christ. To rely upon self-merit is to despise and abandon grace. It should be added that any who do "fall from grace" do so because they were never, in reality, recipients of grace. Their gospel profession was apparent, not real. The truly regenerate person cannot fall from grace, for grace sustains him.

The hope of righteousness (5:5–6)

Those whose hope of eternal life lies in law-keeping have become "estranged from Christ" (5:4). By contrast, true believers **"through the Spirit eagerly wait for the hope of righteousness by faith"** (5:5). This does not mean that "righteousness by faith" is something future. It means that believers look forward with confidence to *that which is secured* by such righteousness, namely the glorious inheritance of the children of God.

Notice how Paul emphasizes the role of the indwelling Holy

Spirit. It is "through the Spirit" that the believer enjoys such confident expectations. This is consistent with his teaching elsewhere. In Romans 5:5 he explains that hope will not be disappointed because the Spirit has infused the believer's heart with God's own love. That is, the Holy Spirit's presence in our hearts is manifested by this divine love, so that the believer is assured that God's promises will be honored. Indeed, the indwelling Spirit himself is a seal or guarantee of our inheritance (2 Cor. 1:21–22; Eph. 1:13–14; 4:30).[6]

The whole basis of our assurance, then, is the righteousness of Christ. This righteousness is gained by faith in Christ alone. The subjective experience of assurance, like faith itself, is given to us by the indwelling Holy Spirit, who teaches us to cry "Abba, Father!" (Gal. 4:6). His presence within our hearts is the guarantee that God has adopted us and will bring us to glory, for the sake of Jesus Christ. Notice also that the believer waits "eagerly" for the fulfillment of his hope. He has a zest for life, a sense of glorious expectation and excitement, at the prospect held before him. Whatever difficulties life might bring, the one who trusts in Christ has everything to look forward to!

Paul ends this section by returning to the contrast between the fruits of law-works and of faith. What about circumcision? It is irrelevant, for **"In Christ Jesus neither circumcision nor uncircumcision avails anything"** (5:6). What, then, does avail? What is of lasting value? Only **"faith, working through love."** The apostle here begins to unfold the last great theme of his letter, namely love and fruitfulness in the Spirit, a theme which is developed fully from Galatians 5:13 to 6:10. For the moment, however, notice that Paul expects faith to secure not only righteousness but also fruitfulness. Faith is not a hidden attribute, but *works* through love; that is, faith manifests itself in visible ways, not least in active love (1 John 3:18). Paul commends the Thessalonians for their "work of faith, labor of love, and patience of hope" (1 Thess. 1:3). Faith is opposed to works as a means of justification. But genuine faith produces works that glorify God (see Eph. 2:8–10).

Summary

In Christ, the believer enjoys a manifold liberty. He is free from the curse of the law, from the curse of Adam (mortality and corruption), from the fear of death, from spiritual death, from condemnation, from the power of sin, and from the authority of Satan. Positively, he is free to enjoy, now and eternally, all that Christ has purchased for him by his death and resurrection.

Having put off the yoke of bondage to law, Christians must stand fast in the liberty afforded by Christ, and not become enmeshed in any system which teaches them to earn merit with God. We "stand fast" when we make Christ, crucified, risen, and exalted, the centre of our lives and message. To submit to law as a means of pleasing God is to reject God's grace and abandon Christ.

The sign of circumcision, which marked out the physical descendants of Abraham, has been replaced by faith, the characteristic of his spiritual offspring. This faith, imparted by the indwelling Spirit of God, brings righteousness, hope, assurance, love, and fruitfulness of life.

Notes

[1] "In the stead of sin and death, he giveth unto us righteousness and everlasting life; and by this means he changeth the bondage and terrors of the law into liberty of conscience and consolation of the gospel" (Luther, *Galatians*, p. 444).

[2] "Positively, then, freedom, as Paul sees it, is the state in which a person is living and walking in the Spirit (Gal. 5:25), so that he produces the fruit of the Spirit (5:22, 23), and with joy and gratitude does the will of God (5:14; Rom. 8:4), in principle fulfilling the law of Christ (Gal. 6:2), even 'the law of liberty' (James 1:25)" (Hendriksen, *Galatians and Ephesians*, p. 192).

[3] "When they call on you to submit to circumcision and other ritual observances, in order to obtain the favour of God, tell them that 'being justified by faith, ye have already peace with God through our Lord Jesus Christ, and have access into the grace wherein ye stand, and rejoice in the hope of the glory of God' " (Brown, *Exposition of Galatians*, p. 109).

[4] "Christ won this liberty for us on the cross; the fruit and possession of it are bestowed on us through the gospel. Paul does well, then, to warn the Galatians not to be entangled again with the yoke of bondage; that is, not to allow a snare to be laid for their consciences ... If we let men bind our consciences, we shall be despoiled of an invaluable blessing and at the same time an insult will be offered to Christ, who is the Author of freedom" (Calvin, *Galatians ... Colossians*, p. 93).

[5] "The general principle of this exhortation is applicable to Christians in all ages, both in regard to religious doctrine and duty. Let them assert their freedom, and guard against the admission of any principle, or the submission to any imposition, that may entangle their consciences and strip their obedience, even to Christ's law, of that childlike character which the faith of Christ in its purity, and the ordinances of Christ in their simplicity, are so well calculated to produce and cherish" (Brown, *Exposition of Galatians*, p. 110).

[6] See Andrews, *The Spirit has Come*, pp. 108–19

26
False Teachers

Please Read Galatians 5:7–12

Paul now turns his guns upon the false teachers themselves. While still chiding the Galatians for their gullibility, he reserves his *condemnation* for those who were leading them astray. The apostle is confident that his readers are truly converted and that they will demonstrate this by responding to his letter in a positive way. But false teachers will be judged by God, not by man.

Hindered from running (5:7)
"You ran well," writes Paul. **"Who hindered you from obeying the truth?"** (5:7). Using one of his favorite metaphors, the apostle likens the Christian life to a race. To the Philippians he testifies, "I press toward the goal for the prize of the upward call of God in Christ Jesus" (Phil. 3:14). The writer to the Hebrews uses the same imagery: "Let us lay aside every weight, and the sin that so easily ensnares us, and let us run with endurance the race that is set before us, looking unto Jesus, the author and finisher of our faith" (Heb. 12:1–2).

Like a race, the Christian life has a starting-line, namely the point at which we first put our trust in Christ. There is also a finishing-tape, or goal, toward which the believer must press with resolve and energy. This "finishing-line" is our arrival in the presence of Christ in glory, and marks the end of our earthly pilgrimage. There is a prize awarded to all who reach that goal, namely "the upward calling of God in Christ," that is, the Father's summons of the soul to glory. As in a race, the Christian runner must lay aside every encumbrance; he cannot run the race carrying the baggage of sin and earthly ambition. Above all, to run effectively, the believer must fix his gaze on Christ, refusing all the diversionary tactics of Satan.

This was the Galatians' problem. Having started well, in a Christ-centered manner, they had allowed themselves to be distracted. Where once they found illumination by the Spirit of Christ, they now relished the earthly wisdom of their false instructors. Where once their goal was Christ alone, they now sought status under the covenant of works. Where once they looked to him, they now found confidence and comfort in the rituals and precepts of the law.

Satan is constantly creating diversions to turn the believer aside from the race of faith. Some of the hindrances he puts in our way are the same as had deflected the Galatians: deferring to fallible human guides instead of to the Spirit-taught Scriptures; becoming sidetracked by doubtful doctrines that are empty of Christ; believing that legalistic and nomistic practices can somehow enhance our acceptance with God beyond the acceptance we already have in Christ. These errors are current in our day as they were in Paul's. But we face many other distractions. The modern emphasis on experiences and "spiritual gifts"; the seductive appeal of the "health, wealth and happiness" gospel; the distraction of intellectualism, when men love doctrine for its own sake, rather than because it exalts Christ; a desire for the praise of men rather than the praise of God; the fear of men in place of the fear of God—these are all hindrances that deflect us from our true goal, which is Christ.

"Who hindered you from obeying the truth?" (5:7; cf. 3:1). Paul equates running badly with failing to obey the truth. No doctrine is true unless it relates in some way to Christ and honors him, for he is "the way, the truth, and the life" (John 14:6). Obeying the truth therefore means submitting to those teachings which exalt Christ and his redeeming work.[1] By the same token these doctrines diminish men, setting at naught their posturing, their pretentions, and their works.

A false persuasion (5:8–9)

Paul admonishes his readers: **"This persuasion does not come from Him who calls you"** (5:8). What persuasion? Clearly, the Judaizers' idea that to follow Christ one must submit to the law of Moses. This doctrine, avers the apostle, does not come from God (the one who calls them). He only calls men "in the grace of Christ" (1:6), never by the works or religious observances of men.

Here is a most valuable test, which can be applied to all or any teaching purporting to be Christian. Any belief or "persuasion" which does not testify to "the grace of Christ," is not from God. Here are twin pillars of the truth, namely the person and work of Christ, and the grace of God in Christ. They support and underpin all truly Christian teaching. No matter how attractive or pious a doctrine may appear, it is not to be received as coming from God unless it passes this double test, namely:

1. Does it make Christ central, and glorify him?
2. Does it exalt the grace of God, over against the activity of man?

Whether it be instruction in salvation, in worship, in service, or in living for God, its precepts are only to be received if they flow from the grace of Christ. Had the Galatians applied this test to the teachings of the Judaizers, they would soon have realized that they detracted from Christ's perfect, finished, and sufficient work of atonement.

Paul goes on, **"A little leaven leavens the whole lump"** (5:8). This is a warning, reminiscent of that given by Jesus to his disciples: "Beware of the leaven of the Pharisees and the Sadducees" (Matt. 16:6). Christ's words may have been a general alert against the attitudes and expectations of these religious leaders. However, the context in Matthew is more specific, namely their request that he "show them a sign from heaven" (Matt. 16:1–4). By this request they revealed both their unspirituality and their unbelief (they needed proof of Christ's claims). Paul's use of the metaphor has a similar aim. He warns his readers that the Judaizers are carnal, not spiritual, and that (in their unbelief) they have failed to understand the meaning of Christ's atonement. Their teaching or "persuasion" is therefore faulty and distorted. Such distortions of the gospel can easily sidetrack believers into fruitless byways. Like leaven in bread, a small amount of false teaching can have a disproportionate effect.

This principle is as true today as ever. Because even a little error can affect the whole body of Christ, we need to be constantly watchful. The idea that doctrine does not matter has gained considerable currency in recent years. Christianity is more than doctrine, people tell us, and we should seek unity in a common experience of God and of his gifts. Yet a right understanding of the gospel is essential to salvation! And *sound* doctrine, which exalts and centralizes Jesus Christ, who is "the image of the invisible God" (Col. 1:15), can never be boring or redundant.

Confidence in the Lord (5:10)

Paul's next statement comes as a surprise: **"I have confidence in you, in the Lord, that you will have no other mind"** (5:10). How can he possibly express confidence in the Galatians? Had they not turned from his teaching to "another gospel"? Had they not called in question his apostolic authority, and acted foolishly? Yes, indeed, but we need to understand Paul's perspective here.

As we noticed earlier, the apostle was sure that his readers were genuine believers. As such, they could not, in the end, depart from the truth. Their preservation would not, of course, be due to themselves, but rather to the keeping power of God. Nevertheless, it was reasonable for Paul to express confidence that they would return to the true gospel. His confidence lay in their union with Christ, and thus in God, who bestowed this standing upon them in election, calling, and regeneration. Speaking from this viewpoint, therefore, he makes clear that his confidence in them was "in the Lord," not in themselves. He was confident that God would enlighten them through his teaching, and bring them back to the path of gospel obedience. They would then have "no other mind [opinion]"; that is, they would agree with and submit to the truth taught by Paul. If they did not do so, it would mean they were not, after all, real believers.

There are some valuable applications here for us. Despite the enormous problems he had with the Galatians, Paul remained optimistic. But this was not because Paul was an optimist by temperament. His loving spirit expressed in this passage is based upon the great doctrine of the perseverance (or preservation) of the saints. It is not a sentimental glossing-over of their errors, nor does it arise from a tolerance of false teaching, as must be plain from the epistle as a whole. In spite of all that had happened, Paul could regard the Galatians with affection and equanimity because he believed in the power of God and the election of grace (Rom. 11:5). Christian ministers and workers often become alarmed and discouraged by the failings of those to whom they minister. But ultimately God is responsible for their salvation. It was he who chose his people, and it is he who will bring every one of them to glory. Our responsibility is to follow Paul's example, to "Preach the word … convince, rebuke, exhort, with all longsuffering and teaching [doctrine]" (2 Tim. 4:2). But salvation and preservation are of the Lord.

The offense of the cross (5:10–12)

Though confident regarding the Galatian believers, Paul condemns their false teachers. **"He who troubles you shall bear his judgment, whoever he is"** (5:10). What is the nature of this judgment? Hear the words of Jesus Christ: "Whoever causes one of these little ones who believe in Me to sin, it would be better for him if a millstone were hung around his neck and he were drowned in the depth of the sea" (Matt. 18:6; the preceding verses 3–4 make it clear that the expression "little ones" means all believers, not just children). This was precisely the offense of the Judaizers. They had led the Galatian believers astray from the truth, and they would be judged by God. That judgment would be so severe that death by drowning would be preferable, were such an option available. These are solemn warnings to any who set themselves up as teachers, knowing nothing of the truth as it is in Christ. It does not matter who they are. Whether they are respected figures in the religious world, or boast high academic credentials, or have a saintly disposition so that all men speak well of them—if they injure God's children by false teaching, they will be severely judged.

Paul cannot resist inserting a further proof of the Judaizers' error. **"If I still preach circumcision, why do I still suffer persecution? Then the offense of the cross has ceased"** (5:11). Possibly the false teachers had misrepresented Paul, alleging that, like them, he also preached circumcision and submission to the law. By this subterfuge they could claim apostolic authority for their errors. If this is the case, he puts them right in no uncertain manner. It is more likely, however, that Paul's statement here is rhetorical. Let me paraphrase it like this:

If it is right to preach circumcision, I would certainly do so, and thereby escape the opposition of the Jews. Why do you imagine I continue to suffer their persecution, when I could avoid it simply by proclaiming Moses and the law? What offends them is my insistence that salvation stems from "the cross," that is, the atoning work of Christ, rather than from obedience to the law. If I were to preach the law instead of Christ, then the cause of offense would have been removed. But I must preach Christ and him crucified, because there is no other way of salvation.[2]

Later, in Galatians 6:12, Paul suggests that one of the motives behind the Judaizers' crusade was a fear of persecution: "These compel you to be circumcised, only that they may not suffer persecution for the cross of Christ." Taken together, these verses throw an interesting sidelight on the false teachers. They were syncretists, seeking to join the old covenant with the new; men-pleasers, aiming to cause offense to no one. They wanted to follow Christ without inviting persecution from their fellow Jews.

This outlook is common today. It shows itself in areas as diverse as inter-faith worship (at one extreme) and the reluctance of many evangelicals to declare the gospel of God's sovereign grace, lest others be offended. Those who do hold to this gospel often preach it in coded language, so that only the initiated know what is being said while the remainder sleep on. By this means they upset no one and enjoy a tranquil, though less-than-faithful, ministry. Paul was prepared to suffer the consequences of his clarity. Are we?

The concept of the "offense of the cross" is an important one in Paul's thinking. In Romans 9:33 he cites a combination of Isaiah 8:14 and 28:16: "Behold I lay in Zion a stumbling stone and rock of offense, and whoever believes on Him shall not be put to shame." While others stumble over it, therefore, believers rejoice in the cross. "God forbid that I should glory except in the cross of our Lord Jesus Christ," declares Paul as he concludes the epistle (6:14). By contrast, those who do not understand the gospel find the cross embarrassing and offensive. To the Jews it was a stumblingblock; to the Gentiles, foolishness. But to those who are called of God, Christ crucified is the "power of God and the wisdom of God" (1 Cor. 1:23–24).

The offense of the cross is part and parcel of the genuine gospel. We must not try to avoid it. There is always the risk of popularizing our message to win a greater following, of sidestepping the offense in order to please men. Many do so, preaching a message heavy on God's beneficence and light on Christ's atonement. They avoid offending people's sensitivities, tiptoeing around the great doctrines of substitution and the sure redemption of the elect. The cross becomes a mystical symbol, a sentimental martyrdom. No! Christ died for our sins. He was made sin that we might be made righteous. His atonement perfectly secured the eternal redemption of his elect people. In him the believer died to sin, rose to newness of life and is exalted to heaven. The blood of Christ is truly precious, for by it we are redeemed indeed (1 Peter 1:18–19).

In light of this glorious gospel of the finished work of Christ, the apostle longs to see all false teaching demolished. He wants to see all that detracts from the glory of God's grace excised from the body of Christ. So he adds, **"I could wish that those who trouble**

you would even cut themselves off!" (5:12). They seek to mutilate your flesh in circumcision, says Paul. They would do better to sever their own connection with God's people and trouble them no more.

Summary
The life of faith is a race, and hindrances to progress abound. Nevertheless, although he exhorts them strongly, Paul is patient with erring believers. He is confident that God will restore them, because he knows that the elect cannot, ultimately, be deceived. However, those who lead others astray by false teaching will be judged severely.

To run well in this race means "obeying the truth"; that is, submitting to those teachings which exalt Christ and his work, while diminishing the works of man. The preaching of "Christ and Him crucified" offends unbelievers, especially those who think themselves religious. This cannot be avoided, since the "offense of the cross" is a necessary feature of the true gospel.

Notes

[1] "By this 'truth' is meant God's special revelation as embodied in the gospel ... That *truth* is full of practical implications. It concerns both doctrine and life. It not only tells men what to believe but also how they should conduct themselves. It reveals to them that God gave his Son as a complete and perfect Saviour, and that, out of gratitude for the salvation that is freely given to all who embrace him by a living faith, the redeemed should spend their days showing forth God's praise in thought, word, and deed" (Hendriksen, *Galatians and Ephesians*, p. 201).

[2] "When, therefore, he says that now, if the preaching of circumcision be received, the stumbling block of the cross will no longer exist, be means that the gospel will no longer be harried by the Jews, but will be given a place with their entire agreement; for they will not take offence at a pretended and spurious gospel, compounded of Moses and Christ, but will tolerate such a mixture, because it will leave them in possession of their earlier superiority" (Calvin, *Galatians ... Colossians*, p. 99).

27
The Law Fulfilled by Love

Please Read Galatians 5:13–15

Paul returns to the theme of liberty in Christ. We are free from bondage, from the law, and from its curse. We are free! But there is another danger, namely that of lawlessness (or "antinomianism"). Liberty is not the same as libertarianism. Freedom from the law does not mean freedom to indulge the old nature, or to sin with impunity. The believer must "pursue ... holiness, without which no one will see the Lord" (Heb. 12:14). But (and here lies the important distinction) this practical righteousness is to be attained through the Spirit, not through the law.

These verses begin one of the most important passages in Scripture on the Holy Spirit and the believer. It deals with practical holiness, victory over sin, and spiritual fruitfulness. This subject occupies the remainder of Galatians 5 and extends into chapter 6. In these initial verses, however, Paul lays the foundation. The new life, into which the Christian has been delivered, by the death of Christ and the power of God, is a life of love.

Called to liberty (5:13)
"**You, brethren, have been called to liberty; only do not use liberty as an opportunity for the flesh**" (5:13). Paul implies that freedom from the law can be misused. Without the external compulsion and restraint of rules and regulations, the old nature ("the flesh") can, in principle, run riot. The epistle of Jude also highlights the problem of libertarianism in the early church, speaking of those who were "turning the grace of God into licentiousness" (Jude 4). How does Paul deal with this danger? He does not reimpose the law, or some substitute for it, but simply instructs the Galatians to make a better choice.[1] It lies within their ability, and

their desire, to reject the sinful tendencies of the old nature; to refuse temptation and choose to do good rather than evil (though, as we have seen, not to the point of sinless perfection).

There is parallel teaching in Romans: "Shall we sin because we are not under law but under grace? Certainly not!... For just as you [once] presented your members as slaves of uncleanness ... so now present your members as slaves of righteousness for holiness" (Rom. 6:15–19). Believers, like all mankind, were once slaves of sin, unable to refuse its demands, try as they may. But all this has changed. They have been delivered from sin's bondage into the glorious liberty of the sons of God. Sin no longer has dominion over them (Rom. 6:14), and they are now free to obey righteousness. This is the essence of their God-given liberty, and only those who *do* "follow holiness" are truly exercising the liberty that Christ has given them. To use this liberty as an excuse to indulge the old nature is, therefore, a contradiction in terms. Any who do so have not understood the meaning of Christian liberty, for liberty and lawlessness are bitter enemies, not companions.

The believer's power to reject sin derives from the indwelling Spirit of God. As Paul explains elsewhere, "If you live according to the flesh you will die; but if by the Spirit you put to death the deeds of the body [the old nature] you will live. For as many as are led by the Spirit of God, these are sons of God" (Rom. 8:13–14). Thus practical holiness is the result of the indwelling Spirit, but notice that we have our part to play. It is we, says the apostle, who must mortify the sinful tendencies of the old nature. This requires positive action, not passivity, on the part of the believer. But equally, we must do it "by the Spirit," relying on his strength and guidance, or else we shall fail.

Called to love (5:13–15)
Therefore, exhorts Paul, **"Do not use liberty as an opportunity for the flesh, but through love serve one another"** (5:13). It would appear that the Galatians were indulging the flesh, particularly, in wrong attitudes to one another. In the churches to which Paul was

writing, there were bitterness and strife, backbiting and criticism. This is clear from verse 15: **"If you bite and devour one another, beware lest you be consumed by one another!"** Was this problem entirely distinct and separate from their doctrinal deviations? Probably not.

Those who embrace the law are in danger of neglecting the Spirit. One of the problems with living by law is that once the explicit duties of the law have been fulfilled, the person feels that nothing more is required. By contrast, those who cultivate the fruit of the Spirit seek to imitate Christ, whose Spirit inhabits their hearts and minds (Gal. 2:20). They run life's race looking to Jesus, the author and perfecter of their faith (Heb. 12:2). Their actions and attitudes are dictated by the Spirit within, rather than by external rules. Of course, these actions and attitudes must be validated by Scripture. Some think they are being guided by the Holy Spirit when, in fact, they are being led astray by a "lying spirit." This was happening in the church at Corinth, and Paul had to teach them to recognize what was from the Holy Spirit and what was not (1 Cor. 12:2–3; see also 1 John 4:1–6). Nevertheless it remains true that the believer is led by the Spirit of Christ in his actions and attitudes.[2]

Chief among the fruits of the Spirit is love, as we shall see later. Thus Paul exhorts his readers, "Through love serve one another" (5:13). An active preoccupation with love is the antidote, not only to feuding between Christians but also to the demands of the old nature. The love invoked here is not human affection, but the very love of God which, says Paul, "has been poured out in our hearts by the Holy Spirit who was given to us" (Rom. 5:5). Many talk glibly about love between believers, but in truth it is a rare commodity. What are its ingredients, and how may we recognize it?

Firstly, as Paul emphasizes here, such love cannot remain a mere attitude; it must reveal itself in action, namely the service of others. Motivated by this love, we shall "do good to all, especially to those who are of the household of faith" (6:10). This requires us to be thoughtful, anticipating the needs of others. We shall be on the lookout for opportunities to render service, not waiting for the minister or someone else to point them out. Our service to others will not be condescending, but "in lowliness of mind," as we "esteem others better than [ourselves]" (Phil. 2:3–4). We shall exhibit a "spirit of gentleness" in our dealings with others (6:1). Our self-giving will be marked by a generosity of heart and mind. Having received freely from God, we shall know how to give freely (Matt. 10:8).

It is commonly taught that our faith in Christ should not rest upon feelings, but on the objective truths of the Word of God. This is correct. But we must be careful not to "throw out the baby with the bathwater." We must not imagine that feelings and emotions are redundant, being somehow contrary to faith. Such thinking leads to a barren, intellectual religion of which the Scriptures know nothing. It deprives believers of authentic spiritual experience, and may set them seeking spurious excitement and false emotion. True Christian experience involves the whole person—affections, emotions, mind, and will. "The kingdom of God is not food and drink, but righteousness and peace and joy in the Holy Spirit" (Rom. 14:17), writes the apostle, and prays, "May the God of peace fill you with all joy and peace in believing, that you may abound in hope by the power of the Holy Spirit" (Rom. 15:13). Love is an emotion; joy is a feeling; peace is an experience!

Love, therefore, is not a theological concept, but a warm reality that moves us to action. Paul commands the Galatians to love, and thus to serve: **"All the law is fulfilled in one word, even in this: 'You shall love your neighbor as yourself'"** (5:14). The mutual service Paul wants to see is prescribed in the law; indeed, says the apostle, it encompasses the law. Yet, ironically, such love can never be a reality if it is based on duty to an external rule. Here lies the weakness of the law: *it can prescribe love but cannot produce it.* This quality of love must be born of, and energized by, the indwelling Spirit of Christ. It is the "more excellent way" which Paul expounds in 1 Corinthians 13. Without it, the most sacrificial act of service is valueless in God's eyes.

The law fulfilled (5:14)

We cannot leave this passage without looking at one further matter, namely the "fulfillment" of the law in the life of the believer. Paul's proposition is not that believers do the law, but that "The righteous requirement of the law is fulfilled in us" (Rom. 8:4). The distinction is important.[3]

As we have already seen, the apostle's teaching on Christian liberty was frequently misunderstood. Because he proclaimed that "Christ is the end of the law for righteousness" (Rom. 10:4), he was accused of preaching lawlessness and encouraging sin (Rom. 3:8; 6:15). This remains a common source of controversy today, as it has been down the ages. Christians, by and large, reject "legalism," which claims that a person is justified before God by law-works. They agree that righteousness can only be found in Christ, not through obedience to the law. But how do we acquire *practical* righteousness? How does the believer, justified as he is through the work of Christ, live out his life in a manner pleasing to God? Some teach that, for the believer to honor God, his practical life must be regulated by the moral elements of the law of Moses. In other words, the Ten Commandments must be his "rule of life." Galatians offers no support for this idea.

Paul's attitude to the law, as we have seen, is very clear. Its purpose is never to justify, nor to help a man please God in lesser ways. "What purpose then does the law serve," he asks? It is "our tutor to bring us to Christ, that we might be justified by faith" (3:19–25). Elsewhere the apostle clarifies his position: "Do we then make void the law through faith? Certainly not! On the contrary, we establish the law" (Rom. 3:31); that is, the law is established in the purpose for which it was designed, namely to bring men to a knowledge of sin and drive them to Christ for relief (Rom. 3:20; 1 Tim. 1:8–10).

However, there is another sense in which the law is "established" by the gospel. Paul speaks of the law being *fulfilled* in the believer: **"All the law is fulfilled in one word, even in this: 'You shall love your neighbor as yourself'"** (5:14). This may be compared with Romans 8:3–4: "He condemned sin in the flesh, that the righteous requirement of the law might be fulfilled in us who do not walk according to the flesh but according to the Spirit" (see also Rom. 13:8).

It is clear from the context, both in Galatians and Romans, that these references are to practical Christian living. The righteous requirement of the law is actually satisfied, or "fulfilled," in the lives of those who "walk according to the Spirit" or are "led by the Spirit" (Rom. 8:14).[4] This fulfillment of the law's requirements is pragmatic, not perfect. This will emerge very clearly as we proceed in Galatians 5. The believer is indwelt by the Holy Spirit, who instructs and leads him in the path of practical righteousness (Rom. 8:9–14). But we also inhabit the fallen mind and body ("the flesh"), in which sin still resides. "If I do what I will not to do, it is no longer I who do it, but sin that dwells in me" (Rom. 7:20). There is therefore a conflict between the Spirit and the flesh, between the new man and the old nature, and this prevents the believer from perfectly obeying God's will. This is why our obedience as Christians can never be such as to obtain favor in God's sight; the righteousness and obedience of Christ, which *were* perfect, remain our only ground of acceptance with God. Whatever we may accomplish in serving Christ, we must call ourselves "unprofitable servants" (Luke 17:10). The danger of nomism is that we might forget this basic truth and seek holiness by our Christian works, when Christ alone is our sanctification (1 Cor. 1:30).

Nevertheless, in a pragmatic sense, the righteous requirement of the law is fulfilled in the believer. The believer, led by the Spirit, does bear fruit in harmony with the law in terms of practical righteous living. How he does so will emerge more fully when we consider the final section of Galatians 5. This righteousness of life is not mere "uprightness" of character. Foremost among its marks is love, from which all else flows. Without this essential ingredient, all our good deeds amount to nothing, as Paul declares so eloquently in 1 Corinthians 13.

Summary

Having declared that the believer is free from the law, Paul addresses the opposite danger, namely that of lawlessness ("antinomianism"). Freedom from the law, he declares, does not mean freedom to indulge the old nature, but rather the opportunity to bear the fruit of the Spirit in righteous living.

The new life, into which the Christian has been delivered, by the death of Christ and the power of God, is a life of love. An active preoccupation with love is the antidote to the demands of the old sinful nature.

Love is not an abstract theological idea, but a warm and compulsive emotion. It is "poured out" in the heart of the believer by the Holy Spirit. However, genuine love cannot remain a mere attitude or inner experience; it will reveal itself in action, namely the service of others.

The law prescribes love but cannot produce it. The love that Christians are to display can only be born of, and energized by, the indwelling Spirit of Christ. Nevertheless, when this divine love is present in our hearts, we shall fulfill the essential requirements of the law (not perfectly, but in a pragmatic sense) by bearing the fruit of the Spirit.

Notes

[1] "What fear may we suppose there was among the Jews, when the gospel freed all men from the law of Moses? What scope did not this great liberty appear to give to evil men? Yet the gospel was not, on that account, taken away; instead the godly were told not to use their liberty to indulge the flesh ..." (Luther, *Bondage of the Will*, p. 94).

[2] "When men become Christians by the belief of the truth, they are introduced into the state, and formed to the character, of spiritual freemen. Their conscience is delivered from the yoke of human authority, and their obedience, even to the Divine law, flows not from the mercenary spirit of a slave, but from the generous spirit of a son" (Brown, *Exposition of Galatians*, p. 125).

[3] " 'Doing' the law is what is *required* of those 'under the law'; 'fulfilling' the law is, for Paul, the *result* of Christian living *the norms of which are stated in quite different terms* [from those of the law]'

    (i) Paul never derives appropriate Christian behaviour by simply applying the relevant precepts from Torah [law];

    (ii) Paul never claims that Christians 'do' (ποιειν) the law; they—and they alone—are said to 'fulfil' (πληρουν) it;

    (iii) Paul never speaks of the law's fulfilment in prescribing Christian conduct, but only while describing its results"

    (Stephen Westerholm, cited in Longenecker, *Galatians*, p. 243).

[4] "The whole will of God, containing our duty towards men, is reducible to this one thing, *love*; for whatsoever God hath commanded us to do towards men, is but a branch from this root, and must flow from love as its principle" (Poole, *Commentary*, p. 657).

28
Led by the Spirit

Please Read Galatians 5:16–21

"I say then," declares the apostle, "**Walk in the Spirit and you shall not fulfill the lust of the flesh**" (5:16). Here lies the secret of practical holiness, of a life that honors God. Such a lifestyle is not an optional extra for the believer, nor is it reserved for the ultra-spiritual. Paul's exhortation is addressed to the same imperfect people who earned his rebuke in the previous verse!

In this well-known passage, Paul reaches the climax of his epistle and provides the clearest possible teaching on the inward, spiritual nature of the Christian life. While these verses are essentially simple, and eminently practical, they are also theologically profound. They go to the heart of the matter, God's ongoing work of grace in the believer.

Has Paul finished, then, with the questions of law and faith? Does he now change the subject as he nears the end of his letter? By no means. If we read the epistle in this way (as many do) we are missing its whole point. Paul's message is that the law and the flesh are co-conspirators against grace and the Spirit, and his dissertation on walking in the Spirit makes a seamless whole with what has gone before. It flows naturally from the epistle's twin themes of justification by grace through faith and the bankruptcy of the law. This can be seen from the way he constantly refers back to the subject of law throughout these closing chapters (see 5:14, 18, 23; 6:2, 12, 13, 15).

Because of the importance of this section of the epistle, we shall devote two chapters to it. The present chapter covers verses 16–21, while the remaining verses of Galatians 5, including Paul's famous statement on "the fruit of the Spirit," will be the subject of chapter 29.

The Spirit against the flesh (5:16–17)

The words, **"I say then"** (Gal. 5:16), announce a new section of the epistle, but also serve to link what follows with what has gone before. What *has* gone before? There are two answers. Firstly, the whole epistle up to this point. The teaching that follows is a logical sequel to Paul's condemnation of law-works as a means of pleasing God. He is about to provide a positive answer and antidote to the fatal love affair between the flesh and the law (see 3:2–3). Secondly, however, Paul links what he is about to say to the immediately preceding verses, in which he condemns strife and exhorts to love. In those verses he set before his readers the Christian ideal. Now he explains how it can be attained.

"Walk in the Spirit," commands the apostle (5:16). The verb employed means "walk about" and thus "conduct yourselves" or simply "live." The emphasis is upon the practical, day-to-day life of the believer, upon his conduct and behavior. This simple statement conveys a profound truth. The outward conduct of the believer is to be dictated and controlled by an inward, spiritual principle. It is not to be dictated by external laws, social conventions, herd instinct, peer pressure, the expectations of others, or the fear of what people will think. Nor will it be controlled by the sinful desires of the old Adamic nature. Instead, the true child of God is "led by the Spirit" (Rom. 8:14; Gal. 5:18). His actions stem from a principle radically different from that which energizes the natural man or the old nature. This is true *even when the outward actions of believer and unbeliever appear to coincide,* as when giving to charity or being neighborly.

Biblical ethics, therefore, are spiritual in the most fundamental sense. That is, they derive from the reality of the indwelling Spirit of Christ. They are not merely "spiritual" with a small "s"; they are Spiritual, with a capital "S." Here we see the outworking of the believer's identification with Christ, which Paul has already defined in unforgettable terms in Galatians 2:20: "It is no longer I who live, but Christ lives in me; and the life which I now live in the flesh [my day-to-day practical life] I live by faith in the Son of

God who loved me and gave Himself for me." The Holy Spirit indwells believers and guides them in their thinking, their attitudes, and their behavior. He pours out God's love in their hearts, so that they are motivated by love rather than selfishness and covetousness. He leads them into a growing understanding of truth through the Holy Scriptures, so that the Bible, in its entirety, becomes their "rule of life" as they seek the glory of God in all that they do.

Attached to this injunction, and stemming directly from it, is a necessary consequence: **"You shall not fulfill the lust of the flesh"** (5:16). It is important to realize that this is not another command, "Do not fulfill ...," as suggested by the KJV margin. It is not even a promise. It is a statement of sober fact. Those who walk in the Spirit *will not* fulfill the lusts of the flesh.

As we have seen before, "the flesh" here means that unregenerate human nature with which we were born. The "lusts of the flesh" should not be equated merely with the "sins of the flesh," since they also encompass the "desires of the ... mind" (Eph. 2:3). As we shall see shortly, jealousy and selfish ambition are just as much works of the flesh as are adultery and uncleanness. As a result of regeneration, the believer has a new nature, embodied in the "new man ... created in righteousness and true holiness" (Eph. 4:24). But he is still encumbered with the old nature, which is called "the flesh" by association, because it resides in his mortal body and mind. Other terminology used by the apostle to describe "the flesh" includes "sin that dwells in me" (Rom. 7:16, 20), "the law [principle] of sin which is in my members" (Rom. 7:23), and "this body of death" (Rom. 7:24). Nowhere, incidentally, does the Bible confuse the sinful desires of the old nature with God-given natural appetites which are an integral part of our physical humanity. These appetites in themselves are neutral, being numbered among our "members," which can be used either as instruments of lawlessness or of holiness (see Rom. 6:19).

Inevitably, there is conflict between the new man and the old nature. Since the Holy Spirit indwells the new man, this struggle can also be represented (as it is here) as a conflict between the flesh and the Spirit himself. **"The flesh lusts against the Spirit, and the Spirit against the flesh"** (5:17). A clearer translation might be, "The flesh desires what is contrary to the Spirit, and the Spirit what is contrary to the flesh."[1]

This conflict is lifelong, since it must persist until the physical body and mind (in which "the flesh" resides) are discarded in death. Those who claim that believers can attain sinless perfection in this life delude themselves. As Paul explains, the flesh and the Spirit **"are contrary to one another, so that you do not do the things which you wish"** (5:17). Far from achieving perfection, believers are continually conscious of temptations, sin, and distractions from the path of righteousness. We have spiritual enemies without, namely the world and its god, Satan. But what grieves and hinders us most is the enemy within, that is, the flesh.[2]

However, the thing works both ways. While the flesh hinders our discipleship to Christ, so the Spirit hinders our surrender to the flesh! As Burton remarks, "Does the man choose evil, the Spirit opposes him; does he choose good, the flesh hinders him."[3] Thus the true Christian can never totally fulfill the desires of the flesh. He is prone to sin, but this is against his Spirit-born desire. He continues to walk with God, confessing his sin, mourning his failure, and seeking the ongoing cleansing of the blood of Christ (see 1 John 1:7–9).

This inability of the believer to surrender to the flesh is part of what Paul means when he says in verse 16, "You shall not fulfill the lust of the flesh." It is impossible for one who is indwelt by the Holy Spirit to abandon himself to the rule of sin (1 John 3:6, 9). However, there is more to it than that. It is only as we "walk in the Spirit" that the sinful desires of the flesh are effectively subdued. How, then, may we walk in the Spirit? What instructions does Paul give that we might do so? The answer to these questions follows in verses 18–25.

Ruled by the law or led by the Spirit? (5:18)

We might think that, by this time, Paul has left behind him the debate about the law and moved on to the quite different subject of practical holiness. Certainly, Galatians is often read as if this were the case. But if this were so, it would be impossible to explain the verse that now follows: **"But if you are led by the Spirit, you are not under the law"** (5:18). Here the apostle defines the relationship of the believer to the law *in the context, not of justification, but of personal holiness*. What connection is there, then, between righteous living and freedom from law?

This verse has important implications. It strengthens the view, expressed earlier in this commentary, that Paul's concern was not only with apostate legalists, but also with the threat which the law, when misapplied, poses to genuine believers. Commenting on this passage, Longenecker writes, "The phrase ... 'under the law' is undoubtedly to be read, as elsewhere throughout the Galatian letter ... as referring to the nomistic lifestyle advocated by the Judaizers ..."[4] What, then, is the apostle telling us? Very simply that, for the believer, the indwelling Spirit has supplanted the external law as the controlling principle that guides his conduct.

Had Paul intended to teach that the law, or any part of it, should be the Christian's "rule of life," here was his opportunity to do so. What does he say? He tells us that those led by the Spirit are not beholden to the law with respect to righteous living. Indeed, he seems to go further; being led by the Spirit and being ruled by the law are mutually exclusive in the area of Christian conduct. Of course, as we have already seen, those who are Spirit-led will fulfill the righteous requirements of the law. They will love God; they will not hate, murder, steal or lie; they will not covet. But this will not be because they subject themselves to the law, but because they are guided by the indwelling Spirit in conformity to the *whole* of God's Word and the example of Christ.

I referred earlier to the "love affair" between the flesh and the law. Unregenerate human nature craves law, for law salves the conscience and feeds the pride of man. Witness the self-congratulations of the Pharisee in Luke 18:11: "God, I thank you I am not like other men ... I fast twice a week; I give tithes of all that I possess." On the other hand, the absence of law leads the unregenerate to sin without constraint, although even they have consciences which, in the providence of God, restrain their worst excesses and allow stable societies to exist. But the Christian ethic is not a middle way between law and licentiousness. It is a higher way that avoids both errors. Led and empowered by the indwelling Spirit of God, and taught in the objective principles of Holy Scripture, the believer seeks to conform his life to the will of God.

The works of the flesh (5:19–21)

Left to itself, fallen human nature bears its own fruits. These are **"the works of the flesh"** which, declares the apostle, **"are evident"** (5:19). That is, when these works are seen among men, no one doubts their cause and origin. They flow "from within, out of the heart of men" (Mark 7:21–23). Of course, many try to deny the obvious. Such antisocial actions, they say, are caused by unemployment, poverty, social deprivation, lack of education, and political mismanagement. But the true reason is clear to any honest person: people sin because they are sinners.

What are these "works of the flesh"? Paul provides a comprehensive catalogue. It is not, of course, exhaustive, but serves to illustrate the scope and nature of man's sins. First are the sexual sins, **"adultery, fornication, uncleanness, licentiousness"** (5:19). These are placed first, not because they are necessarily the worst sins, but because they are the most common. Sex, remember, is God-given. "Marriage is honorable among all, and the bed undefiled; but fornicators and adulterers God will judge" (Heb. 13:4). As Hebrews makes clear, it is not sex that is sinful, but rather its misuse. We live in a society where sex outside marriage is considered normal and acceptable behavior. Even so-called churches have ceased to regard fornication, and even homosexual activity, as sinful. But God has not changed the rules; sexual immorality will be judged.

Next in Paul's blacklist come the religious sins of **"idolatry"** and **"sorcery"** (5:20). Both were rife in New Testament times, and nothing has changed since then! Idolatry may be less obvious today, but it occurs whenever men worship gods of their own making. These gods may even bear a superficial resemblance to the true God, but he alone reveals himself in Jesus Christ. Similarly, our modern world has seen a resurgence of witchcraft, divination, astrology, spiritism, and other forms of sorcery. Movements as diverse as Nazism and the New Age movement exhibit occult tendencies. The human heart prefers these things to truth.

The hatred of man for man features next among the works of the flesh. This gives rise to **"hatred, contentions, jealousies, outbursts of wrath, selfish ambitions"** and **"dissensions"** (5:20). The veneer of civility that often hides these tendencies from view is fragile. Witness the behavior of the average motorist when something annoys him, or of commuters trying to board a crowded train! Closer to home, these things are all too often found within the church itself. The Galatians were "biting and devouring" one another (Gal. 5:15), and we can be guilty of the same sins. Too often there are dissensions and selfish ambition among Christians, to the sorrow of our Lord. We shall only learn to deal with these things when we recognize them for what they are, the works of the flesh.

"Heresies" stand alone in Paul's bleak catalogue (5:20). The reference is to gross distortions and denials of the truth of the gospel. Only religious people can commit heresy, yet to accuse anyone of heresy today is considered uncharitable and unchristian. Any profession of religion, however far-out it may be, is accepted as valid. No one, we are told, has all the truth; that can only be arrived at by a synthesis of diverse opinions. Not so, says Paul. Truth and error can be recognized. The latter must be opposed and the former proclaimed.

However, we must also beware of the opposite extreme. Christians often accuse one another of heresy or error when none exists, or where a little understanding would clear the air. We quarrel and separate over minute and unscriptural distinctions. But for the grace of God, every man would become his own denomination. The Scriptures exhort us to walk "with all lowliness and gentleness, with long-suffering, bearing with one another in love, endeavoring to keep the unity of the Spirit in the bond of peace" (Eph. 4:2–3).

Finally Paul cites **"envy, murders, drunkenness, revels, and the like"** (5:21). These are the more public works of the flesh, the visible fruit of unrighteousness, which disrupt society and create a climate of fear. They can be restrained by human laws and punishments; but only grace can deal with their root cause.

In the believer, the flesh has just the same tendencies as in the unregenerate. However, being also indwelt by the Spirit, the Christian is not controlled by the flesh and is kept by the power of God from most sinful behavior. Although, therefore, the believer is not without sin, the distinction is such that Paul dares to use behavior as a test of a person's spiritual state. Thus, having itemized the works of the flesh, he concludes, **"I tell you beforehand, just as I also told you in time past, that those who practice such things will not inherit the kingdom of God"** (5:21). Although a person is not justified by works, good works will be the sure consequence of regeneration. The true Christian will be marked out by a Christ-honoring life. As Paul explains elsewhere, "We are his workmanship, created in Christ Jesus unto good works, which God has before ordained that we should walk in them" (Eph. 2:10, KJV).

Summary

Believers do not live morally perfect lives. This is because they still carry with them the old nature or "the flesh." There is conflict between this old nature and the indwelling Spirit of Christ, and they are unable to fulfill perfectly either the desires of the flesh or the directions of the Spirit.

Nevertheless, it remains true that believers are led by the Spirit in their practical lives, and are not beholden to the law. It is therefore possible for them to walk (live) in the Spirit, and avoid sin. So confident is Paul of this that he uses a person's lifestyle to diagnose his spiritual condition. Those who do the works of the flesh show they are not heirs of God's kingdom.

The "works of the flesh" are evident. They proceed from within the human heart and take many forms, including sexual sin, hatred and its effects, religious sins, heresies, and public offenses which disrupt social order.

Notes

[1] Longenecker, *Galatians*, p. 245.

[2] "Hence we observe ... *Believers have experience of the power and efficacy of indwelling sin*. They *find* it in themselves; they find it as a *law*. It hath a self-evidencing efficacy to them that are alive to discern it. They that find not its power are under its dominion" (Owen, *Temptation and Sin*, p. 159).

[3] Burton, *Galatians*, p. 302.

[4] Longenecker, *Galatians*, p. 246.

29
Walking in the Spirit

Please Read Galatians 5:22–26

Having listed the works of the flesh, Paul turns to the evidences and manifestations of the indwelling Spirit: **"The fruit of the Spirit is love, joy, peace, long-suffering, kindness, goodness, faithfulness, gentleness, self-control"** (5:22). These things, he declares, fulfill all the requirements of the law and characterize the true followers of Christ. Notice that the fruits of the Spirit are attitudes that control and dictate actions, rather than the actions themselves. Thus the believer's manner of life flows from a genuine inner principle, not from adherence to an external law.

Spiritual fruit (5:22)

The flesh produces "works," but the Spirit bears "fruit." Paul's choice of words is deliberate and full of insight. Fruit is that which arises naturally from the intrinsic character of a tree or plant. Of course, the works of the flesh also stem naturally from man's sinful condition. Paul is not denying that. But he wants to emphasize the positive truth that fruitfulness in Christian living is the direct result of the Spirit within.

The Lord Jesus employs the same idea in the Sermon on the Mount: "Do men gather grapes from thornbushes or figs from thistles? Even so, every good tree bears good fruit, but a bad tree bears bad fruit ... Therefore by their fruits you will know them" (Matt. 7:15–20). The visible fruit discloses the unseen nature of the tree. Again, in John 15:4–5, he teaches the same truth: "As the branch cannot bear fruit of itself, unless it abides in the vine, neither can you, unless you abide in Me. I am the vine, you are the branches. He who abides in Me, *and I in him*, bears much fruit; for without Me you can do nothing" (emphasis added; the indwelling Spirit and the indwelling Christ are one and the same).

In the same way, the good works done by believers flow naturally from the activity of the Spirit within. It is by this "fruit" that the Holy Spirit's presence is demonstrated and his power declared. One who is led by the Spirit cannot avoid bearing fruit, but those who are not so led can never produce it, no matter how hard they try. This important distinction has been largely forgotten in our day. Many are accepted as true believers on the basis of their religious profession, doctrinal beliefs, or church affiliation. But this is not enough. Scripture demands living evidence of regeneration. It is true that in the last analysis only "The Lord knows those who are His" (2 Tim. 2:19), but the necessity of fruit-bearing is underscored in no uncertain terms. "Every branch in Me," said Christ, "that does not bear fruit He [the Father] takes away" (John 15:2). This does not mean that a believer can lose his salvation. It simply means that someone who *claims* to be a Christian but does not bear the fruit of the Spirit in his life is a fraud and will be rejected by God.

Spiritual fruit is not only the evidence of spiritual life. Even more important is the fact that it glorifies God. "By this," said the Lord Jesus, "My Father is glorified, that you bear much fruit; so shall you be My disciples" (John 15:8). Again, Christ commands his followers, "Let your light so shine before men, that they may see your good works and glorify your Father in heaven" (Matt. 5:16).

Spiritual attitudes (5:22)

Paul proceeds to list the fruits of the Spirit. In doing so, he does not write about specific acts such as almsgiving, hospitality, forgiveness and the like, but rather about the basic *attitudes* from which such actions flow. There is, therefore, a difference in kind between the fruits of the Spirit and the works of the flesh, where specific actions are described (adultery, for example). The indwelling Spirit does not compel us to carry out particular actions, as if we were robots under alien control. He rather induces in our hearts and minds these Christlike attitudes, which then issue in specific acts that glorify God.

It is the believer himself who is responsible for translating these attitudes into good deeds. As Paul exhorts later, "As we have opportunity, let us do good to all" (6:10). Exhortations like this, which abound in Scripture, would not be necessary if Christians automatically produced good works without conscious thought or effort. Some commentators so emphasize the naturalness of bearing fruit that they portray the believer as altogether passive in the process. Nothing could be further from the truth. It is we who must "do good." The Spirit within gives us the attitudes, desires, and intentions to do so, but it is our responsibility to put these intentions into effect.

Fruit is visible (5:22)

Whenever the New Testament uses the metaphor of fruit, it refers to something that can be seen. How else could we "know" men by their fruits? (Matt. 7:20). Obviously love, joy, and peace can all be private, inward experiences. But in calling them **"the fruit of the Spirit,"** Paul is making an important point. If genuine, these inward experiences will express themselves in outward actions. The reality of the Spirit within will be exhibited in visible effects. These effects, notice, are not what are called elsewhere the "gifts" or "manifestation of the Spirit," such as miracles or tongues (1 Cor. 12:4–11). Those things had their place in the New Testament church (though it was nothing like the prominent place that some would have us believe). What Paul is talking about here are Spirit-given attitudes which issue naturally in Christ-honoring lives. It is when others "see your good works," said the Lord Jesus, that they will "glorify your Father in heaven" (Matt. 5:16).

Does this mean that Christians are to show off? Should we emulate the Pharisees who prayed on street corners and sought to impress people with their religious deeds? Of course not. The whole point of "fruit-bearing" is that it is not self-conscious, but natural and spontaneous. The Pharisees' problem lay not so much in what they did but in their insincerity. That is why Christ condemned them as hypocrites, which means literally "play-actors," for everything they did was outward show. I can tie bunches of grapes on the branches of a thornbush and pretend it is a vine, but this will fool no one for long. True fruit-bearers seek God's approval, not men's, and tend to shrink from human admiration.

What kind of fruit? (5:22)

What, then, are these fruits? The list begins with **"love, joy, peace."** Notice that all are divine attributes before they become human attitudes. "God is love," John tells us (1 John 4:8). Paul declares that God is "blessed," which simply means "happy" or "joyful" (1 Tim. 1:11; 6:15). The same apostle also speaks of "the peace of God" (Phil. 4:7). Thus the attitudes produced in the believing heart derive from God himself. They are not intensified or accentuated human emotions. They are the direct result of our being made "partakers of the divine nature" through the indwelling of the Holy Spirit (2 Peter 1:4). Nevertheless, although they are no mere human feelings, they do no violence to our personalities, but rather blend with, and sanctify, our own affections.

Thus believers exhibit not just love, but "the love of God which is poured out in our heart by the Holy Spirit who is given to us" (Rom. 5:5). This is a selfless love, for it "does not seek its own" (1 Cor. 13:5). It is patient, kind, contented, humble, polite. It rejoices in truth, has broad shoulders, is optimistic, hopeful, and enduring (1 Cor. 13:4–7). This love mirrors the love that God showed toward us, in that "while we were still sinners, Christ died for us" (Rom. 5:8). It reveals itself first in our love to God himself, which we shall not be able to hide from those around us. We shall love his name, his word, his house, his worship. Then it will be manifested toward Christ's people. They will be a special object of our love, for they are our spiritual family. We shall love our human families with a more than human love (Eph. 5:22–6:4). Finally, we shall love all men for Christ's sake, seeking to lead them to Christ by making known to them the gospel of his grace.

The believer's "joy" will be more than natural happiness. It will be the joy of the Lord. "These things I have spoken to you," said the Lord Jesus, "that My joy may remain in you, and that your joy may be full" (John 15:11). In some circumstances it will so abound that it becomes "joy inexpressible and full of glory" (1 Peter 1:8). In all cases it will be "joy ... in believing" in Christ (Rom. 15:13). Nor will this joy be concealed, for what is hidden is not "fruit." Our joy in Christ will be evident to those around us. Likewise, the "peace" of the believer, deriving from "the God of peace" (Rom. 15:33), will be the "peace of God which surpasses all understanding" (Phil. 4:7); that is, it will be experienced even in circumstances that would normally destroy a person's peace of mind. To that extent, it will be inexplicable to others. It will be peace with strength, for it will "guard our hearts and minds through Christ Jesus" (Phil. 4:7).

"**Long-suffering,**" or patience, will also extend beyond natural limits. Witness the patience of Job in his suffering, and his unswerving faith in the wisdom, sovereignty, and beneficence of God. "Though He slay me, yet will I trust Him," he cries (Job 13:15). Some of us are naturally impatient. The fruit of the Spirit will be seen in a patience that denies our natural tendencies, that waits upon God and trusts his promises, though their fulfillment be delayed.

"**Kindness, goodness, faithfulness**" and "**gentleness**" will characterize our dealings with others, just as they typify God's dealings with his elect. A Christian should be incapable of treating others unkindly, for he has himself, undeservedly, received the "kindness and love of God" (Titus 3:3–4). "Goodness" signifies that our words and actions will never be motivated by evil desires or selfish intentions, but only by love that God imparts. "Faithfulness" reflects the believer's loyalty to his Master, just as Jesus Christ himself was faithful to his Father's will (Heb. 3:2). Our "gentleness" toward others will echo Christ's gentleness to us, so that Paul exhorts the Corinthians "by the meekness and gentleness of Christ" (2 Cor. 10:1). Finally, "**self-control**" will be the product of a heart and mind which are themselves under the control of Christ. Paul speaks of "bringing every thought into captivity to the obedience of Christ" (2 Cor. 10:5).

"**Against such** [things] **there is no law,**" adds the apostle. He may have been quoting Aristotle who, speaking of those who showed exemplary virtue, said, "Against such people there is no law." The quote, dating from 4 B.C., may have become a common maxim.[1] Whether or not this is the case, Paul's point is that such Spirit-led behavior transcends the requirements of any law, even that of Sinai. Thus "the righteous requirement of the law [is] fulfilled in us who ... walk ... according to the Spirit" (Rom. 8:4). Paul's conclusion also means that the fruit of the Spirit cannot be interpreted as a *new* law imposed upon believers, replacing that of Moses. The whole point of this passage is that spiritual fruitfulness supersedes external law as the spring and basis of moral action.[2]

Walk in the Spirit (5:24–26)

The apostle returns to the exhortation to "walk in the Spirit" with which he began the passage (5:16). **"Those who are Christ's,"** he explains, **"have crucified the flesh with its passions and desires"** (5:24). This could be a reference to the absolute death of the "old man," something accomplished for all time when Christ died on the cross (Rom. 6:6; see also Gal. 2:20; Col. 3:9). It is more likely, however, that it refers to the believer's action in "mortifying" the sinful tendencies of the flesh. "If you live according to the flesh you will die," avers the apostle, "but if by the Spirit you *put to death the deeds of the body*, you will live. For as many as are led by the Spirit of God, these are sons of God" (Rom. 8:13–14, emphasis added).

The believer has a new nature, the "new man ... created according to God, in righteousness and true holiness" (Eph. 4:24). But although the "old man" is dead, the old nature ("the flesh") lingers on. It is therefore a lifelong responsibility of the believer to "go on putting to death" the sinful tendencies of the flesh and thus to live a life that honors Christ. If anyone habitually fails to do this, and is led by the desires of the flesh rather than the Spirit, then great doubt is cast upon that person's profession. "Those who are Christ's" manifest their reality by "crucifying the flesh," that is by keeping control of the sin that still dwells within them.[3] How do they do it? By the Spirit, replies Paul. By exercising themselves in the things of the Spirit and using all the means of grace that God has provided for us. Above all, it is our faith in Christ that will "quench all the fiery darts of the wicked one" (Eph. 6:16).

That this is what Paul is teaching here is confirmed by the verse that follows: **"If we live in the Spirit, let us also walk in the Spirit"** (5:25). Those who are Christ's are indeed "alive in the Spirit." The Spirit of God has imparted spiritual life, and that by his own indwelling of the believer. Indeed, the "new man" consists in the indwelling of Christ by the Spirit (see 2:20). How then should such a person "walk" or behave? Surely in a manner consistent with his spiritual state. It is the life of the Spirit that should shine through that of the believer, not the desires of the flesh. "Since we are alive in the Spirit," says Paul, "let us demonstrate that fact by living in a Spirit-led manner."[4]

To illustrate his point, Paul concludes this section with a brief but down-to-earth exhortation: **"Let us not become conceited, provoking one another, envying one another"** (5:26). He wants us to understand that "walking in the Spirit" involves such basic matters as our attitudes toward ourselves and others. As regards ourselves, we must mortify the natural conceit that is part of our fallen nature; we are still sinners and have nothing to boast about before God. As regards others, we are to avoid the spite and envy that are so universal among the unregenerate.

Summary

The fruits of the Spirit are attitudes that control and dictate actions, rather than the actions themselves. Thus the believer's manner of life flows from a genuine inner principle, not from adherence to an external law. It is the believer himself who is responsible for translating these attitudes into good deeds.

The fruits of the Spirit are divine attributes before they are human attitudes, and fruitfulness in Christian living is the direct result of the indwelling Holy Spirit. Such fruitfulness provides visible evidence of spiritual life and so brings glory to God. It is the responsibility of the believer to mortify the sinful tendencies of the flesh and thus live in a manner that honors Christ.

Spirit-led behavior transcends the requirements of any law. Spiritual fruitfulness supersedes external law as the spring and basis of moral action.

Notes

[1] Longenecker, *Galatians*, p. 264.

[2] "And all these are 'the fruit of the Spirit,' the natural produce that appears in the lives of Spirit-led Christians. No wonder that Paul adds again: *against such there is no law* (verse 23). For the function of law is to curb, to restrain, to deter, and no deterrent is needed here" (Stott, *Message of Galatians*, p. 149).

[3] "The word crucified is used to indicate that the mortification of the flesh is the effect of Christ's cross. This work does not belong to man [unaided by the Spirit], but it is by the grace of Christ that we have been planted into the fellowship of Christ's death, so that we might no longer live to ourselves" (Calvin, *Galatians ... Colossians*, p. 106).

[4] "The death of the flesh is the life of the Spirit. If God's Spirit lives in us, let him govern all our actions. There will always be many who impudently boast of living in the Spirit, but Paul challenges them to prove their claim. As the soul does not live idly in the body, but gives motions and vigour to every member and part, so the Spirit of God cannot dwell in us without manifesting Himself by the outward effects. By 'life' is here meant the inward power, and by 'walk,' the outward actions. Paul means that works are witnesses to spiritual life" (Calvin, cited in Wilson, *Galatians*, pp. 112–13).

30
The Spirit of Meekness

Please Read Galatians 6:1–5

We saw in the last chapter that the fruits of the Spirit are attitudes rather than actions. However, attitudes beget actions, and Paul proceeds to urge upon his readers the practical consequences of fruit-bearing. In doing so, he selects two areas of special significance to the Galatians, namely pride and humility (6:1–5), and perseverance in doing good (6:6–10). It is the first of these subjects that concerns us in this chapter.

Paul has already begun to apply his teaching on spiritual fruit in the closing verses of Galatians 5: **"Let us not become conceited, provoking one another, envying one another"** (5:26). Some commentators feel that this verse marks the beginning of the apostle's application and that, logically, it should be seen as the true start of the next section of the epistle. However, the form of address with which Galatians 6 begins, **"Brethren,"** itself suggests the commencement of a new passage. This minor dilemma is best resolved by realizing that the closing verse of Galatians 5 is *both* a postscript to the teaching on the fruit of the Spirit, *and* a springboard for the exhortations that follow.

Restoring those who fall (6:1)
Paul has already mentioned the dangers of conceit; he now addresses the subject of pride and humility on a wider front. He evidently felt that this was an area where the Galatians were particularly vulnerable. Their ill-judged pursuit of the law made them prone to the sin of the Pharisees, that is, spiritual pride. To make his point, the apostle invokes a situation in which a Christian has fallen into some unspecified but public sin. His fellow-believers, of course, would not dream of behaving as he had done. They are

shocked. They feel both injured and superior. Righteous indignation wells up within their hearts. Surely such a sinner should feel the full weight of church discipline and the disapproval of his peers. Yet Paul cautions them.

"**Brethren, if a man is overtaken in any trespass, you who are spiritual restore such a one in a spirit of gentleness, considering yourself, lest you also be tempted**" (6:1). Those who sit in judgment upon others need to exercise special care. A situation like this offers much scope for the works of the flesh, not in the offender but in his fellow-believers! It is fertile ground for the sins of censoriousness, self-righteousness, and spiritual conceit. "Righteous indignation," implies the apostle, is not in order, for in such circumstances it is more likely to stem from spiritual pride rather than a truly righteous heart. Of course, sin must be repudiated, others warned, and the sinner must be shown the error of his ways. But we must never forget that the purpose of such action is to *restore* the offender, not destroy him.[1] Remember how Paul himself dealt with the Corinthian fornicator: "Out of much affliction and anguish of heart I wrote to you, with many tears ... the punishment which was inflicted by the majority is sufficient for such a man ... you ought rather to forgive and comfort him, lest perhaps such a one should be swallowed up with too much sorrow" (2 Cor. 2:4–7).

Do we deem ourselves spiritual? Then let us demonstrate that we are Spirit-led by our gentleness, our humility, our watchfulness, and our desire that God should be glorified in the offender's restoration.

The law of Christ (6:2)
Paul continues, "**Bear one another's burdens, and so fulfill the law of Christ**" (6:2). This can be regarded as a generalization of the previous verse. Those who seek a sinner's restoration will certainly involve themselves in his problems. In that sense, they will bear his burden. But the injunction has a far wider application. "Let each of you look out, not only for his own interests, but also

for the interests of others," Paul writes to the Philippians, and proceeds to cite the ultimate example of Christ, who bore our burden of sin (Phil. 2:4–8). To fulfill the "law of Christ" thus requires us to have the mind of Christ in our dealings with others (Phil. 2:5).

"The law of Christ" stands in contrast to the law of Moses.[2] It is an inner principle rather than an external precept, and is fulfilled as we bear spiritual fruit. Why has Paul waited till now to use this important term, with its powerful connotations? If used earlier, would it not have strengthened his argument, that the covenant of Sinai has been replaced? The answer may be that the expression could have been misunderstood had it been introduced at an earlier point in the epistle. Enamored as they were with law, the Galatians might have perceived the "law of Christ" as yet another set of rules, different perhaps from Sinai's, but of the same essentially external nature. It is only now, after Paul has shown that Christian morality stems from the indwelling of the Holy Spirit, that he dares use the word "law" to describe this inward, motivating principle. Whether this is the case or not, it serves to remind us that the believer is not without law. He is no longer under the law of Moses, but is controlled and motivated by a higher principle, namely, "the law of the Spirit of life in Christ Jesus" (Rom. 8:2).

Self-examination (6:3–5)

Paul continues his warning against self-righteousness: **"If anyone thinks himself to be something, when he is nothing, he deceives himself"** (6:3). Self-esteem is proper, and important for our mental well-being. But such is man's fallen nature that self-esteem is easily distorted into self-importance. Perhaps the Judaizers had encouraged such attitudes, for the Galatians would have felt flattered by the attention they received from their false teachers. Certainly the Judaizers' legalistic teaching, with its emphasis upon the works of man, was fertile soil for self-righteousness (and remains so today).

We have to keep a balance. Certainly, God's children are important and special in his sight, but only as the objects of his grace, not for anything in themselves. We dare not think ourselves "to be something," that is, having some merit, attainment or standing of our own. We possess all these things only in Christ, for in ourselves we are "nothing." To think otherwise is to deceive ourselves, and such self-delusion is dangerous, blinding us to the true nature of salvation. Self-importance in anyone is obnoxious; in a believer it is a denial of the gospel.

As an antidote to self-importance, Paul advises self-examination: **"Let each one examine his own work, and then he will have rejoicing in himself alone, and not in another"** (6:4). The words, "not in another," carry a meaning in the Greek that is not apparent in translation. They signify that we are not to evaluate our own behavior *by comparison with others whom we consider to be wrongdoers.*[3] Thus the apostle is still speaking in the context of the trespasser referred to in verse 1. Comparing ourselves with those we deem inferior may boost our egos, but it will do nothing to promote holiness.

Forget the sins of others, advises Paul. Consider your own manner of life! Put your own actions under the microscope of Scripture to establish their spiritual quality. If they pass the test, then you really will have something to rejoice (or "boast") about. If not, then you will be too busy putting your own life in order to worry about the shortcomings of your fellow-believers. **"For each one shall bear his own load"** (6:5); that is, we are each responsible to God for our own lives. At the judgment seat of Christ we shall answer for our own stewardship, not for others. We are building on the foundation of Christ, Paul reminds the Corinthians, but "Let each one take heed how he builds upon it" (1 Cor. 3:10).

Summary

Paul identifies self-righteousness as a problem among the Galatians. This is a work of the flesh, not the fruit of the Spirit. He drives his point home by reference to the actual or hypothetical case of a sinning believer. If his fellow-believers are truly spiritual, they will restore him with gentleness and humility.

We should not evaluate our own discipleship by comparing ourselves with others less worthy than ourselves. That way lies self-deception. Rather we should be watchful, judging our own actions by the standards God has provided. Only then can we be confident that our actions are pleasing to God.

Notes

[1] "This word restore means to mend, to bring something or someone back to its or his former position of wholeness or soundness. Thus it is used with respect to mending nets (Matt. 4:21; Mark 1:19) and perfecting human character (2 Cor. 13:11; 'be perfected')" (Hendriksen, *Galatians and Ephesians*, p. 232).

[2] "The word 'law' when applied to Christ represents an argument [i.e., Paul is making a point]. There is an implied contrast between the law of Christ and the law of Moses, as if he said, 'If you desire to keep a law, Christ enjoins on you a law which you can only prefer to all others; and that is to cherish kindness towards each other.' On the other hand he says that when everyone compassionately helps his neighbour, the law of Christ is fulfilled. By this he means that everything that is foreign to love is unnecessary; for the composition of the Greek word expresses an absolute completion" (Calvin, *Galatians ... Colossians*, p. 110).

[3] "The substantial use of the adjective *heteros* ('other') has in mind 'someone else' than those spoken to in the directive. The articular form of the substantival adjective ... restricts those in view to either (1) a particular wrongdoer with whom someone in the church may compare himself, or (2) a general class of wrongdoers with whom someone in the church may compare himself" (Longnecker, *Galatians*, p. 277).

31
Sowing to the Spirit

Please Read Galatians 6:6–10

Having warned the Galatians concerning spiritual pride and self-congratulation, Paul now makes a more positive application of his teaching on the fruit of the Spirit. Just as Jesus Christ "went about doing good" (Acts 10:38), so also the believer is to practice good works. Indeed, declares the apostle in yet a further warning, only those who *do* produce such fruit will **"reap everlasting life"** (6:8). This does not, of course, suggest that we are justified, or even sanctified, by good works. It simply re-emphasizes that saved people will, necessarily, demonstrate their salvation by fruitful lives. "We are His workmanship, created in Christ Jesus for good works, which God prepared beforehand that we should walk in them" (Eph. 2:10).

Supporting the ministry (6:6)

What kind of good works is Paul looking for? He gives an example: **"Let him who is taught in the word share in all good things with him who teaches"** (6:6). While the word "let" is grammatically an imperative, Paul's words come across as an exhortation rather than a commandment. As Brown comments, "The general principle conveyed in the passage is ... 'that Christian teachers should be supported by the *voluntary* contributions of those whom they instruct' " (emphasis added)."[1] This exhortatory approach to Christian morality is consistent with Paul's teaching on spiritual fruit-bearing and is a denial of legalistic religion. Too many Christians do good out of a sense of obligation, or because their leaders demand it from them, rather than from the abundance of the heart. But this is not the apostle's way: "Let each one give as he purposes in his heart, not grudgingly or of necessity; for God loves a cheerful giver" (2 Cor. 9:7). Willingness is the touchstone of reality (Exod. 35:29; 2 Cor. 8:3, 12). In Proverbs we read, "Honor the LORD with your possessions and with the firstfruits of all your increase" (Prov. 3:9). Financial giving does, indeed, honor the Lord, but only as it fulfils certain principles.

1. It must be done for the sake of the Lord Jesus Christ, who "though He was rich, yet for your sakes ... became poor, that you through His poverty might become rich" (2 Cor. 8:9).

2. As noted above, it must be willing and part of a larger attitude of self-giving (2 Cor. 8:5, 12). It is not the amount given that matters, but the cost to the giver (remember the widow's mite, Mark 12:42–44).

3. It should be for a legitimate purpose, namely one countenanced by Scripture. In the final analysis, there are only two such purposes for Christian giving: the furtherance of the true gospel and the relief of the poor. Concerning the latter, see Galatians 2:10. The former is the subject of Paul's exhortation here in Galatians 6.

This third criterion is worthy of elaboration. Many appeals for money are made to the Christian public which do not meet this standard. I remember many years ago a well-known evangelist had the idea of holding simultaneous evangelistic crusades in several cities. He would preach in one city, immediately travel with his entourage to a second city, move on to a third, and so on, only to repeat the circuit several times within the space of a few weeks. Of course, such a scheme was very costly, but people supported it because of its novelty value. To me, this seemed little more than an expensive gimmick and a misuse of the Lord's money.

More seriously, vast amounts of money are spent by Christian missions and other organizations on furthering their own influence and material wealth. It is not only cults and televangelists who build up vast real-estate empires on the giving of their followers. Respected churches and missionary societies are not immune from the temptation to lay up treasure on earth in the form of elaborate buildings and institutions, or to spend large sums on administration, conferences, and surveys which do nothing to promote the gospel of Christ.

Most serious of all, the "gospel" that is often supported by Christian giving is not the true gospel of the grace of God in Christ. There are churches which are themselves doctrinally conservative which support overseas missionaries whose message is man-centered, and whose influence is antagonistic to the gospel of grace. Why? Because the home churches, impressed by PowerPoint presentations of starving natives, busy clinics or crowded churches, often forget to ask the missionary, "What is your *message*?"

Paul's formula is very simple: those who are "taught the word" should share their material wealth with "him who teaches." In other words, the congregation should support its minister(s) financially, and do so (as the word "share" implies) at the same standard of living as they themselves enjoy. This was the principle that God laid down for the support of the Levites by the remaining tribes of Israel in Old Testament times (though the New Testament transmutes obligation into willingness). Where pioneer missions are involved, and until there is a congregation to support the preacher, the sending church or churches should bear this responsibility. But let us also notice that when Paul and Barnabas were sent out by the church at Antioch (Acts 13:3), they did not spend the first six months securing pledges for their support! On the contrary, they departed immediately for Cyprus, to preach the Word of God. They knew they had been sent out, not only by the church, but by the Holy Spirit, who was well able to care for their needs as they arose (Acts 13:4–5).

Sowing and reaping (6:7–8)

Rather than give further specific examples of Christian fruit-bearing, the apostle now states a general principle of profound importance: **"Do not be deceived, God is not mocked; for whatever a man sows, that he will also reap. For he who sows to his flesh will of the flesh reap corruption, but he who sows to the**

Spirit will of the Spirit reap everlasting life" (6:7–8). What is this principle, and how does it help us bear fruit?

In this context, the metaphor of sowing refers to behavior. To "sow to the flesh" is to indulge sinful human nature or, as Paul puts it in Ephesians 2:3, to "fulfill the [sinful] desires of the flesh and of the mind." Those who sow to the flesh are motivated in their thoughts and actions by indwelling sin, even though they may profess to be Christians. They evidence "the works of the flesh" described in Galatians 5:19–21. Paul therefore states that no amount of professed religion can deliver such people from the wrath of God and eternal loss. Their sinful fruits betray their unregenerate nature, and God is not deceived by their claim to be his children. They *themselves* may be deceived, implies the apostle, but their false profession of faith in Christ is an affront to a holy God, who will not tolerate such mockery.[2] Those whose discipleship is a sham will reap the whirlwind of God's judgment.

It is clear that Paul is not just making a general point, but addressing the particular problems of the Galatian churches. Legalists and libertarians alike are indicted here for, though they are outwardly very different, they are inwardly the same; both follow the flesh, not the Spirit. What is the answer to this problem? It is given in the latter part of verse 8: "He who sows to the Spirit will of the Spirit reap everlasting life."

As before, sowing means living, acting, behaving. If our actions arise from the leading of God's Holy Spirit, then we are proven to be God's children. "For as many as are led by the Spirit of God, these are sons of God" (Rom. 8:14). The works that we do cannot give us "everlasting life," for that is the gift of grace, but they do provide the evidence that we are heirs of God through Christ (4:7). Genuine believers do live in obedience to the Spirit, although not perfectly, for they are sinners still. We may know them by their fruits. This is a principle of great importance in a day when "easy-believism" is taught so widely. Assent to certain basic doctrines, combined with an act of "commitment" to Christ, is all that is needed (we are told) to receive eternal life. But the

Bible requires evidence of the new birth, namely that we should be found to be new creatures in Christ. "Old things have passed away; behold all things have become new" (2 Cor. 5:17). Mere profession is not enough.

Do not give up (6:9)

Since spiritual fruit is both essential and inevitable, it is inconceivable that believers will not persevere in good works. Thus Paul continues, **"Let us not grow weary while doing good, for in due season we shall reap if we do not lose heart"** (6:9). He recognizes the human frailty of his readers. We are all prone to give up, to stop trying, in this matter of walking in the Spirit and producing his fruit. It is so much easier to let our sinful natures take over, to drift with the tide of worldliness rather than swim against it. Like the psalmist, we "behold ... the ungodly, who are always at ease," and are tempted to cry, "I have cleansed my heart in vain ... for all day long I have been plagued, and chastened every morning" (Ps. 73:12–14).

Paul's words are both encouragement and warning. We need to look beyond the present problems, and "run with endurance the race that is set before us, looking unto Jesus, the author and finisher of our faith" (Heb. 12:1–2). Psalm 126:5–6 has an application here: "Those who sow in tears shall reap in joy. He who continually goes forth weeping, bearing seed for sowing, shall doubtless come again with rejoicing, bringing his sheaves with him." Sowing to the Spirit may well bring tears, as we battle against the sinfulness of our own hearts and the oppositions of Satan. But God has guaranteed a harvest of joy to those who endure hardship and refuse to give up.

All true believers will "overcome" (Rev. 3:5), but there is also a warning here against falling away. "We shall reap," says Paul, "if we do not lose heart" (6:9). "Losing heart" or giving up, is not something we dare indulge in ourselves, or sympathize with in others. It is a sign of apostasy, an indication that the faith professed is not genuine saving faith. Thus in his closing chapter,

Paul raises again the specter of a lost eternity for those who follow the law and do not rest in Christ.

Do good to all (Gal. 6:10)

Paul sums up: **"Therefore, as we have opportunity, let us do good to all, especially to those who are of the household of faith"** (6:10). By doing good, we imitate Christ and bring honor to his name. We also fulfill his eternal purposes, for "We are His workmanship, created in Christ Jesus for good works, which God prepared beforehand that we should walk in them" (Eph. 2:10). In light of scriptures such as this, the importance of good works cannot be overstated, and it is significant that Paul should elevate good works in Galatians, an epistle which so vehemently rejects justification by the works of the law.[3] However, a little thought will show us how appropriate this is. Just as there are spurious "gospels," so there are spurious works. The works that God requires have certain marks, as follows:

1. They glorify God (John 15:8).
2. They conform to Scripture (2 Thess. 3:14).
3. They stem from the indwelling Spirit (Gal. 5:25).
4. They are motivated by love for God and for his Son (2 Cor. 5:14–15).

By contrast, the works of the law, with all their appearance of piety, seek to glorify and justify man, stem from the flesh, and are motivated by love of self (2 Tim. 3:2). It is essential that we know the difference!

Paul says, "As we have opportunity ..." Such opportunity will arise naturally, in the providence of God, and does not have to be forced. No one likes "do-gooders," people who actually impose upon others in their search for self-justification. The believer's good works will be characterized by humility, self-effacement, and discretion. Nevertheless, we must be alert to the opportunities that God provides! We are often so immersed in our own affairs that we fail to notice the needs of others. A self-centered Christian is a contradiction in terms.

Finally, Paul singles out "those who are of the household of faith" for special attention. An old proverb says that "Charity begins at home," and this is Paul's point. It is particularly easy to do good to members of our immediate family, since we know their needs and wishes so well, and spend much time with them. If we cannot show kindness to them, we shall hardly do so to strangers. So it is in the Christian family, the church or "household of faith." Our brothers and sisters in Christ have special claims upon us: upon our affection, our time, our support, our sympathy, our company. It should be a manifest and outstanding mark of any local church, that its members love one another, "not … in word or in tongue, but in deed and in truth" (1 John 3:16–19). If this love is absent from a church, as is sadly so often the case, is it any surprise that God's blessing is also absent?

Summary
The fruit of the Spirit is further illustrated by the work of Christian giving. Discernment is needed to support the true gospel and those who preach it, rather than spurious causes that do not further the work of Christ.

Paul also states a general principle of Christian living: those who are truly regenerate will "sow" to the Spirit, living in a manner that glorifies God, and will "reap" everlasting life. But those whose profession is false will indulge their unregenerate nature and will reap corruption. It is vital, therefore, that we should not lose heart, but by perseverance in doing good should demonstrate the reality of our faith. Our fellow-believers should, particularly, be the objects of our love and care.

Notes

[1] Brown, *Exposition of Galatians*, p. 149.

[2] "What the apostle is saying is that men may fool themselves, but they cannot fool God. They may think they can escape the law of seedtime and harvest, but they cannot" (Stott, *Message of Galatians*, p. 166).

[3] Commenting on "Do good to all" (Gal. 6:10), Betz says, "The Christian community is obliged to disregard all ethnic, national, cultural, social, sexual, and even religious distinctions within the human community. Since before God there is no partiality, there cannot be partiality in the Christian's attitude towards his fellow man" (*Galatians*, p. 311).

32
Glorying in the Cross

Please Read Galatians 6:11–18

The epistle to the Galatians is a fighting letter and, true to form, it does not fade quietly away at its close. Paul has been contending earnestly for the true faith, and it is fitting that he should end with a clarion call. **"God forbid,"** cries the apostle, **"that I should glory except in the cross of our Lord Jesus Christ"** (6:14). In the final eight verses of the epistle, Paul refers or alludes three times to the cross of Christ. There can be no doubt that he intended to leave his readers with their gaze fixed upon "Jesus Christ and Him crucified" (1 Cor. 2:2), for here lies the remedy for all error.

How to win followers (6:11–12)

These verses deal with what could be called "the battle for the mind," that is, the competition of religious leaders for the allegiance of professing Christians. To seek a following is not, of course, an activity unique to religion, for it is the essence of all political ambition. Paul here unmasks the motivation of the Judaizers and contrasts it with his own.

It was common in Paul's day for letters to be penned by an amanuensis, or scribe, but for the author himself to add a conclusion (or "subscription") in his own handwriting. This appears to have been the apostle's practice. What is different about the Galatian epistle is that Paul draws special attention to the fact: **"See with what large letters I have written to you with my own hand"** (6:11). There has been much speculation about the significance of these words. One idea is that Paul suffered from poor eyesight (cf. 4:15) and therefore used large characters when writing in his own hand. However, most commentators believe that Paul was simply emphasizing how strongly he felt about his message to the Galatian churches. Burton says, "The size of the letters would have somewhat the effect of bold-face type in a modern book."[1]

However, taken in its immediate context, Paul's emphasis may have had a more pointed purpose, namely to underscore the difference in attitude between himself and the Judaizers. "I am deeply and personally concerned for your spiritual welfare," he seems to be saying. "That is why I have written this impassioned and sometimes painful letter to you. Compare this with the attitude of your false teachers, who seek your allegiance only for their personal ambition and gratification." Thus Paul's attitude to the Galatians was that of a concerned parent, desiring only their good. To this end he had written a letter to them in which he sets forth the true gospel and exposes error. He rests his teaching on the principle laid down by Christ himself: "You shall know the truth, and the truth shall make you free" (John 8:32).

We should also be careful to follow this principle. Too often we seek to put people right, or win their approval, by unspiritual means. We impose unscriptural rules and regulations to keep people "in line." We use peer pressure or a dominant personality to ensure allegiance to our particular cause or church. We manipulate people by giving or withholding the approval they crave from their leaders. Not so the apostle, whose only weapon is the truth. He is content to believe that only "the truth in Christ" (1 Tim. 2:7) can make men free to serve the living God.

How different was the approach of the Judaizers! Their desire was **"to make a good showing in the flesh"** (6:12), that is, to win the applause of their fellow Jews by bringing the Gentile churches under the law of Moses. How they would be praised for their missionary zeal! Their work, unlike Paul's, would be hailed as really effective, since it expanded Judaism and pandered to national pride. But it was all outward show, a work of the flesh, and not of God's Spirit.

We must always be alert to the dangers of personal pride and self-aggrandizement in Christian service. Success and reputation can easily go to our heads. We need to seek the praise of God rather than that of man, for the latter can be a snare. A preacher I know is frequently introduced in the most glowing terms, for he is a notable servant of God. But when he rises to preach he studiously avoids responding to such praise, his first words being the announcement of his text. Is he being ungracious? Not at all. He is reminding us that we have not come to admire a man, but to worship God.

Despite their "good showing" in the eyes of their admirers, the truth about the Judaizers was unsavory. They were motivated by the fear of their fellow Jews. **"They try to compel you to be circumcised, only that they may not suffer persecution for the cross of Christ"** (6:12). To proclaim "Jesus Christ and Him crucified" was to set aside the law of Moses, to banish Judaism and thus to arouse the anger of the Jews, especially the influential Zealots. By imposing the law and circumcision upon Gentile Christians, the Judaizers could claim to be maintaining the cause of Judaism. They could thus enjoy a reputation among believing Jews for their missionary zeal, while at the same time avoiding the ire of the Jewish establishment, and the persecution that went with it. No doubt the Judaizers had some doctrine of the cross, for the death and resurrection of Christ must have had a place in their scheme. But they did not teach an atonement which rendered the law redundant, along with its temple, its priesthood, and its perpetual sacrifices. They could not proclaim that Christ had "offered one sacrifice for sins forever [and had] sat down at the right hand of God ... [having] perfected forever those who are being sanctified" (Heb. 10:12–14). The total and eternal efficacy of the death of Christ as an atonement for the sins of the elect (who alone are set apart or "sanctified") is a doctrine that even today brings ridicule and persecution upon those who hold and declare it. Yet this is the truth that sets men free.

To preach "the cross of Christ," therefore, is to do more than make mention of Christ's death. It is to proclaim that there is no salvation apart from that obtained by Christ for his elect through his vicarious and perfect atonement for sin. No role is left for man to play. "When He had *by Himself* purged our sins, [He] sat down at the right hand of the majesty on high" (Heb. 1:3, emphasis added). Many think they preach the cross of Christ who do not do so.

Glorying in the cross of Christ (6:13–14)

Paul draws a further contrast between himself and the Judaizers. They **"glory in your flesh"** (6:13), but the apostle glories **"in the cross of our Lord Jesus Christ"** (6:14). The verb "to glory" is not one we use much today, but several different words are needed to express its content in modern terms. It signifies pride, pleasure, satisfaction, rejoicing, and exultation. It suggests that the heart and mind are so taken up with the object of glorification that a person is all but lost in its contemplation.

The object of the Judaizers' glorification was a Gentile church which had (as they hoped) embraced the old covenant through circumcision and submission to the law. **"They desire to have you circumcised that they may glory in your flesh"** (6:13). They rejoiced to see the Gentiles brought into the Jewish fold, and were full of self-congratulation for their success. Paul comments, wryly, that the Judaizers were not really interested in the law, for **"Not even those who are circumcised keep the law"** (6:13). Their real concern was not for their message (the law), but only for results and the self-esteem they brought. "Success" is a heady wine for Christian leaders today, as it was then. We are all in danger of glorying in success, in large congregations, in fruitful evangelism, in visible "results." The converse is that we become discouraged when our churches are small and we struggle against indifference or opposition as we seek to make Christ known. Both attitudes are wrong, for they both stem from the false perspective that the work is ours, not God's.

Paul corrects our thinking: **"But God forbid that I should glory except in the cross of our Lord Jesus Christ"** (6:14). There was so much, humanly speaking, in which Paul might have found satisfaction. He could have gloried in his learning, his literary gifts, his power as a preacher, his travels, his evident success as a missionary, the esteem in which he was held by countless believers, his high standing as an apostle. But Paul sought and found his joy and satisfaction in Christ. He saw the emptiness of boasting in his own achievements or in the praises of men. The only achievement worthy of his boasting was the saving work of Christ. In that alone could he find comfort, joy, satisfaction, and rest. How could Paul's sufferings compare with the suffering of Christ upon the cross, where he bore the sins of his people? What are the feeble attainments of man in comparison with the eternal purpose and efficacy of the atonement? Where was the similarity between the apostle's achievements and the glorious victory of Christ over sin, Satan, and death itself? Whom had Paul saved? No one. Whom had Christ saved? Those that his Father had given him before time began (John 6:39), a great multitude that no one can number. If anyone is to glory, then "He who glories, let him glory in the Lord" (1 Cor. 1:31).

Paul's glorying, then, was in **"the cross of our Lord Jesus Christ, by whom** [or which] **the world has been crucified to me, and I to the world"** (6:14). Being "crucified ... to the world" does not mean, of course, that Paul had been cut off, or isolated in some way, from the world around him. On the contrary, he was actively engaged in evangelizing that world and its peoples. His words here relate to the things the world holds dear or precious. Among men, such things as riches, reputation, achievements, social standing, and success are greatly valued. Men covet the praises of their fellow men, and none did so more than the Judaizers! The believer, however, is dead to such blandishments, desiring the praise of God rather than the plaudits of man. He is dead, therefore, to the opinions and values of the world, though alive to the will and requirements of God. What has brought about this difference? The cross of Christ.

Paul's statement here echoes one of the pivotal verses of the epistle, Galatians 2:20, where he writes, "I have been crucified with Christ; it is no longer I who live, but Christ lives in me; and the life which I now live in the flesh I live by faith in the Son of God, who loved me and gave Himself for me." To be "crucified to the world," therefore, is no negative stance, but an inevitable result of our identification with Christ in his death and resurrection. Through these, the believer has been delivered from the power of sin and from conformity to "this present evil age" (1:4). He has been made free to live to God, in newness of life, by the indwelling Spirit of Christ. As Paul exhorts the Romans, "I beseech you therefore, brethren, by the mercies of God, present your bodies a living sacrifice, holy, acceptable to God, which is your reasonable service. And do not be conformed to this world, but be transformed by the renewing of your mind, that you may prove what is that good and acceptable and perfect will of God" (Rom. 12:1–2).

A new creation (6:15–16)

Paul continues to underscore the transformation that has taken place in the life of the believer as a result of his union with Christ. **"For in Christ Jesus neither circumcision nor uncircumcision avails anything, but a new creation"** (6:15). In these closing verses, the apostle powerfully reasserts the main theme of his epistle. Religious externals mean nothing; the indwelling of the Spirit of Christ, bringing new life to the soul, is everything.

It may seem strange, especially in light of Galatians 5:2, that Paul here treats circumcision as a matter of indifference. There is no inconsistency, however. In the earlier verse he condemned circumcision because, in submitting to it, the Gentile believers were placing themselves under the old covenant, thus turning their backs on the new! But now Paul refers to the fact that circumcision is merely an outward symbol which retains no significance under the new covenant. True believers, whether Jew or Gentile, are united in Christ, and all difference between them has been expunged. What *does* matter is that each of them has become "in Christ Jesus … a new creation." As Paul says elsewhere, "If anyone is in Christ, he is a new creation; old things have passed away; behold, all things have become new" (2 Cor. 5:17). Through union with Christ in his death and resurrection, and by the instrumentality of the indwelling Holy Spirit, believers are new creations. They are no longer under the judgment of God, but have passed from spiritual death to spiritual life. They possess eternal life. They are children and heirs of God. They are led by God's Spirit and walk in the light, bringing forth his fruit in their lives. They are citizens of heaven, not of earth.

Thus Paul rejects all religion that is merely outward, consisting in rituals, rules, law-keeping and human contrivances. True faith in Christ is inward, "the life of God in the soul of man." It is a work of God, transforming the life and fixing the affections on Christ. So it is that Paul can write, **"As many as walk according to this rule, peace and mercy be upon them, and upon the Israel of God"** (6:16). The only "rule" that is valid in the sight of God is just this principle of new life in Christ. Those who evidence it in their life or "walk" are the beneficiaries of the "peace" that Christ has made in the blood of his cross, and the subjects of God's everlasting "mercy" toward undeserving sinners. Thus can Paul pronounce with all sincerity the benediction: "Peace and mercy be upon them."

The benediction also embraces "the Israel of God" (6:16). Some take this to signify a separate category of believers, namely Jewish Christians, but this is unlikely to be Paul's intention. For one thing, he has just been emphasizing the unity of Jew and Gentile in Christ, and is unlikely here to imply that a division of some sort still exists. It is more likely that Paul is driving home once again one of the main messages of the epistle, namely that the true descendants of Abraham, the heirs of faith, are not those who follow the law but those who embrace the gospel "rule" that he has just enunciated. Thus the "Israel of God" is the church of Christ, made up of all who walk by the rule of faith in Christ.

The marks of the Lord (6:17–18)

Paul concludes his letter with a warning and a benediction. How typical this is of the whole epistle! The warning is as follows:

"From now on let no one trouble me, for I bear in my body the marks of the Lord Jesus" (6:17). At the outset of the epistle Paul wrote of the Judaizers, "There are some who trouble you" (1:7). Now he states what has been implicit throughout, that whoever troubles the churches of Galatia, troubles the apostle also. This is because his own heart is bound up with the churches founded through his God-given ministry. Their enemies are his enemies, and it is no light thing to oppose the appointed messenger of God!

Earlier in the epistle, Paul took pains to emphasize that his apostleship and gospel were from God, not from man. Now he adds a further token of his God-appointed ministry: "I bear in my body the marks of the Lord Jesus." What does he mean by this? Although the word translated "marks" is the Greek word *stigmata*, Paul is not referring to anything mystical or bizarre. Rather, he is talking about the physical scars he bore from beatings and other injuries sustained in the course of his preaching ministry. He enumerates some of his sufferings in 2 Corinthians 6:4–10: "In all things we commend ourselves as ministers of God: in much patience, in tribulations, in needs, in distresses, in stripes, in imprisonments, in tumults, in labors …" Later in the same epistle he provides an even more harrowing catalog of his afflictions in the service of Christ: "In stripes above measure, in prisons more frequently, in deaths often. From the Jews five times I received forty stripes minus one …" (2 Cor. 11:22–33). Significantly, in this latter passage, Paul is contrasting himself with certain "false apostles" who sought to bring his readers "into bondage" (2 Cor. 11:13–20).

Paul saw his sufferings not just as misfortunes that had to be endured. In the sovereign providence of God, they served a genuine and necessary purpose. Writing to the Colossians, he puts it thus: "I now rejoice in my sufferings for you, and fill up in my flesh what is lacking in the afflictions of Christ, for the sake of His body, which is the church, of which I became a minister according to the stewardship from God which was given to me for you, to fulfill the word of God" (Col. 1:24–25). In Paul's mind, the things he suffered were a necessary part of his ministry, enabling him to follow in the footsteps of Christ who "loved the church and gave Himself for it" (Eph. 5:25). This is why he perceived his scars as a proof of his ministry and thus of his God-given authority as a teacher of the truth. By implication, therefore, he warns the Galatians that those who oppose or "trouble" him are actually opposing the truth of God, and will be judged for their presumption.

Yet, typically, Paul's final words are words of benediction, not of blame: **"Brethren, the grace of our Lord Jesus Christ be with your spirit. Amen"** (6:18). In spite of all the grief they had caused him, he addresses the Galatians, tenderly, as "brethren." He has never lost sight of the fact that his readers are believers in Christ, whatever their frailty, and in spite of the threat of apostasy that hung over them as long as they persisted in error. His one concern is to restore them to faith in Christ alone, and to that end he commits them to "the grace of our Lord Jesus Christ." Paul understands that, in the last analysis, it is only the grace of God in Christ that can establish them in the truth. God's servants can proclaim that truth, but only God's grace can apply it with saving and preserving power.

Summary

Paul expresses his concern for the Gentile churches by presenting the truth of Christ. By contrast, he exposes the unworthy motivation of the Judaizers, who cared nothing for the church, or even for the law itself, but rather sought personal advancement and the approval of the Jews.

His opponents gloried in their influence and their apparent success in converting Gentiles to Judaism. Paul gloried only in the cross of Christ, by which true believers have been reconciled to God and delivered from this "present evil age," from its power and the condemnation under which it lies.

Through the atoning work of Christ, and its application by the Holy Spirit, the elect become new creations in him. This alone is authentic Christianity. External religion, such as advocated by the

Judaizers, avails nothing in the sight of God. Paul warns his readers not to oppose his teaching, for to do so was to oppose the God whose messenger he was. He commends them to the grace of Christ, for that alone can save and preserve their spirits to eternal life.

Notes

[1] Burton, *Galatians*, p. 348.

Bibliography

Andrews, E. H., *The Spirit has come,* Evangelical Press, 1991 (previously published 1982 under the title *The promise of the Spirit*).

Bolton, Samuel, *The True Bounds of Christian Freedom* Banner of Truth, 1964 (originally published 1645).

Berkhof, L., *Systematic Theology,* Banner of Truth, 1959 (originally published 1941).

Betz, H. D., *Galatians: a Commentary on Paul's Letter to the Churches in Galatia,* Fortress, Philadelphia, 1979.

Boston, Thomas, *Human nature in its fourfold state,* Sovereign Grace Book Club, Evansville, 1957.

Brown, John, *An Exposition of Galatians* (Christian Classics Edition, P.O. Box 2722 Grand Rapids, Michigan, undated).

Bunyan, John, *The Pilgrim's Progress,* Nelson Classics edition (originally published 1678).

Burton, E. de W., *A Critical and Exegetical Commentary on the Epistle to the Galatians,* ICC Edinburgh; T. & T. Clark, 1921.

Calvin, John, *The Epistles of Paul to the Galatians, Ephesians, Philippians and Colossians,* Torrance edition, Oliver & Boyd, 1965.

Cross, F. L., *The Oxford Dictionary of the Christian Church,* OUP, 1958.

Denney, James, *The death of Christ,* IVP 1951.

Eadie, John, *Galatians,* Zondervan (undated).

Fausset, A. R., *Galatians,* JFB; Collins, 1874.

Gill, John, *Exposition of the Old and New Testament,* The Baptist Commentary Series, 1809; reprint by The Baptist Standard Bearer Inc. 1989.

Hendriksen, William, *New Testament Commentary, Galatians and Ephesians,* Banner of Truth, 1968.

Kistemaker, Simon J., *Exposition of the Epistle to the Hebrews,* Evangelical Press, 1984.

Lightfoot, J. B., *St Paul's Epistle to the Galatians,* Oliphants edition, 1957 (originally published 1865).

Lloyd-Jones, D. M., *Romans,* vol. 3, Zondervan, 1973.

Longenecker, Richard N., *Paul, Apostle of liberty,* Harper and Row, New York, 1964.

Longenecker, Richard N., *Galatians* (World Bible Commentary 41), Word Books, Dallas, 1990.

Luther, Martin, *The bondage of the will,* Weimar Edition of Luther's works XVIII (597 ff), James Clarke, 1957.

Luther, Martin, *A Commentary on St Paul's Epistle to the Galatians,* James Clarke, 1953 (originally published 1535).

Murray, John, *Redemption Accomplished and Applied,* Banner of Truth, 1961.

Owen, John, *Temptation and Sin,* Sovereign Grace Book Club, 1958.

Poole, Matthew, *Commentary on the Holy Bible,* vol. 3, Banner of Truth, 1963 (originally published 1685).

Ramsey, W. M., *St Paul the Traveller and the Roman Citizen* (reprint), Grand Rapids, 1949.

Reisinger, John G., *Tablets of Stone,* Crowne Publications, Inc., USA, 1989.

Shedd, W. G. T., Dogmatic Theology II, New York, 1891–1894.

Stott, John, *The Message of Galatians,* IVP, London, 1968.

Wilson, Geoffrey B., *Galatians, a Digest of Reformed Comment,* Banner of Truth, 1973.

www.ingramcontent.com/pod-product-compliance
Lightning Source LLC
Chambersburg PA
CBHW071156300426
44113CB00009B/1224